'To our children, Isabelle, Nicola, Julia and Isaac'

THE KINGDOM, THE POWER AND THE GLORY:
WESTERN YOGA

CRAIG J. LEGGAT AND SALLY M. BLAIR

BALBOA.PRESS
A DIVISION OF HAY HOUSE

Balboa Press books may be ordered through booksellers or by contacting:

Balboa Press
A Division of Hay House
1663 Liberty Drive
Bloomington, IN 47403
www.balboapress.com.au
AU TFN: 1 800 844 925 (Toll Free inside Australia)
AU Local: 0283 107 086 (+61 2 8310 7086 from outside Australia)

Print information available on the last page.

ISBN: 978-1-5043-2203-4 (sc)
ISBN: 978-1-5043-2223-2 (e)

Balboa Press rev. date: 08/19/2020

INTRODUCTION

THIS BOOK IS about how to make your life better by using a very ancient and very wise tradition. The tradition has many names. One name is the Western tradition. Another name is the Western Mystery Tradition. Another name is Western Yoga or the Yoga of the West. I will call it Western Yoga.

Western Yoga is very different from the yoga that originated in India.

Western Yoga is based on The Tree of Life. Three of the parts of the Tree of Life are The Kingdom, The Power and The Glory. You have heard those words before.

Western Yoga is founded on those words[1].

The cover of the book you are reading has a photograph of a painting of the Tree of Life by the brilliant American artist Patricia Waldygo[2].

As you will see from the front cover, the Tree of Life consists of ten spheres arranged in a particular pattern. In this book I will take you through seven of the spheres. The spheres are also known as paths. The ten paths are connected by another twenty-two paths, making a total of thirty-two paths[3].

Western Yoga was created and developed in the schools of the Chaldeans and the Sumerians located in the Fertile Crescent between the Mediterranean Sea and the Persian Gulf. Those schools taught values, ethics, morality, philosophy, politics and theology thousands of years before Jesus Christ, Siddhartha Gautama the Buddha[4], Confucius[5] and Muhammad[6] the prophet of Islaam.

Western Yoga was taught by Pythagoras[7], Socrates, Plato, Aristotle and others.[8] Western Yoga is a merger of the best of Jerusalem and the best of Athens[9]. Western Yoga has been the foundation of western culture for more than three thousand years.

Western Yoga considers that our human existence has a transcendent purpose and that our lives reveal that purpose to us.

Western Yoga states 'As above, so below' to describe the idea that we are created in the image of a creator with a mind and a soul. Our mind and soul reflect the mind and soul of the creation process, according to Western Yoga.

Western Yoga and its Tree of Life have been described as 'an attempt to reduce to diagrammatic form every force and factor in the manifested universe and the soul of man; to correlate them one to another and reveal them spread out as on a map so that the relative positions of each unit can be seen and the relations between them traced. In brief, the Tree of Life is a compendium of science, psychology, philosophy and theology.'[10]

Western Yoga considers that because you have a soul you participate in the creation of humanity itself. This brings with it great personal responsibility to select values and to act on those values. That is because we can create hells on earth, like our own family sized versions of Auschwitz.

The values in the Tree of Life stand in stark and joyful contrast to the post-modern Nihilistic view that human life has no meaning or purpose and that human values are invented by oppressive, elite and powerful hierarchies.

Nihilism and post-modernism

A leader of the Nihilistic movement was Sergey Nechayev, born in Russia in 1847. Nechayev's great influence on Vladimir Lenin and on Joseph Stalin is well chronicled[11].

Nechayev was the main author of the revolutionary pamphlet 'Catechism of a Revolutionary'. That pamphlet was the blue-print for the Nihilistic movement.

The pamphlet included the proposition that human beings ought to have 'no private interests, no affairs, no sentiments, ties, property not even a name of his own... severed every link with the social order and with the entire civilized world. He is its merciless enemy and continues to inhabit it with only one purpose – to destroy it.'[12] Lenin and Stalin adopted and promoted those ideas and brought about hell on earth for millions of people in Russia.

Nechayev wrote [13] 'The only form of revolution beneficial to the people is one which destroys the entire State to the roots and exterminated all the state traditions, institutions and classes in Russia... the nobility, the bureaucracy, the clergy, the traders and the parasitic kulaks.'

To give the devil his (or her) due, parts of Nechayev's Catechism have a superficial attraction. In particular, paragraph 22 which states 'The Society has no aim other than the complete liberation and happiness of the masses – ie of the people who live by manual labor.' While such an aim (happiness) can be criticized validly[14], an aim of liberation and happiness would certainly appear to be preferable to an aim of unhappiness and subjugation.

The Nihilistic and post-modern value, that life is without objective purpose and meaning, was recognised by Shakespeare. Shakespeare has Hamlet state[15] 'There is nothing either good or bad but thinking makes it so.' Michel Foucault and Jacques Derrida, took Hamlet's lead into the territory of post-modernism/post-structuralism.

Nihilism, yoga and the beach

As a teenager in the 1970's, my exposure to nihilism and its accompanying existential crisis, caused me to leap whole heartedly into the yoga of the east. I was searching for values to replace those that I had thrown out with the western bath water.

I moved to Avalon Beach on Sydney's glorious peninsula of northern beaches. Shared a house with Geoff and Collette Searle who ran, with Geoff's parents, the Avalon Beach health food store. Geoff spoke highly of a yoga teacher who lived in nearby George Street.

The yoga teacher was a middle-aged woman named Mary Thompson. Mary was married to Dr Brian Thomson. Mary and Brian had three sons. The eldest son named Charles was a couple of years younger than me. Mary had been given the name Sita (a Hindu goddess) by her yoga teacher Swami Satyananda Saraswati from the Bihar School of Yoga in India. Brian had been given the name Rama (a Hindu god) by Swami Satyananda. The Thomson house was filled with the smell of sandalwood incense and books on yoga by Swami Satyananda. I felt like I had found my tribe. My discovery was being repeated by myriad young people all around the western world.

I noticed a micro-tell of angst on yoga teacher Sita's face when I asked about her sons. It was apparent the three boys, aged about 6 to 12 years, were living spartanly in Swami

Satyananda's ashram in the middle of rural India while Sita and Rama were living luxuriously in Avalon Beach, Australia. I soon set off to join the sons in rural India.

For the next 40 plus years I learned and practiced yoga and then taught yoga and then taught yoga teachers how to teach yoga. I also studied and practiced law, married and raised and continue to raise our four children with my wife Sally who was then a lawyer and is now a clinical psychologist in private practice. Many nights in the yoga ashram there would be a time after dinner when Swami Satyananda would sit and talk. The Sanskrit word for such a session was 'satsang'. The root word 'sat' means true or truth, and 'sanga' means community. During one such satsang, Swami Satyananda looked at the large number of western learner yogis sitting at his feet and said words to the effect 'I really do not know why you come here. You have your own yoga of the west. It suits you better.' I discovered many decades later that Swami Satyananda was referring to the Tree of Life.

One of the values that I was taught in Swami Satyananda's yoga school was 'vairagya'. Swami Satyananda described[16] that value in the following manner:

'In Sanskrit it is called "vairagya" … which describes the attitude of the mind which is beyond both interest and no interest. Detachment is that inner attitude which, no matter what one's outer actions may seems to indicate, is neither for nor against events of the world. It can be understood as the attitude that sees no real difference between "good" and "bad".'

This is the approach described by Hamlet that I set out above - 'There is nothing either good or bad but thinking makes it so.'

A cursory examination of the internet reveals the central and profound role of 'vairagya'[17] in the yoga of east, as taught in the west. The website Fitness Health 101.com states:

'Concepts of Yoga – There are generally considered to be 12 major concepts associated with Yoga. Yoga concepts were derived from the original meanings of the words that make up these concepts… the intent is to summarize the 12 major concepts of Yoga into an understandable format that you can easily implement in your daily life to enhance the overall quality of your lifestyle…Vairagya concerns itself with the disinterest in anything of the current life. This concept requires the participant to distance himself from anything that they enjoy in their mortal life in order to better prepare for the afterlife.

This includes the indifference of possessions, enjoyed feelings and the enjoyment of any emotional action or response.'[18]

In my view, there is a problem with the yoga of the east, for those born in and living in the west. The problem is the value of 'disinterest' in the yoga of the east.

The problem had been recognised about seventy years earlier by Violet Firth, a Welshwoman. Ms Firth changed her name to Dion Fortune and under that name wrote many books about western yoga. Dion Fortune wrote[19]:

'...is it therefore desirable to try and implant Eastern ideals in a Westerner? Withdrawal from the earth-plane is not his line of progress. The normal, healthy Westerner has no desire to escape from life, his urge is to conquer it and reduce it to order and harmony. It is only the pathological types who long to "cease upon the midnight with no pain," to be free from the wheel of birth and death; the normal Western temperament demands "life, more life."'

Ms Fortune wrote:

'... there is a Western Tradition .... completed by an oral tradition... used as the bases of the practical work of the Yoga of the West. The adepts of those races whose evolutionary destiny is to conquer the physical plane have evolved a Yoga technique of their own which is adapted to their special problems and peculiar needs.'[20]

My present view is consistent[21] with that advanced by Ms Fortune. For human beings in the West, the Tree of Life provides values and ethics that are preferable to those taught by teachers of the yoga of the East.

There is common ground between the 'vairagya' of the yoga of the East ('disinterest in possessions and the enjoyment of any emotional action or response') and the Nihilistic Catechism of Sergey Nechayev referred to earlier.[22]

This is, of course, not to equate the yoga of the East with the despotic nihilism of Stalin, but rather to point out common ground between the two. The common ground may explain, to some extent, the attraction to the young people of the West (who included me) to exploring the edges[23] of life via the yoga of the East, post-modernism and Nihilism.

Western Yoga

Western Yoga values emotional attachment to family, friends and society.

Western Yoga uses the delightful description 'the path of the hearth fire' to describe this valuing of attachment and friendship. The path of the hearth fire describes a comfortable and loving family home. There is a fire place with a blazing fire providing warmth and security. Hot food and drink are being shared. Stories are being told. Children and elders, and all in between, converse and discuss and argue and laugh and teach each other. The hearth fire provides a place where human beings can thrive. The path of the hearth fire is the path where the sufferings of the world are walked and endured with the knowledge that everybody suffers, in some way, at some time, and for many people, in many ways and at many times. The blazing light of the hearth fire values the path that leads away from the tragedy, malevolence, sorrow and suffering of life. The path of the hearth fire leads to a better life. The path of the hearth fire is the path where anxiety, bitterness, hopelessness and resentment can be confronted and made better, by taking on responsibility, by creating meaning, by aiming for and re-creating the hearth fire.

As part of my exploration of Western Yoga I studied with a school Dion Fortune had established and which is still thriving quietly today[24]. The path of the hearth fire was an important symbol for the school and one of the school's numerous written examinations required me to write a poem about the path of the hearth fire. My examination paper included the following:

> Beth of the twelfth,
> thank-you for your advice,
> "The hearth fire is where life begins its physical manifestation."
> I have struggled for so long,
> ignoring the pull at my heart strings,
> from the hearth fire.
> The lonely times cloistered in detachment from the world,
> when all along you were there providing warmth
> and the secret mysteries of the flames.
> The transmutation of the dense wood into the useful heat.
> The practical gifts of heating water and cooking food and
> providing solace and inspiration.
> The Eastern denigration of the hearth fire
> misplaced in my Western mind and Western heart.

Beth of the twelfth, thank-you for your vision in the flames,
the apparitions transparent but grounded in the hearth.
My house now built around the hearth fire.
A house now sound for the spirit to inhabit and thrive in useful service.

The path of the hearth fire symbolises the values of western civilization. The values have been taught continuously in the west since the times of the Chaldeans and the Sumerians, referred to above. The values are embedded in the Tree of Life. The values differ markedly from the values at the core of nihilism and from the values at the core of the yoga of the east[25].

The values, ethics and morality, the richness and the depth of wisdom in the Tree of Life is an antidote to the nihilism of the last 150 years. A similar view has been expressed by Dr Jordan Peterson in his book '12 Rules for Life: An Antidote to Chaos'. Dr Peterson writes 'We must have the meaning inherent in a profound system of value or the horror of existence rapidly becomes paramount. Then, nihilism beckons, with its hopelessness and despair.'[26] The profound system of value has been recorded by Western civilization in the Tree of Life.

Western civilization is based on the philosophies developed by Socrates, Plato and Aristotle, and those philosophies are based on the Tree of Life and what is known as the Western mystery tradition. Accordingly, in order to understand the values of western civilization, it is necessary to understand the Tree of Life and its role in the teachings of Pythagoras, Socrates, Plato and Aristotle.

Fundamental to Western Yoga and to the Tree of Life is the ideal that every human has a soul and that every human is created in the image of the creator (or the creation process). As noted above, the Tree of Life records this in summary form as 'As above, so below'. I will explore this later in more detail. A modern philosopher, A.H.Almaas, has written[27] about the importance to Western civilization of Socrates' view of the soul:

'Ancient Greek conceptions of soul are the primary sources of all Western views of soul, including those of Islam and Judaism. In fact, it is Socrates who is credited to be the father of the Western conception of soul, for he was the first to recognise that a human being is his soul.'

As we will explore, Socrates was a pupil of Pythagoras. Pythagoras, Socrates, Plato and Aristotle studied and taught the Tree of Life. The values of Western civilization are based on Western Yoga and its Tree of Life.

As I mentioned earlier, I am married to Sally Blair. Sal works as a clinical psychologist. It was Sal who first introduced me to Dion Fortune and the path of western yoga. At the end of many of the chapters in this book, Sal has provided insightful commentary on themes found in the chapter.

CHAPTER ONE

PATH 1 – The Kingdom

THE FIRST PATH of the Tree of Life, that we will explore, is known as The Kingdom[28]. The Kingdom sits at the very bottom of the Tree of Life. The path to the left of The Kingdom is known as The Power. The path to the right of The Kingdom is known as The Glory. It is a self-evident, but little-known fact, that the Lord's Prayer[29] which includes 'For yours is the kingdom and the power and the glory' was written by someone well acquainted with the Tree of Life[30].

The Tree of Life considers the world to be a place of physical action. The Tree of Life calls this place The Kingdom. It is the planet Earth. The Kingdom is located at the very foot of the Tree of Life. On one side of the Tree of Life is severity/order. On the other side is mercy/chaos. In the middle is equilibrium.

Dr Jordan Peterson has adopted a similar model. In '12 Rules for Life'[31] he summarises the approach he took in his book 'Maps of Meaning' in the following manner - 'Order and chaos are the yang and yin of the famous Taoist symbol...For the Taoists, meaning is to be found on the border between the ever-entwined pair. To walk the border is to stay on the path of life, the divine Way.'

The Tree of Life adopts that approach, but one that has more layers, as you will see. Severity is on the left side of the Tree of Life as you look at a picture of the Tree of Life. Severity is coloured black. Severity is made up of three paths or spheres[32] which sit suspended one above each other. The combined impact of the paths is to create 'order', or 'severity' as the term is used in the Tree of Life. Mercy is on the other side of the Tree of Life. Mercy is coloured white and is made up of three paths which sit suspended one above each other. Those paths create Mercy also known as 'chaos'. In between order and chaos is the middle pillar of equilibrium. At the foot of the pillar of equilibrium is the path or sphere of Earth known as The Kingdom. As noted earlier, suspended above The Kingdom and at the base of the Mercy / Chaos is The Power, and its opposite at the base of Severity / Order is The Glory. Hence the significance, noted above, of the Lord's Prayer which states 'yours is The Kingdom and The Power and The Glory'.

Demeter is the goddess associated with this Path of the Kingdom on the Tree of Life. The colourful, lusty and adventurous tales of Demeter have been studied by humans since at least 1,500BC. Demeter's adventures teach us about our deepest emotional needs, our most cherished longings and our share in the cyclical nature of life.

The raunchy tales of the goddess Demeter and their relevance to the Path known as the Kingdom were subjects taught in the western mystery schools of Pythagoras, Socrates, Plato and Aristotle.

Pythagoras, Socrates, Plato and Aristotle

Pythagoras, Socrates, Plato and Aristotle studied, trained and taught, in the western mystery schools[33]. The Tree of Life was a focal point of the western mystery schools[34].

The western mystery schools also taught politics and the importance of politics to western civilization and human flourishing. One of the greatest books written about politics is the one thousand page two volume work of Professor Alan Ryan titled 'On Politics: A History of Political Thought: From Herodotus to the Present'[35]. Professor Ryan was born in London in 1940 and was Professor of Political Theory at Oxford University for most of his professional life. From 1988 to 1996 he was Professor of Politics at Princeton University. It has been written of this book that 'If you want to understand why we think as we do, go back to the Ancient Greeks. Alan Ryan brilliantly explains why that is true – and why it matters.'[36] And 'With an unmatched magisterial command, Alan Ryan powerfully reminds us how the leading thinkers since classical times can and must inform our debates over how to envision the better world we must build.'[37], '...an unparalleled guide for our times to the Western tradition of political thought.'[38]

I found it fascinating that Professor Ryan had concluded, in his 72nd year, after a lifetime spent examining politics, that:

'Perhaps prayer rather than politics is the answer to the human condition.'[39]

The idea that 'perhaps prayer rather than politics is the answer to the human condition' is very similar to the view expressed by Jordan Peterson when he wrote[40] 'Maybe the environmental problem is ultimately spiritual. If we put ourselves in order, perhaps we will do the same for the world.'

Similarly, Ryan writes[41] 'The final thought that "Republic" inspires is that Plato's account of the ideal polity belongs to <u>soul craft</u> rather than to statecraft; it is not a picture of political life at all.' (emphasis added).

As noted in the introduction to this book, the idea of a 'soul' is an integral part of Western civilization. The reason why that is so will be explained in this chapter.

Professor Ryan's view that 'perhaps prayer rather than politics is the answer to the human condition' arose when he asked the question 'This is a book about the answers that historians, philosophers, theologians, practicing politicians, and would-be revolutionaries have given to one question. How can human beings best govern themselves?'[42]

What do we aim for, to make our lives better?

To understand the aims and values of western civilization it is necessary to understand the values in the Tree of Life as taught by Pythagoras, Socrates, Plato and Aristotle.

Almost all accounts of the history of political thinking begin with Plato, according to the considered opinion of Professor Ryan.[43] However, for Plato himself, it was the trial of Socrates that commenced the history of Western political thinking.[44] Accordingly, in order to understand the aims and values of Western political thinking it is necessary to explore Socrates. A great way to explore Socrates is through the book of Professor Gregory Vlastos titled 'Socrates: Ironist and moral philosopher'.[45] Professor Vlastos was born in 1907 in Turkey. He obtained a PhD from Harvard University and was Stuart Professor of Philosophy at Princeton University between 1955 and 1976 and thereafter at Berkeley. However, it is prudent to dig even more deeply and explore the relationship between Socrates and the earlier Pythagoreans. That is because, as Professor Vlastos notes, Plato came to Italy to study with the Pythagoreans.[46]

Pythagoras

Encyclopedia Britannica states summarily 'Pythagoras (born c 570 BCE) ... formulated principles that influenced the thought of Plato and Aristotle and contributed to the development of mathematics and Western rational philosophy... Pythagoras, however, is generally credited with the theory of the functional significance of numbers in the objective world and in music.'

Bertrand Russell in 'History of Western Philosophy' (1946) writes 'Pythagoras... was intellectually one of the most important men that ever lived...Mathematics, in the sense of demonstrative deductive argument, begins with him, and in him is intimately connected with a peculiar form of mysticism.' Roger Penrose in 'The Road to Reality: A Complete Guide to the Laws of the Universe' (2005) writes 'Although mathematical truths of various kinds had been surmised since ancient Egyptian and Babylonian times, it was not until the great Greek philosophers Thales of Miletus (c.625-547 BC) and Pythagoras of Samos (c.572-497 BC) began to introduce the notion of mathematical proof that the first firm foundation of mathematical understanding – and therefore of science itself – was laid.'

Professor Charles H Kahn, from the University of Pennsylvania, writes in 'Pythagoras and the Pythagoreans – a Brief History'[47] '... there is room for wide scholarly disagreement in evaluating the personal contribution for Pythagoras himself and the intellectual level attained in the early school. Burkert sees Pythagoras as essentially a religious or cultural leader, a guru rather than a scientist or philosopher, and he has been followed here by Carl Huffman in his important studies of Philolaus (1993) and Archytas (forthcoming). By contrast, a defense of the more traditional picture of Pythagoras as a great intellectual innovator has been presented in Leonid Zhmud's learned book 'Wissenschaft, Philosophie und Religion im fruhen Pythagoreismus (Berlin, 1997). The position to be argued for here reaches conclusions closer to those of Zhmud.'

Kahn also writes[48] 'Pythagoras is not only the most famous name in the history of philosophy before Socrates and Plato; he is also one of the most fascinating and mysterious figures of antiquity. Pythagoras was celebrated in the ancient tradition as a mathematician and a philosopher of mathematics, and his name is still linked to a major theorem in plane geometry. Aristotle claims that Plato's own philosophy was profoundly influenced by Pythagorean teaching and later authors regard Pythagoras as the creator of the Platonic tradition in philosophy. In the literature of late antiquity Pythagoras appears as a unique genius, the founding father for mathematics, music, astronomy and philosophy.'

Kahn writes[49] of the legends of Pythagoras that '... he was seen in Croton and Metapontum at the same time... Pythagoras could recall his previous incarnations, including the Trojan hero Euphorbus mentioned by Homer. His learning was universal. He first studied geometry and astronomy with Anaximander, then hieroglyphic symbolism with the priests of Egypt and the science of dreams with Hebrew masters. He studied also with the Arabs, with the Chaldaeans of Babylon… The story of Pythagoras' studies with the priests of Egypt is mentioned by Isocrates in the early fourth century BC and hinted at even earlier by Herodotus.'

The 20th century teacher known latterly as Osho (and formerly as Bhagwan Shree Rajneesh) wrote[50] 'The mandala meditation was the technique given to Pythagoras. Pythagoras went with this technique to Greece. And, really, he became the fountainhead, the source, of all mysticism in the West.'

Moshe Idel was Emeritus Max Cooper Professor in Jewish Thought at the Hebrew University in Jerusalem, Israel. Idel has taught at Harvard, Princeton and Yale. Idel has written[51] 'Both Luke and Philo… are very authoritative testimonies that Moses was very learned in all Egyptian doctrines. And all the Greeks who have been considered superior – Pythagoras, Plato ….used the Egyptians as masters… Pythagoras transferred many things from the Mosaic law into his own philosophy.' This is describing the merger of Jerusalem and Athens that I referred to earlier.

Johann Reuchlin was a Christian scholar born in Germany in 1455. Reuchlin wrote[52] extensively about the Tree of Life. Reuchlin wrote, in the dedicatory epistle of the book 'De arte cabalistica' to Pope Leo X, 'I have therefore written of the symbolic philosophy of the art of (the Tree of Life) so as to make Pythagorean doctrine better known to scholars.'

Khan writes[53] 'There is independent evidence for the unusual role of women as active participants in the Pythagorean community: Pythagoras' wife and daughter were both renowned for their wisdom.' As you will come to read, the Tree of Life values equally the female and the male. In this manner, Pythagoras and the Pythagorean community were living the values described in the Tree of Life.

Reuchlin has written[54] 'anyone of outstanding knowledge or intelligence was said to have studied under Pythagoras. Thus the principle school of Italian philosophy got its name. The Pythagorean Numenius agrees with this favourable account. In volume I of his book "On Good" he says that Plato and Pythagoras expounded in Greek what had been discovered by the Brahmans, the Magi, the Egyptians and the Jews'.

Reuchlin concluded[55] that the Tree of Life was 'the source for Pythagoras'. The primary teaching of the Tree of Life was 'as above, so below'. The teaching included the ideals that a human being was made in the image of god, that a human being had a soul and that life on earth was a place of action where a human could make her or his life better by taking personal responsibility for co-creating human life.

Socrates

What is known about Socrates is complicated by the fact that he made no writings. At least no writings that anyone has ever seen, ever. What we know about Socrates comes from the writings about him by Plato and others. Socrates was born about 470 BC in Athens. He trained initially as a stonemason. For many years he was a citizen-soldier, known as a Hoplite, who fought in the unsuccessful Peloponnesian War, armed with a spear and a shield. The Peloponnesian war was between Athens and Sparta and continued for more than 25 years.

Socrates was considered to be very wise. Plato wrote in his book titled 'Apology' that Socrates' friend Chaerephon asked the Oracle[56] at Delphi if there was anyone wiser than Socrates and that the Oracle said that no-one was wiser than Socrates[57]. This was no small accolade, for the reasons that follow. The role of the Oracle of Delphi was an interesting civic position. It was held by the High Priestess of the Temple of Apollo at Delphi who held the rank and title of Pythia. The Pythia was considered to be the most powerful woman of the classical world. The role was abolished in the 4th century AD by the Roman Emperor Theodosius the First. The role of Pythia was held by three women at any one time. They shared the task of providing prophecy, which task was performed once a month but only during the nine warmest months of the year. Carved into the entrance to the Delphic Temple were two phrases. One of which was 'gnothi seauton' which means 'know thyself'. Cicero stated that no important political decisions were made unless the Oracle agreed that the decision was appropriate.

Ryan, the academic political scholar, describes Socrates as 'a mystic'[58] and notes[59] that on a number of occasions Socrates is recorded as saying that it is not he who is speaking but a force beyond his control. This is consistent with the description provided by Vlastos[60] that in Plato's 'Apology', Plato records Socrates saying 'I came by this reputation (the wisest person in Athens), O Athenians, only by a sort of wisdom. What sort? Exactly that which is, no doubt, human wisdom. It looks as though in this I really am wise. But those of whom I spoke just now would be wise in a wisdom that is more than human – I don't know how else to speak of it.'

Vlastos records[61] Plato's attribution to Socrates that 'I believe I am one of few Athenians, not to say the only one, to engage in the true political art and of the men of today I am the only one who does politics. And now, most excellent man, that you are beginning to engage in the city's affairs and you invite me to do the same, reproaching me for not doing so, shall we not examine each other and ask "Come, has Callicles made any of the citizens a better man? Is there anyone – alien or citizen, slave or freeman – who previously a bad man, unjust, intemperate, foolish – has become a good and honorable man because of Callicles?' Vlastos considers[62] that the above passage demonstrates that 'No one who heard Socrates say this could be left in doubt that by "the true political art" Socrates could only mean the art whose exercise improves the moral character of one's fellow-townsmen...' This reminds me of Jordan Peterson's approach[63], to the effect that improvement of one's moral character is the antidote to chaos and a proper aim for human political aspiration. Ryan notes[64] that Socrates stated, with admirable prescience, that women should receive exactly the same education as men. This is utterly consistent with the equality between female and male displayed by the Tree of Life.

Socrates' political and philosophical views are also recorded in the 'Republic' which was written by Plato around 380 BC. The Republic is made up of ten books. Book 1 investigates the moral domain. Socrates' goal is 'to determine the conduct of our life – how each of us should conduct himself to live the most advantageous life'.[65] Books 2 to 5 deal with questions such as 'What is a state?', 'What is a perfectly good state?', 'What is the institutional structure of its society?'. Books 4 to 10 identify a theory of the ideal state, among other matters. It is evident that a hierarchy of aims, goals, paths and values, to make life better, are being described by Socrates.

After the trial and execution of Socrates in 399 BC, Plato and many of Socrates' followers went into voluntary exile. Several years later Plato returned to Athens and founded the Academy in 387 BC.[66] The Academy has been recognised as 'the first philosophical school'[67]. Plato taught there for the rest of his life. The motto of the Academy was 'Let nobody approach who does not know geometry'. The Academy continued for more than 900 years, until 529 AD. Socrates' life's work of creating an aim and goal in order to answer his question 'how to live the most advantageous life' shows how Socrates aimed high to make his life better by taking on high values and high personal responsibilities.

Plato

Plato was born in Athens in 427BC and died in 347BC. Plato scholar Julia Annas states that there is 'nothing implausible' in the idea that Plato travelled to and studied in Egypt searching for the wisdom that the Greeks considered came originally from older Eastern countries[68]. Reuchlin has written[69] that 'Numenius the Pythagorean aptly described Plato as none other than Moses speaking Attic Greek'. Plato's two most famous books are 'Timaeus' and 'Republic'. In 'Timaeus' Plato sets out his metaphysical thinking. In 'Republic' Plato sets out his political thinking. Plato's book 'Laws' contains elements of both metaphysical thinking and political thinking.

Plato considered that wisdom arose from 'dialegesthai' (discussion) and that required a particular type of thinking which he called 'dialectic'. A regular topic that was discussed in a dialectic manner by Plato in Timaeus is the Tree of Life / Cabalistic[70] concept of 'Forms'. Forms function as patterns which manifest in The Kingdom but the Forms 'are, without coming to be'. Annas has written[71] 'This is the important metaphysical difference between Forms on the one hand and, on the other, the items around us which are said to "participate in" Forms, or be "likenesses" or "images" of the them.' This is a description of the manner in which the 10 paths of the Tree of Life interact and in particular how Forms function as patterns which manifest in The Kingdom but which do not themselves come into being in The Kingdom.[72]

Ryan makes the perceptive observation that 'If the premise is accepted (ie Plato's premise) that the crucial task of politics is to align the social, economic and political order with a divinely appointed natural order('As above, so below'), a central role must be found for whoever understands that order, if not as the day-to-day ruler of a society, then as a spiritual guardian of the day-to-day ruler. How that authority is to be exercised is a question that roiled medieval Christendom and remains unanswered in the Muslim world. In Medieval Europe the question whether popes could depose kings was one aspect of it; in the modern world Iran is an avowed theocracy, while Israel is avowedly but uneasily not one.'[73] (Words in parentheses have been added by me).

The Tree of Life demonstrates that the expansion associated with the paths on the left of the Tree of Life, needs to be balanced by the conservation associated with the paths on the right side of the Tree of Life. In this way there was to be an equilibrium in the middle pillar, from time to time, when the pendulum swings back and forth across the middle pillar. Jordan Peterson has reached a similar conclusion[74] albeit not by recourse to the Tree of Life. Ryan provides a description of Plato's idea that is consistent with both the

Tree of Life and Jordan Peterson, when Ryan writes 'If utopia could be created, surely it would endure forever. Not so, says Plato… Decay follows a cyclical path. First, honor superseded wisdom as the basis of authority; the wise elite will become a "timocracy", or an aristocracy based on honor; this in turn will degenerate into an oligarchy where rich men oppress their inferiors.'[75] This is describing the way the paths on the right of the Tree of Life turn towards stolid inertia over time. And how the paths on the left of the Tree of Life can ameliorate that problem, but at the risk of overshooting into chaotic unbridled fecundity.

Plato returns time and again in his writings to the theme of how people can live a good life. Plato considers that a good life is the product of using your attributes, your talents, like a craftsperson uses tools and materials. Plato describes our 'virtues' like courage and wisdom as 'divine goods'. He describes health and wealth as 'human goods'.[76]

Plato considered that human beings not only possessed a soul but that such soul was an immortal soul.[77] Almaas has written that 'Plato did not use reason to prove the existence of the divine; he used it as a facet needed for the development of a way of knowing that can experientially penetrate to the divine.'[78] This reminds me of Dion Fortune's statement to the effect that the Tree of Life is used to train the mind not to inform it.

The importance of 'soul' to Plato is apparent when Annas writes[79] 'Further, Plato never doubts that when I ask what I, myself, really am, the answer will be that I am my soul, rather than my animated body. Hence Socrates, on his deathbed, jokingly reminds his friends that they will not be burying him, only his body.' Plato wrote in 'Phaedo' (78b-84b) of the soul being akin to the objects of pure thought which are unaffected by any of the sources of change in the world of our sensory experience[80].

Almaas has written[81] about the importance to Western civilization of Plato's view of the soul:

'Ancient Greek conceptions of soul are the primary sources of all Western views of soul, including those of Islam and Judaism. In fact, it is Socrates who is credited to be the father of the Western conception of soul, for he was the first to recognise that a human being is his soul.'

And:

'Plato basically systematized the Socratic way of philosophy in his metaphysical system, where he established a clear and distinct supersensible dimension, that of the eternal ideas, the counterpart to the physical and the sensory. The ideal or intelligible dimension is composed of eternal realities, perfect and heavenly, and the soul is "the intelligible and immaterial aspect of man, and it is as eternal as the intelligible is eternal." (Giovanni Reale 'A History of Ancient Philosophy: Plato and Aristotle, p.140). He believed that the soul is eternal, and saw this as necessary for her to be able to know the immutable and eternal ideas. This means that he believed the soul to originate from this spiritual dimension…"We have now learned, not only that Plato considers the soul to be immortal but that he considers it to be in some essential way akin to the eternal Forms, changeless, simple, without parts, ever the same… we shall find the soul gradually absorbing all of man that is not sheer physical matter." (G.M. Grube 'Plato's Thought, p.129).'

Reuchlin has written[82] about Plato's 'Timaeus' that 'I think so highly of these words of Plato, as the instructions of a man who was truly wise, that I have considered it worthwhile to keep them with me as a kind of oracle. And if there are any fundamental beliefs, any fixed points in (the Tree of Life) then these are they.'

Plato continued the lineage of the Tree of Life from Pythagoras to Socrates and then to Plato. The principal value passed down the line was the fundamental role of the immortal human soul that absorbed the experiences of life in The Kingdom and was capable of being made better by confronting and fixing our anxieties, hopelessness, resentfulness and bitterness by deciding to pursue and aiming at the highest goals.

Aristotle

Aristotle was born in 384 BC. He moved to Athens in 367 BC, at around 17 years of age, to study with Plato at Plato's Academy[83]. Aristotle lived there for 20 years. Aristotle was a prolific writer. He wrote more than 150 books. Topics included constitutional history, astronomy, mathematics, law, politics, ethics, zoology, biology, chemistry, space and time[84]. Dante described Aristotle as 'the master of those who know'[85]. The lineage from Pythagoras to Aristotle, via Socrates and Plato is well established[86].

What is also well established is Aristotle's view that it is important for human beings to value 'reputable opinions' for ethical and moral guidance. In his book entitled 'Topics' he advises that we ought to collect 'reputable opinions' and use them as starting points to develop a vision for our lives. By 'reputable opinions' Aristotle is referring to the aims, goals, paths and values of Western civilization including that of his teacher Plato, and Plato's teacher Socrates, influenced by the thinking of Pythagoras and the Pythagoreans.

This is apparent when Aristotle writes in his book 'On the Soul'[87], 'For our study of soul it is necessary...to call into council the views of those of our predecessors...The doctrine of the Pythagoreans seems to rest upon the same ideas...In the same way Plato in the Timaeus...'.

As noted by Jonathan Barnes[88], 'He (Aristotle) was highly conscious of his own position at the end of a long line of thinkers; he had a strong sense of intellectual history and of his own place therein.' Aristotle considered, in his book 'Nicomachean Ethics', that reputable opinions may prove to be the end-points as well as the starting-points for the creation of ethical and moral values 'for if the difficulties are solved and the reputable opinions remain, sufficient prove of the matter will have been given.'[89]

Aristotle was known to be a fastidious collector of proverbs[90]. Aristotle considered that proverbs contained wise ethics, morals, aims, goals and paths. Aristotle considered[91] that respect for tradition, and valuing tradition, was important for the steady growth of knowledge about ethics and morality. The approach lauded by Aristotle, of valuing ethics and morality and building incrementally on those traditional values, contrasts sharply with the nihilism of Nechayev, described earlier when Nechayev wrote[92] 'The only form of revolution beneficial to the people is one which destroys the entire State to the roots and exterminated all the state traditions, institutions and classes in Russia... the nobility, the bureaucracy, the clergy, the traders and the parasitic kulaks.' At the considerable risk of oversimplifying 'identity politics', the extreme left might be characterised as having adopted a Nihilistic Nechayevean Pillar of Chaos and Mercy approach. Whereas the extreme right has adopted an equally unbalanced Pillar of Severity approach. The Middle Pillar on the Tree of Life is the Pillar of Equilibrium and that is the zone to be pursued.

Our Tree of Life team of Pythagoras, Socrates, Plato and Aristotle are shown in a famous painting entitled 'The School of Athens'. It was painted by Raphael in about 1510 for the library of Pope Julius the second. The painting has as its focal point Plato and Aristotle. Plato is standing and holding his book the 'Timaeus' and pointing upwards. Socrates stands to Plato's right separated by seven men and women. Aristotle is standing next to Plato, very slightly in front of Plato. Aristotle's right arm is resting against Plato's left arm. Aristotle is looking at Plato. Aristotle is holding the book Aristotle wrote called 'Ethics' and Aristotle is gesturing outwards. Pythagoras is seated in the left foreground. Socrates, Plato and Aristotle are shown between Pythagoras and Euclid in the right foreground[93]. The painting is described by Annas in the following manner: 'The contrasting gestures indicate that Aristotle is more concerned to understand the world around us in terms of philosophical principles, while Plato is more austerely focused on the abstract and theoretical principles themselves.'

The painting is important because it records and recognizes your heritage. The painting is like a photo from a family album. These are the people on whose shoulders you can stand today.

Ryan writes[94] that 'when the cultural renaissance of the twelfth century reinvigorated classical scholarship in western Europe, it was Aristotle's 'Politics'[95] rather than Plato's 'Republic' that scholars turned to for political illumination'. In 335 BC Aristotle founded his own school, the Lyceum, in Athens.[96] Aristotle tutored Alexander the Great[97]. Ryan states that Aristotle's 'political analysis is an engrossing mixture of practical wisdom and an almost Platonic attempt to show that the best state is best "by nature".'[98]

The relationship between Aristotle and the Constitution of the United States of America is described by Ryan in the following manner[99]:

'Aristotle bequeaths to posterity the thought that the extent and the nature of authority that sustains human associations are determined by the functions for which the association exists, that is, by the nature of the association. Locke's analysis of the authority of government in his 'Second Treatise', published in 1690, relies on just this thought two millennia later; whether through Locke's influence or by some other route, the thought itself is enshrined in the American Constitution with its commitment to limited government, and the measuring of authority by the goals to be sought.'

Aristotle shared the aim of Plato to create public-spirited citizens.[100] Aristotle argued for private production and common use.[101] In that regard Ryan has written[102]:

'He (Aristotle) saw a truth that the state of much public space reinforces today; we think it belongs to nobody, and we neglect it. For a man to have an incentive to provide for his family, he must think of it as *his* family; to have an incentive to look after his farm and crops in the most productive way, he must see them as his. Aristotle argues for private production and common use.'

Aristotle's views on the nature of citizenship, the qualities of good constitutions and the causes of revolution are topics that have kept his work in circulation for more than two and a half thousand years.[103] Seymour Martin Lipset, the world famous Professor of Government and Sociology at Harvard University, has acknowledged[104] our debt to Aristotle in identifying and creating the conditions for stable liberal democratic government.

How did Pythagoras, Socrates, Plato and Aristotle think thoughts that were of such value as to remain in circulation for more than two and a half thousand years? The answer might be found in Iain McGilchrist's masterpiece 'The Master and his Emissary – The Divided Brain and the Making of the Western World'[105]. The book has been described as 'the most comprehensive, profound book ever written on brain laterality'[106].

McGilchrist suggests that during the lifetimes of those ancient Greeks there was a development in human beings of enhanced frontal lobe function.[107] The enhanced frontal lobe function, McGilchrist states, created the circumstances for 'increased independence of the hemispheres, allowing each hemisphere to make characteristic advances in function, and for a while to do so in harmony with its fellow'[108]. However, since that time, McGilchrist states 'there has been a relentless growth of self-consciousness, leading to increasing difficulties in co-operation … the balance of power has shifted … further and further towards the part-world created by the left hemisphere.'[109]

What McGilchrist is describing is an evolutionary process that occurred in the hemispheres of the human brain during the period in which Pythagoras, Socrates, Plato and Aristotle were living. The process was one in which their left and right cerebral hemispheres operated in unprecedented harmony. Human beings who lived subsequently operated with a left hemisphere dominance that precluded the harmonious interaction of left hemisphere and right hemisphere that was characteristic of the thinkers of ancient Greece. If McGilchrist is correct, that may provide an explanation as to the longevity of the teachings of those teachers. That is, those teachers had an advantage that we do not have. Those teachers were able to perceive and deliberate with a left and right hemisphere that was characterised by greater harmony than we have ready access to today. Because those teachers had that advantage they were able to perceive and articulate matters in extraordinary depth. We will explore McGilchrist's work in more detail in chapter two.

Polybius and Cicero

The Tree of Life teachings of Pythagoras, Socrates, Plato and Aristotle, and in particular the importance of the soul and the importance of the betterment of the soul, arising from the values of meaningful, ethical and moral actions carried out in The Kingdom, was continued by Polybius and Cicero.

Plato and Aristotle provided the foundations for one of Western civilization's most important and famous features, known as the doctrine of the separation of powers.[110] [111] The doctrine of the separation of powers is a central feature of stable democratic government. The separation of powers is the separation of the executive, judicial and legislative branches into distinct and separate institutions. 'It is no accident, then, that so many who gathered at Philadelphia to declare independence and a decade later to draft a constitution were men who had apprenticed themselves to … Plato, Aristotle, Polybius and Cicero, and who could debate at length on the various constitutional forms of the classical world before they chose one for the new American nation. We owe our very existence as a people in part to classical learning.'[112]

The influence of the United States federal model (the doctrine of the separation of powers) on the Australian Constitution and on the decisions of the High Court of Australia, the nation's constitutional court, is well recognized[113]. The Australian Constitution came into legal being as part of a British Act of Parliament in 1900. That was necessary because at the time Australia was a collection of six self-governing British colonies. Similarly, Canada was created by an act of Parliament of the United Kingdom called the British North America Act 1867. At the time Canada was a self-governing British colony. The Canadian Constitution adopts the doctrine of the separation of powers of the executive, the legislative and the judicial. New Zealand's Constitution Act 1986 uses the same doctrine of the separation of powers. A South African academic has written 'There is virtually no constitution, written or unwritten in the modern world, that is not structured, in one way or another, on the basic doctrine of (the separation of powers).'[114] A famous Australian High Court judge has written 'Roman law is the fruit of the researches of the most learned men, the collective wisdom of the ages and the groundwork of the municipal law of most of the countries in Europe.'[115]

Inherent to the legal doctrine of the separation of powers is the legal concept of the individual and the legal obligations and legal rights of the individual. As Ryan notes[116] 'The individual Roman was free from personal oppression by any other Roman; the story of Saint Paul's dealings with the Roman legal authorities in Acts of the Apostles suggests how important that was.' Ryan is referring to Saint Paul's assertion of his citizenship 'civis Romanus sum' when he was faced with scourging and brutality at the hands of soldiers enforcing law and order. See Acts 16:22 to 29. President John F. Kennedy invoked the phrase and the legal concept when he stated famously in 1963 'Two thousand years ago, the proudest boast was 'civis Romanus sum'. Today, in the world of freedom, the proudest boast is "Ich bin ein Berliner".'[117]

The writings of Polybius and Cicero, including in particular De Republica, De Legibus and De Officiis, provide important historical resources for understanding the Roman legal and political system and the important legal and philosophical concept of the self and the soul (the 'I am') for citizens of the world. As Ryan notes 'Cicero's skill was to combine ideas about virtue from Stoic, Platonic and Aristotelian sources while glossing over their differences, and to make them applicable not to the Roman statesman but to the citizens of the world.'[118]

Jordan Peterson has identified[119] the importance to Western civilization of the development of the concept that humans are created in the image of the divine and that there is 'a spark of the divine' in every human, so that one can say of one's self 'civis Romanus sum'. Consistent with Jordan Peterson's approach, it has been written by A.H.Almaas that:

'Ancient Western thinkers understood human subjectivity or consciousness to include a spiritual dimension. Socrates originated the understanding of soul as comprising all of the individual consciousness; Plato and others further developed it.'[120]

Almaas has also written[121] 'this notion of soul originated with Socrates and subsequently became the primary Western conception'... 'The original Socratic concept of soul became what we now call self, denuded of the substance and richness of its original meaning. The ancient concept of soul included both of the modern concepts of self and soul, but excluded the body. For these ancients, especially for those following Socrates, the individual self was inseparable from its essential and spiritual elements.'[122]

In De Republica and in De Legibus, Cicero explains Roman constitutional theory and tackles the nature of law and the rule of law. The writing imitates the style of Plato's Republic and Plato's Laws and uses a Socratic dialogue. Cicerco focuses on the relationship between the law of nature, which Cicero equates with divine law, and the law of a particular state. As Ryan notes 'His (Cicero) account of the law is ... law is the deliverance of right reason... it treats everyone equally; the mere say-so of any particular group of people does not suffice to make their decrees law. This last claim is the crux of Cicero's natural law theory. Laws must be properly made and for the right reasons to be laws at all. It became the basis of one of the most important – and hotly disputed – claims of medieval and subsequent jurisprudence: injusta lex nulla lex est. A law that violates justice is not a law at all. It is the view that sustains the claim that Nazi legislation depriving Jews of all civil and political rights could not have been a valid law, because it was too unjust to count as law at all...'[123]

You will recall that the context in which we are looking at Cicero is that he is part of a lineage that taught the Western mystery tradition and its Tree of Life. You will recall also that the right wing (so to speak) of the Tree of Life (when dealing with the Tree subjectively as described below) is the pillar of severity and the left wing is the pillar of mercy. That structure is embedded in Cicero's concept of the nature of law, which as we have seen, is foundational to the legal constitutions of the Western world, as is apparent from the analysis by Ryan:

'Justice (that is the pillar of severity) is the desire to give each man his own, to preserve as common what is common, and to keep private what is private; and Cicero raises all the still familiar questions about how we should distinguish between justice (the pillar of severity) and benevolence (the pillar of mercy) – the line between giving people what they are entitled to (the pillar of severity) as opposed to giving them what they are not entitled to but what we are prompted to give them out of generosity (the pillar of mercy).'[124] (The words in parenthesis have been added by me).

The fundamental manner in which the values of the Tree of Life and its teachers Pythagoras, Socrates, Plato and Aristotle have provided the foundation for Western civilisation and for the values of Western civilization is apparent from the descriptions above. In particular, you can decide to create, live and labour in a hierarchy of ethical and moral values as the way to make your life better. The Tree of Life teaches that 'as above, so below' means that you have a soul which is divine and which can be made better by aiming at the highest goal you can manage. In that way your life has a transcendent purpose, your potential is unlocked through the voluntary assumption of responsibility and the sacrifice of nihilistic and hedonistic short term values. The realisation that you are participating in the creation of humanity itself brings with it a massive realisation of responsibility. You can create, in your own family, your own gulags and Auschwitz's. You can make your life better by confronting anxiety, bitterness, hopelessness and resentment by creating meaning through taking on responsibility for making your life better in The Kingdom. Traveling knowingly the very well-trodden paths on the Tree of Life, while aiming for the highest ethical and moral goals you can manage, is the way to get your life together, to make your life better and is an antidote to the nihilism and meaninglessness associated with post-modernism.

Exploring The Kingdom (path 1) on The Tree of Life

As described above, The Kingdom is located on the Tree of Life in the centre or middle pillar known as the Pillar of Equilibrium. As one looks at the Tree, on the left hand side is the Pillar of Severity and on the right hand side is the Pillar of Mercy. That is how the Tree is structured when viewed by an objective bystander. Interestingly, when using the Tree for personal subjective practices one stands with one's back to the Tree so that on one's right hand side is the pillar of severity and on one's left hand side is the pillar of mercy[125]. This subjective alignment accords with the language of political left and political right. From a subjective perspective The Kingdom is located between the left hand side of the body and the right hand side of body, that is The Kingdom is located in the position of one's spinal column and located above The Kingdom is one's gut, one's heart and one's head. Putting that another way, the structure of the Tree of Life, when considered from a subjective perspective, includes the proposition that one's head, one's heart and one's gut contribute to one's actions in The Kingdom in which one acts. And that the place of action is in The Kingdom in the Pillar of Equilibrium located between the Pillar of Severity and the Pillar of Mercy. Jordan Peterson has reached the same conclusion albeit by a different model[126].

Aristotle wrote at length[127] about what it is to be a successful human being. He concluded that to be in 'eudaimonia' is to make a success of life. Eudaimonia means flourishing, in 21st century parlance. Eudaimonia is not a synonym for happiness. There is a connection between Eudaimonia and happiness but that connection is indirect. Aristotle concluded that Eudaimonia is 'an activity of the soul in accordance with excellence'[128]. Importantly, eudaimonia refers to engagement in activity, it is not a feeling, it is not a state of mind. The activities to be pursued are those activities in which your soul excels.

Artistotle wrote that humans 'are not isolated individuals, and the human excellences cannot be practiced by hermits'[129]. The approach described by Aristotle serves to highlight the difference in emphasis between Western civilization and the vairagya of the yoga of the East.

Western Myths teach the values of Western Civilisation

One really good way to work with the Tree of Life is the contemplative exercise known as 'pathworking' or as Carl Jung called it 'active imagination'[130]. The purpose of active imagination is to provide practical experience of the values contained in the Tree of Life[131].

Modern psychology considers that we all have instinctive forces operating inside of us. The gods and goddesses are archetypes and symbols of our instincts. The stories about their deeds teach us about values.

Dr Liz Greene has written[132] that:

'Myth portrays universal truths and fundamental human patterns which do not alter, and which stand outside the trends of any particular time… Myths are archetypal, timeless and universal…They arise from deep levels of the psyche that the ego cannot control…'

One good way of exploring and understanding the deeds and nature of gods and goddesses, like Demeter, is by reading the fantastic book by Robert Graves 'The Greek Myths', Penguin Classics Deluxe Edition,1955 and 2012, Penguin Publishing Group, Kindle Edition. The following material is assembled from that book[133].

The brilliant children's author Rick Riordan, the author of the series 'Percy Jackson and the Olympians', of which there are more than 20 million copies in print, wrote the introduction to the most recent edition of Robert Graves 'The Greek Myths'. Riordan wrote that 'In the end, that is why these myths have survived and continue to speak to us. They provide a road map for the human condition—our own lives reflected in the looking glass of the gods.'[134]

The Kingdom and the goddess Demeter

Demeter's adventures teach us about our deepest emotional needs, our most cherished longings and our share in the cyclical nature of life.

Demeter is the goddess of fertility, of grain and agriculture. Demeter has been a goddess for about 9,000 years, from the time when humans started growing and eating corn.

Once upon a time there was a very beautiful goddess named Demeter. When Demeter was young a ray of sunshine used to follow her around like the way limelight follows an actor on a stage. Demeter was always found bathing in this stream of bright sunshine. Demeter would sing merrily as she walked bare footed among the ploughed fields that were being made ready for the planting of crops. Wherever Demeter walked bright green moist seedlings would burst forth from her footprints on the ground. Demeter literally dripped and oozed holy love. Demeter was pure goodness and goodness was the fabric of everything about her and around her. Demeter was divine love personified and was surrounded by and immersed in divine love. Demeter's life was lived in a bubble of divine love and the bubble enclosed the whole of the world.

Demeter fell in love with the god Zeus. Zeus was a very handsome and powerful god and he adored Demeter. Zeus would spend hours and hours each day ploughing Demeter's paddock, as the Ancient Greeks used to say in their metaphoric manner. Demeter became pregnant. Rivers of tears of golden joy were cried when their daughter Persephone was born. Persephone was a breathtakingly beautiful young goddess. Persephone also radiated divine love. Sadly, not long after Persephone's birth, Zeus commenced ploughing the paddocks of a great many other goddesses and mortal women.

Demeter started to feel a lack of love from Zeus. Then Demeter started to feel unlovable at her very core. Demeter felt like the divine fabric of love that had been all around her had moved on somewhere else. Demeter felt like she was missing part of herself, that she was incomplete. Demeter started to feel that the goddesses and mortal women Zeus was now ploughing day and night were more interesting, more important and more valuable than her. Demeter felt like she was vanishing and fading into the background. Demeter felt she was less lovable than other goddesses and mortal women and that felt very, very painful for Demeter. Whereas Demeter previously loved being the focal point of the bright sunlight, with eyes on her wherever she went, Demeter now felt only pain and numbness. Demeter started to feel comfortable in the background and very frightened whenever the sunlight singled her out and shone on her. Demeter became numb through and through. Demeter started sleeping longer and longer and longer, hiding away from Zeus and Persephone and life itself.

Demeter would find a dark secluded nook in her royal palace and would hide away. Sometimes Demeter would hide away in her nook for many days. Demeter found she could no longer decide what to do with her days. And very often after Demeter had made up her mind to do something she then was unable to follow through and do it. Demeter became indolent and slothful. It was not as though Demeter was entirely inactive but rather that she could no longer work out what was essential for her to do, and if eventually she decided to do something she could not follow through and keep on track. Demeter thought to herself 'I am unlovable. I am missing a part of me. I am not fully formed.' Day by day Demeter ate more and more and more and slept more and more and more and her body became very, very heavy and leaden. Demeter started to collect more and more things and her once beautiful palace became cluttered, dank and dark.

Demeter's daughter Persephone grew into a very beautiful young woman. Persephone was like Demeter had been in her younger days. Persephone glowed in the limelight of the bright sunshine. Persephone dripped divine love and people crowded around her to be bathed in the fabric of divine love. Suitors came from the four corners of the earth seeking to win Persephone's heart. Sadly, this blissful oasis of holy love was about to be shattered. Demeter had a brother in law named Hades. Hades was the king of the underworld. He lived underground in the underworld. The underworld was devoid of holy love. The underworld was bleak and cold and lacked beauty. Hades desperately wanted Persephone to come and live in the underworld to add holy love, colour and beauty to the otherwise drab underworld. Hades was the eldest brother of Zeus. Hades asked his brother Zeus for Persephone's hand. Zeus did not want to offend Hades. Zeus lacked the courage to refuse his elder brother. Zeus said to Hades 'I neither give nor withhold my consent.' This emboldened Hades. He abducted Persephone while she was picking flowers in a meadow and took her in chains to the underworld to be his bride forever and ever.

Demeter was devastated beyond words. Persephone had been the last remnant of the fabric of divine love for Demeter. Demeter's memories of the days when the whole of manifestation was the stuff of love had faded to the point of near invisibility. Demeter found herself doubting there had ever been a time everyone was full of pure goodness. It was only being around Persephone that kept that ember of the memory of holy love alive for Demeter. But now that ember had been stolen by Hades and imprisoned in the underworld.

Demeter felt morose and numb without Persephone. Demeter felt unlovable, by everyone and by everything. Demeter felt that her life was without purpose and without meaning because she was incomplete.

However, at the same time Demeter was descending to the tragic depths of utter despair, something curious started happening to her. Demeter started to spend more and more time reminiscing about and reflecting on the wonderful days when she and Persephone had danced through meadows in the bright sunshine and grains had sprouted green shoots from under their footprints as they danced in the divine love that they wore like an ethereal cloak. As Demeter turned more and more inwards towards the depth of herself she began to get clear what she needed to do. Demeter started to change dramatically. As Demeter remembered more and more about the days when she had oozed divine love from her every pore she felt herself waking up from her self-forgetting indolence.

Demeter started very, very slowly to become joyful again. Demeter started to journey out of her secluded nook. Demeter started to move around her palace. Then one day Demeter ventured out into the blazing sunshine. As Demeter felt the sunshine on her now very pale skin, Demeter started to remember the feelings of divine love. Slowly and slowly, day by day, Demeter ventured into the sunshine and began to feel lovable and loved by the divine sunshine that was bathing her and bathing all those around her. Then one day Demeter walked barefoot across the moist black rich soil of a nearby paddock and Demeter felt divine love flowing through her body and out of her feet. Demeter looked back at her footprints and saw that lush green iridescent shoots of corn had spouted from her foot imprints in the soil. Demeter knew in that moment she would journey to the four corners of the earth in search for her beloved daughter Persephone. Demeter commenced her journey immediately and searched without rest, neither eating nor drinking, and all the time calling out Persephone's name. Demeter's heavy laden body became lighter and lighter as each day passed. But still Demeter was unable to find Persephone.

On one of her journeys, Demeter came in disguise to Eleusis to search for Persephone. Demeter was starting to glow more and more with divine love and people started to congregate around her. The King and Queen of Eleusis invited Demeter to stay on as wet-nurse to their newly-born Prince. Demeter felt great love for the little mortal princeling and decided that she would make the Prince immortal. That night Demeter held the prince over the hearth fire, to burn away his mortality. However, the Queen happened to enter the hall before the process was complete, and broke the spell; so the Prince lost his chance to become immortal and god-like. The Queen and the King were very angry at Demeter because they thought Demeter was a dangerous witch who had tried to murder their son. Demeter fled from Eleusis with the help of a kindly prison guard who understood how Demeter had tried to bestow divine immortality on the baby prince.

Demeter continued to journey all around the world looking diligently but unsuccessfully for Persephone. Sadly, Demeter became very resentful and decided to punish the world. To punish the world Demeter forbade all trees to yield fruit and forbade all herbs to grow. Humans grew hungry and were on the verge of extinction.

Zeus knew he had to do something to stop the human race from starving to death. But Zeus was ashamed to visit Demeter in person at Eleusis because of the way Zeus had treated Persephone. Zeus sent a deputation of the Olympian gods to Eleusis, with conciliatory gifts for Demeter. But Demeter said she would not return to Olympus, and swore that the earth must remain barren until Persephone had been returned.

Only one course of action remained for Zeus. He sent Hermes, the messenger god, with a message to Hades: 'If you do not restore Persephone, we are all undone!' and with another to Demeter: 'You may have your daughter again, on the single condition that she has not yet tasted the food of the dead.'

Unfortunately, unbeknown to Zeus, Persephone had eaten seven seeds from a pomegranate that had grown on a pomegranate tree in Hades' garden. That meant that Zeus' condition could not be met and Persephone could not be released from the Underworld.

On hearing about the pomegranate and Persephone being unable to leave the underworld, Demeter grew more dejected than ever, and said: 'I will neither return to Olympus, nor remove my curse from the land.'

Demeter found a dark, dingy, cramped cave on the outskirts of a remote desert and slumped into sloth. Demeter was convinced she was unlovable and that divine love had abandoned her forever. Demeter's curse was in place and remained in place by slothful default. No crops grew. There was no corn and no wheat. No grains of any kind. The fruit trees were barren. No leaves, no flowers, no fruit. The bountiful, natural fertility of the earth was replaced by inert, infertile paddocks. Years and years went by. Hundreds of thousands of humans died in the infertile wasteland that arose from Demeter's sloth. Humans were faced with starvation and extinction.

Demeter' mother Rhea had been watching quietly for many years as the tragedy unfolded. Rhea knew that she had to intervene in order to save humans from extinction. As Demeter's mother, Rhea knew from past experience that Demeter's resentful, slothful, inert mood could be shifted. Rhea knew that Demeter would move on from her indolence when Demeter felt bathed in divine love. So, Rhea reached an agreement with Hades. The agreement was that Persephone would stay underground in the underworld with Hades for three months every year. In those three months Persephone would bring her vitality and colour to the underworld. However, in the remaining nine months every year, Persephone would rise from the underworld and would live with Demeter above ground.

As soon as Demeter heard of the arrangement, she saw a tiny, tiny beam of sunshine come through a huge stained glass window in her palace. Demeter moved her head so that the sunshine warmed her ear. Demeter felt a tiny tingle of divine love caress her ear and create a super power ability in her ear to listen to her deepest feelings and thoughts. Each day as Demeter listened more and more to her deepest feelings and thoughts she counted down the three months, waiting for the returning home of Persephone. Demeter found herself listening to herself reminiscing about the days gone by when she felt divine love everywhere around her and in her. As Demeter listened to herself more and more, her feelings of numbness and leadenness started to slowly, slowly subside. Demeter's feelings of numbness, leadenness and unlovableness were slowly, slowly, day by day being replaced by a delightful feeling of sharp awareness of what needed to be done and how to do it.

Demeter threw out the dusty furnishings that were cluttering Persephone's bedroom. Demeter set up her throne outdoors. The mortals were amazed at how a beam of sunlight would always shine down on Demeter, even on cloudy days and even when it was raining there was a dazzling ray of sunshine bathing Demeter. Demeter spent weeks and weeks running around the palace grounds watching as peach trees burst from the earth where her footprints had been. Some days Demeter would run across the grass so many times that the gardeners would beg her to stop as they were unable to manage the vegetation that was spouting forth from Demeter's footprints, preparing for the return of Persephone with a growing awareness of the proximity of divine love.

Finally the day came when Hades returned Persephone from the underworld to live with Demeter for the next nine months. On that day the sun shone more brightly than it had ever shone before. The mortals were amazed as the sun made two bright limelights that shone equally on both Demeter and Persephone.

Demeter was amazed to see that Persephone had grown into an even more breathtakingly beautiful goddess. The mortals were amazed to see the striking resemblance between mother and daughter. The resemblance was such that when Demeter and Persephone hugged each other and the two bright limelights of sunshine shining on them merged, it was not possible to tell which goddess was mother and which goddess was daughter.

And so Demeter and Persephone lived happily ever after for nine months every year. Their separation each year for three months of the year felt painful but bearable because they knew they were part of the cycle of divine love. They knew that the whole of manifestation is the stuff of love. They knew they were pure goodness. They knew they lived in pure goodness and that divine love was the very fabric of what they are.

Lessons from goddess Demeter

Demeter's adventures teach us about our deepest emotional needs, our most cherished longings and our share in the cyclical nature of life.

Demeter's values are fertility, creation and an awareness that love is the fabric of what we are. Fertility is the process of bringing something into being. Fertility is the antithesis of inertia and sloth. The best way to bring something into being is by working out your goal and then aiming at the creation of that goal by taking steps towards that goal. The goal does not have to be as high as Demeter's goal was, of bringing her daughter Persephone back from the underworld of Hades. Your goal requires you to make a decision and a choice. You have to identify a target and choose a target, from a huge range of options. Your goal can be as simple as making your bed each day. I have a surfing friend who I will call Jack to retain his anonymity. Jack was brought up by his single mum. Jack's mum taught him the value of making his bed each day. For many years Jack lived in his friend's garages among junk and car parts while he aimed at making a living from surfing competitions and from playing music in his band. Jack's life was a daily struggle. Jack says that what sustained him most during that period was that when he would crawl back into the garage at the end of the day, there to meet him was a neatly, freshly made bed with sheets, pillow and blankets, even if they were on the concrete floor surrounded by oil leaks and rodents. Jack says the daily act of making his bed every morning kept him sane during that challenging phase of life.

Demeter could have succumbed slothfully to pain and resentment when she felt unlovable and unloved by Zeus. After the abduction of Persephone by Hades, Demeter could have slunk slothfully to her basement and stayed there watching re-runs on Netflix, numbing her leaden self. However, Demeter did not do that. Demeter listened to the deep feelings within herself about the whole of manifestation being the stuff of love. Demeter felt lovable and loved, by her mother Rhea who had looked out for her, and with that came a clear knowingness for Demeter of what needed to be done and how to do it. Demeter knew she needed to de-clutter her home and make it ready for the return of Persephone from the underworld. Demeter then took clear and practical steps towards that goal. The goal provided meaning for Demeter. The meaning provided a motive for action, in other words the meaning provided a motivation.

A related lesson we can learn from Demeter's story is that there will be a period of suffering when there is no access to vitality, when the signs of life are no longer apparent. That time will be followed by a longer period when Demeter and Persephone are together. The vitality will re-emerge after its time underground with Hades. In other words, there is an inevitable phase when the joy and grain of life (Persephone) is underground and appears to be without vitality. There is a period of suffering, and that is just how it is. That is the arrangement that was entered into by Rhea, the mother of all the gods, with her children Demeter, Zeus and Hades. Demeter's resentment about the fact that Persephone was with Hades underground, could not change that fact. Demeter's resentment towards Zeus for letting his brother Hades take Persephone could not change the fact that Persephone was underground with Hades. The arrangement had been put in place by Rhea the mother of all gods. However, Demeter could confront that suffering by making the decision to have the goal of finding Persephone and then taking steps towards that goal.

Further, it is apparent from the story that Demeter's suffering, arising from her separation from Persephone, arose from events that Demeter could not control and with which Demeter had not been involved directly. Persephone had eaten the seven seeds from the pomegranate. The consequences that followed for Persephone followed notwithstanding that Persephone did not know at the time that there would be an adverse consequence arising from the eating of the fruit. In other words, Demeter's suffering (and Persephone's suffering) was to a very large extent not of her own making.

Another lesson from the Demeter tale arises from the time when goddess Demeter was put in the role of wet-nurse to the baby Demophoon. A wet nurse lets a baby suckle on her tit so that the baby can obtain breast milk as a source of nutrition. Demophoon was a human baby and like all human babies was therefore going to die one day. Demeter had the power to make Demophoon immortal, that is to become a god and not die, ever. Demeter embarked on the process of making the baby god-like. The process involved subjecting Demophoon to an intensely hot fire to burn away that part of him that was mortal. In other words, Demophoon had an immortal part of himself that was covered by mortal human parts. In order to become god-like Demophoon had to have his human parts burned away so that all that was left was the immortal part. The burning off of the human parts involved a lengthy and painful process for the baby Demophoon. Unfortunately during the process of Demeter subjecting Demophoon to the growth by fire, the process of becoming godlike was interrupted by Demophoon's mother. Eminent psychologists have observed for many years how important it is for a mother to let her son be subjected to the ordeals of life in order for the son to burn off his infantile parts and to become godlike as a consequence of experiencing the ordeals of life. Modern vernacular refers to the painful process of growth in terms of 'a blowtorch to the belly' and 'a baptism of fire'. This is what Demeter was doing for and with Demophoon. Understandably, albeit unfortunately, Demophoon's growth was stunted by his mother's intervention. Jordan Peterson describes a better approach in his chapter about not interrupting kids when they are skateboardriding in his great book '12 Rules for Life' described earlier. Robert Bly in his book 'Iron John' deals with the same issue that befell Demophoon. Bly's book is used by countless men's groups to help men confront and move through the stunted growth that can arise from being taken out of the fire before the fire has done its work and burned off his infantilized parts.

Another lesson from the story is that suffering is part and parcel of The Kingdom, and that the antidote to suffering is to decide on a goal and then keep walking along the path towards the goal. Demeter wanted her daughter Persephone, the nymph filled with the vitality of life, to be around all year long. However, that could not be achieved because that was not the arrangement made by Rhea the mother of all gods. The arrangement was that the corn (Persephone) will remain underground and unseen for 3 months every year. At the end of the 3 month period Persephone (the corn) will emerge from the earth and will be enjoyed by Demeter for 9 months. At the end of that time, the young Persephone will re-join Hecate underground for 3 months before Persephone re-emerges. That is, the ripe corn (Persephone) eventually dries out and the dried out corn (Hecate) can then be planted and used as a seed for the next generation of corn. There is a cycle that was agreed long before you were born. Suffering is part of the cycle. The ancient myth of Demeter uses the metaphor of Hecate as the corn when it is under the ground. Hecate is the old corn. Hecate is a crone. Crone is a very old English word meaning an old woman past her child bearing days. Persephone is the green corn, Demeter is the ripe ear corn, and Hecate is the harvested corn. The goddess in triad – maiden, nymph and crone. Humans have seen this progression and relationship in corn for more than 9,000 years. The ideal of a goddess in triad depicted in the life cycle of corn was well known more than 6,000 years before Jesus described a cognate triad. By this I do not seek in any way to undermine the importance of the ideal of god in triad but rather to point out its consistency with a way of experiencing the world that was well and truly entrenched long before Christianity.

The Golden Bough

My paternal grandfather was born in Glasgow, a tough ship building town on the River Clyde in Scotland. His favourite book was 'The Golden Bough – a study in comparative religion'[135] by James George Frazer, another Glaswegian. Frazer expressed many views about Demeter in 'The Golden Bough'. Here are some of Frazer's views. They will help you build up a picture in your mind of how your ancestors experienced Demeter and how the ideals of Demeter have been consolidated beneficially into western civilization for thousands and thousands of years.

Frazer writes[136] of the timeless tradition where Egyptian corn reapers would sing melancholy chants each year when they were harvesting the ripe corn. The melancholy chant was to announce the death of the corn-spirit. The Egyptians named the corn spirit Osiris. The Ancient Greeks transmogrified Osiris into Demeter.[137]

The goddess triad, of Demeter, Persephone and Hecate, was worshipped and explored at least since 1500 BC as part of what is now known as the Eleusinian mysteries. Frazer writes that the central mystery that was revealed to the initiated was known as the rites of Demeter and as part of that initiation a reaped ear of corn was used as teaching aid and metaphor.[138] Frazer writes that in one of the chambers dedicated to Osiris in the great temple of Isis at Philae, the dead body of Osiris is represented with stalks of corn springing from it, and a priest is watering the stalks from a pitcher which he holds in his hand. The accompanying inscription sets forth that "This is the form of him whom one may not name, Osiris of the mysteries, who springs from the returning waters." Frazer suggests that it would seem impossible to devise a more graphic way of representing Osiris as a personification of the corn; while the inscription proves that this personification was the kernel of the mysteries of the god, the innermost secret that was only revealed to the initiated.[139]

Frazer writes that in Scotland, when the last corn was cut after Hallowmas, the female figure made out of it was sometimes called the Carlin or Carline, i.e. the Old Woman. But if cut before Hallowmas, it was called the Maiden; if cut after sunset, it was called the Witch, being supposed to bring bad luck. In County Antrim, down to a few years ago, when the sickle was finally expelled by the reaping machine, the few stalks of corn left standing last on the field were plaited together; then the reapers, blindfolded, threw their sickles at the plaited corn, and whoever happened to cut it through took it home with him and put it over his door. This bunch of corn was called the Carley which was probably the same word as Carlin.[140] The ancient goddess triad of Demeter, Persephone and Hecate was thereby celebrated, albeit probably unknowingly.

The Bible stories and the values of The Kingdom

A really good way to understand and remember the values of each of the paths on the Tree of Life is by reading Bible stories. My favourite translation of the Bible is by George M. Lamsa. Lamsa has translated from the Aramaic language used at the time of Jesus by the Jews of Palestine. I find Lamsa's translation to be the most authentic. For example, most of the current translations of the Lord's Prayer ask God to 'lead us not into temptation'. This is clearly a very clumsy translation because leading humans into temptation is an unlikely divine action. Lamsa's translation is preferable it says '*And do not let us fall (enter) into temptation*' which makes a lot more sense. On 22 May 2019, the current Pope (Francis) officially approved such a change.

In the book of Matthew the following story is told by Matthew.

There was a wealthy man who had three servants. The man's savings amounted to eight talents. A 'talent' was the name given to the value of a block of gold weighing 35 kilos. Before going away on a long journey, the man gave one employee five talents to manage. The second employee was given two talents. The third employee was given one talent. The wealthy man distributed his investment savings 'to each one according to his ability'.

The servant who had been given five talents to manage, traded the five talents and earned five more. The servant who had been given two talents to manage, traded the two talents and earned two more. The servant who had been given one talent to manage, dug a hole and hid the one talent in the hole for safe keeping.

After a long time the lord of the servants returned and called his servants to account. The first servant returned the five talents and then handed over the five new ones that he had earned by trading. The first servant said 'My lord you gave me five talents and look I have added five more.' His lord said to him 'Well done, good and reliable servant. You have been faithful over a little, I will appoint you over much. Enter into your master's joy.' Then the servant who had been given the two talents came and said 'My lord you gave me two talents and look I have added two more.' His lord said to him ' Well done, good and reliable servant, you have been faithful over a little, I will appoint you over much. Enter into your master's joy.' Then the servant who had received the one talent came up and said to his lord 'My lord I knew that you were a hard man so I was scared and I went and hid your talent in the ground. Here is the very one that you gave to me.' His lord answered saying 'You are a slothful servant. You should have put my money in the exchange and when I returned I would have demanded my own with interest. Therefore I am taking the talent away from you and giving it to the servant who has ten talents. For to him who has, it shall be given, and it shall increase to him. But he who has not, even that which he has shall be taken away from him.' The slothful servant was thrown into the outerdarkness where there will be weeping and gnashing of teeth.

Matthew's story about the slothful servant teaches many values. The primary value is that slothful behaviour is not rewarded and that it is good to use discrimination, prudence and diligence to create and pursue a worthy goal. In that way inertia and slothful behaviour is confronted and overcome.

Sal the clinical psychologist says …

Meaningful engagement in life is the cornerstone for mental health and an individual who is mentally unwell will adopt methods of coping with the pain of their internal thoughts and feelings. These coping technique correspond to the response of an organism under threat, that is, fight, flight or freeze.

The fight response involves an attempt to push back at the negative thoughts and painful feelings which have arisen. This response can include being inappropriately attention or approval seeking, which usually indicates underlying loneliness. Other 'fight' responses include bragging and competitive behaviour which send the message "look at me, I'm doing incredibly!" – to overcompensate for how the individual is really feeling. Other individuals may use over-control techniques involving focusing attention on details, ruminating or exercising extreme control – to avoid criticism, misfortune or perhaps malevolence. Typical over-controlling behaviours include perfectionistic, scolding, worrying, eating disordered, suspicious and compulsive over-control. One interesting type of over-control is known as the "Pollyanna" over-control, where even in the most difficult of circumstances, the individual only sees the positive side, whilst invalidating both their own and other's experiences. Finally, and most commonly seen in forensic criminal settings, are conning and manipulation, bully and attack and predator responses.

The flight response, which is known as avoidance, can take several forms. There are those people who cut off their emotions and discourage others from getting close to them by having a cool, aloof facial expression and body language. Others bubble with a wall of anger, or express irritation and frequent complaints. A third way of distancing yourself is to present a 'spaced out' persona, which discourages intimacy. Some individuals take avoidance literally and head out of town when challenging situations arise ! Alternatively, other choose to anaesthetise, stimulate or distract themselves with drugs, alcohol, pornography, work, gambling, promiscuous sex, overeating, excessive computer games, television or fantasizing.

The freeze response, as the name implies, suggests that the person accepts their negative thoughts and painful emotions without questioning them and in so doing often accepts mistreatment. They do not try to get their healthy needs met. These individuals may take on the persona of a victim with frequent complaining about their life circumstances.

Observing and describing our painful emotions, bodily sensations and thoughts as well as accepting that they have arisen, can be the first step in moving towards an engaged life. This approach acknowledges that pain in life is inevitable but that we turn pain into suffering by non-acceptance and avoidance of that pain. By not being in the moment, we waste life, analyzing past hurts and worrying about future possible outcomes. Ironically, by observing, describing and accepting our difficult thoughts, sensations and feelings (without resorting to dysfunctional fight, flight or freeze responses) their intensity eventually diminishes.

Living in the moment offers a freeing alternative to ruminating on the past and catastrophizing about the future. This approach allows us to act with awareness rather than on autopilot and to use patience, compassion and humour towards ourselves and others in this journey called life.

Summary

- There is a Western tradition of values, ethics, morality, philosophy, psychology, politics and theology.

- Pythagoras, Socrates, Plato and Aristotle form the main part of that lineage which continues to the present day. Some call it the Western mystery tradition. Some call it Western yoga. It is very different to the yoga of the East.

- A seminal concept of the yoga of the East is vairagya. Vairagya is the concept of detachment from life. Vairagya and nihilism are the antithesis of the Western mystery tradition.

- The seminal value of the Western mystery tradition/Western yoga is meaningful engagement in life and family and commerce.

- The Western mystery tradition has, as one of its foundations, the ideal that a human being possesses a spiritual dimension known as a soul.

- Ancient Greek conceptions of soul are the primary sources of all Western views of soul, including those of Islam and Judaism. Socrates is credited as the father of the Western conception of soul.

- Democracy and the legal constitutions of the countries of the West are based on the Western mystery tradition and on the idea of an individual possessing a soul.

- The political scholar Professor Alan Ryan wrote words to the effect that 'perhaps it is prayer rather than politics that provides the answer to human problems'.

- The Western mystery tradition is recorded in an image known as the Tree of Life.

- The Tree of Life is used to train the mind, not to inform it.

- The Tree of Life is made up of 32 pathways, comprising 10 spheres with 22 connecting pathways.

- The Kingdom is the name of the sphere/path in which we live and act.

- The Lord's Prayer was written by someone well acquainted with the Tree of Life and the Western mystery tradition. That is apparent from that part of the text of the Lord's Prayer which states 'for yours is the kingdom and the power and the glory'. The Kingdom, The Power and The Glory are three of the spheres/paths on the Tree of Life.

- The Western mystery tradition and its values of soul, ethics and morality provides an antidote to the chaos inherent in nihilism and post-modernism.

- Each path on the Tree of Life has virtues and vices. The virtues and vices represent the values of Western civilization. These are the lessons that our ancestors learned and now pass on to us.

- The virtues and vices of the paths on the Tree of Life have been taught for thousands of years in the Ancient Greek goddess and god myths and in the Bible stories.

- Demeter is the goddess associated with this Path. The colourful, lusty and adventurous tales of Demeter have been studied by humans since at least 1,500BC.

- Demeter's adventures teach us about our deepest emotional needs, our most cherished longings and our share in the cyclical nature of life.

CHAPTER TWO

PATH 2 – THE FOUNDATION

THE SECOND PATH is The Foundation. It is located on the Central Pillar of Equilibrium immediately above The Kingdom.

The Tree of Life uses Heracles (aka Hercules) to teach us that we need super strength to battle our natural fear that we are not as good as others. There is an unhealthy envy that arises from self-doubt and evaluative comparison[141]. The antidote to that envy is the prudence of self-honesty and self-acceptance.

You will read in this chapter how Heracles had to kill and flay the mighty Nemean Lion. Heracles shot his deadly arrows but the arrows rebounded harmlessly as the mighty Lion yawned. Heracles used his sword which buckled hopelessly. Heracles then used his mighty club which broke into pieces, whereupon Heracles felt weak and inept. Heracles felt envious as he looked upon the strength, bravery and physical magnificence of the Nemean Lion. Heracles then had a dream in which he recalled his divine nature and saw his physical reflection in the face of a huge ocean wave. Heracles saw his massive muscles and knew that he could access his strength to wrestle the Lion, which he then did. It was Heracles's prudent and diligent consideration and reflection about his divine nature, coupled with self-honesty and self-acceptance of his strengths and weaknesses, that enabled him to set aside the debilitating envy he had for mightiness of the Nemean Lion. Heracles needed super strength to battle his natural fear that he was not as good as the Nemean Lion. The unhealthy envy that arises from self-doubt and evaluative comparison is transformed by the prudence of self-honesty and self-acceptance. This is the virtue we can learn from the Path known as the Foundation.

The Foundation collects input from The Power and from The Glory, processes that input and passes it on to The Kingdom. As noted above, the Bible records that process as 'For yours is The Kingdom, The Power and The Glory, for ever and ever.' The process of The Power, The Glory and The Kingdom in the Tree of Life was a breathtaking insight of genius as to the structure of the human brain and the brain's process of thinking. Putting that another way, thousands of years before the discovery of the human brain's two cerebral hemispheres and their role in perceiving and manifesting life, the Tree of Life provided that information and more.

Iain McGilchrist's masterpiece 'The Master and his Emissary – The Divided Brain and the Making of Western World'[142] has been described as 'the most comprehensive, profound book ever written on brain laterality'[143].

McGilchrist has stated[144] '…I believed it to be profoundly true that <u>the inner structure of our intellect reflects the structure of the universe</u>…I believe that our brains not only dictate the shape of the experience we have of the world, but are likely themselves to reflect, in their structure and functioning, the nature of the universe in which they have come about.' McGilchrist summarized that statement by stating[145] '… <u>the brain is not just a tool for grappling with the world. It's what brings the world about</u>.' (Emphasis added). The ability of the brain to bring the world about, is an idea that is at the heart of the Tree of Life. The profound complexity of the human brain is apparent readily from McGilchrist's observation[146] that there are 'more connections within the human brain than there are particles in the known universe'. In other words, "as above, so below".

The left cerebral hemisphere of the brain and the left side of the Tree of Life, known as the Pillar of Severity, perform the same role. The right cerebral hemisphere of the brain and the right side of the Tree of Life, known as the Pillar of Mercy, perform the same role.

Between the left cerebral hemisphere and the right cerebral hemisphere is the corpus callosum. Between the left side of the Tree of Life and the right side of the Tree of Life is the Pillar of Equilibrium. The corpus callosum and the Pillar of Equilibrium perform the same role. We will explore this in this chapter.

Feminine and masculine

The Tree of Life demonstrates a delightfully complex relationship between the feminine and the masculine. We have already seen how the sphere of The Power and the sphere of The Glory contribute to the sphere of The Kingdom. And we have noted previously the manner in which those aspects were recorded in the Lord's Prayer.

The left hand side of the Tree of Life contains three spheres which together comprise the Pillar of Severity. The Pillar of Severity is considered to be feminine[147]. The bottom-most of those three spheres comprising the Pillar of Severity is known as the Glory.

The right hand side of the Tree of Life contains three spheres which together comprise the Pillar of Mercy. The Pillar of Mercy is considered to be masculine. The bottom-most of those three spheres comprising the Pillar of Mercy is known as the Power.

Sitting between the Pillar of Severity and the Pillar of Mercy, is the middle pillar known as the Pillar of Equilibrium. Four[148] spheres together comprise the Pillar of Equilibrium. The bottom-most of those spheres comprising the Pillar of Equilibrium is, as described in chapter one, known as the Kingdom. Sitting above the Kingdom is the sphere known as the Foundation.

The Tree of Life depicts the coming into being of existence as a result of, among other things, the movement of life from the sphere known as the Power in the Pillar of Mercy across to the sphere known as the Glory in the Pillar of Severity. This is a movement from an expansive fecundity of force into a constrained considered cloistered form.

This is a movement from the right side of the Tree of Life to the left side of the Tree of Life. The same transition and effect occurs in the brain.

McGilchrist states[149] there is temporal hierarchy of attention 'with our awareness of any object of experience beginning in the right hemisphere, which grounds experience, before it gets to be further processed in the left hemisphere.'

Not only is there a temporal hierarchy moving from right hemisphere to left hemisphere (Pillar of Mercy to Pillar of Severity) there is also a coming into being from force to form as the cognition moves from the right hemisphere to the left hemisphere.

McGilchrist states[150]:

'Hence the brain has to attend to the world in two completely different ways, and in so doing to bring two different worlds into being. In the one (the right hemisphere / the Pillar of Mercy) we experience the live, complex, embodied world of individual, always unique being, forever in flux, net of interdependencies, forming and reforming wholes, a world with which we are deeply connected. In the other (the left hemisphere/ the Pillar of Severity) we "experience" or experience in a special way: a "re-presented" version of it, containing now static, separable, bounded, but essentially fragmented entities, grouped into classes, on which predictions can be made. This kind of attention isolates, fixes and makes each thing explicit by bringing it under the spotlight of attention.' The commentary in brackets has been added by me.

A narrowing or a spotlighting occurs as the force from the Pillar of Mercy is put into a form in the Pillar of Severity. McGilchrist describes this in the following manner[151] 'Patients with right-hemisphere damage don't seem able to adjust the breadth of the "spotlight" of their attention; they suffer from "an excessive and more or less permanent narrowing of their attentional window". That's what happens when we have to rely on left-hemisphere attention on its own.'

The Tree of Life provides information in relation to the manner in which the Pillar of Mercy and the Pillar of Severity can best be used at the level of the individual (and also at a political or societal level).

The sphere at the foot of the Pillar of Mercy (the right hemisphere of the brain) is known as the Power. In the Tree of Life the sphere of The Power is nature, including that aspect of nature that is "nature red in tooth and claw". Thousands of years of intellectually rich Western philosophy have captured and recorded wisdom in the stories and deeds of gods and angels. In that regard, Dion Fortune writes of the sphere of The Power that it [152] '... is Venus, the Green Nature Ray, elemental force, the initiation of the emotions...instinct'. Haniel is the relevant Archangel. The virtue is unselfishness. The vice is unchastity, lust. The symbol is the lamp and girdle and the rose. McGilchrist states[153] that 'empathy, emotional understanding' are right-hemisphere functions.

The sphere known as the Power is best understood by contrasting it with the sphere known as the Glory. Dion Fortune writes of the sphere of The Glory that [154] ' (The Glory) is Mercury, Hermes, the initiation of knowledge...Intellect, concrete thought, the reduction of intuitive knowledge to form.' This is the Egyptian Thoth the Lord of Books and Learning. The relevant Archangel is Michael. The symbol is the apron and the caduceus. The virtue is truthfulness. The vice is falsehood, dishonesty. The depth of Western wisdom contained in the symbols and deeds of gods and angels is breathtaking and is undervalued at present.

McGilchrist states[155] 'It might be then that the division of the human brain is also the result of the need to bring to bear two incompatible types of attention on the world at the same time, one narrow, focused, and directed by our needs, and the other broad, open and directed towards whatever else is going on in the world apart from ourselves.'

Dion Fortune writes [156]'... these two representing force and form on a lower arc.... (The Power) represents the instincts and the emotions they give rise to, and (The Glory) represents the concrete mind. In the macrocosm they represent two levels of the process of the concretion of force into form.'

The Tree of Life demonstrates that after the life energy has travelled from the sphere known as the Power in the Pillar of Mercy to the sphere known as the Glory in the Pillar of Severity, the energy then moves across and down to the sphere known as the Foundation in the middle Pillar of Equilibrium. From there the energy moves down the Pillar of Equilibrium to the sphere known as the Kingdom. The Kingdom is the domain of action, it is where life takes place. Accordingly, what we perceive in the Kingdom is the result of, among other things, the interplay of the Pillar of Mercy and the Pillar of Severity, blended, condensed, thickened and manifested in the Pillar of Equilibrium in the Kingdom.

McGilchrist puts it this way[157]:

'In reality we are a composite of the two hemispheres, and despite the interesting results of experiments designed artificially to separate their functioning, they work together most of the time at the everyday level. But that does not at all exclude that they may have radically different agendas, and over long periods of time and large number of individuals it becomes apparent that they each instantiate a way of being in the world that is at conflict with the other.'

And:

'... as I also emphasized at the outset, both hemispheres take part in virtually all "functions" to some extent, and in reality both are always engaged.'[158]

Importantly for present purposes, Dion Fortune described the Tree of Life as 'a method of using the mind, not a system of knowledge'[159].

The Tree of Life is considered to be a diagram of both the macrocosm and the microcosm. The Pythagorean schools spoke regularly of the concept of "as above so below"[160]. That phrase describes the macrocosm and microcosm point. Dion Fortune wrote[161] 'As above, so below, man is a miniature microcosm.'

'As above, so below' describes the manner in which the three Pillars interplay to manifest life and also describes the manner in which an individual manifests life by the interplay of the three pillars in the life of the individual. Thousands of years before McGilchrist described the relationship between the two hemispheres and the corpus callosum, the Tree of Life recorded the relationship and far more.

What explains the prescience and depth of wisdom we have seen in the Tree of Life and its use in the schools of Pythagoras, Socrates, Plato and Aristotle? McGilchrist has identified something that may provide an answer. McGilchrist suggests that during the lifetimes of those ancient Greeks there was a development in human beings of enhanced frontal lobe function.[162] The enhanced frontal lobe function, McGilchrist states, created the circumstances for 'increased independence of the hemispheres, allowing each hemisphere to make characteristic advances in function, and for a while to do so in harmony with its fellow'[163]. However, since that time, McGilchrist states 'there has been a relentless growth of self-consciousness, leading to increasing difficulties in co-operation … the balance of power has shifted … further and further towards the part-world created by the left hemisphere.'[164]

What McGilchrist is describing is an evolutionary process that occurred in the hemispheres of the human brain during the period in which Pythagoras, Socrates, Plato and Aristotle were living. The process was one in which their left and right cerebral hemispheres operated in unprecedented harmony. Human beings who lived subsequently operated with a left hemisphere dominance that precluded the harmonious interaction of left hemisphere and right hemisphere that was characteristic of the thinkers of ancient Greece. If McGilchrist is correct, that may provide an explanation as to the longevity of the teachings of those teachers. That is, those teachers had an advantage that we do not have. Those teachers were able to perceive and deliberate with a left and right hemisphere that was characterised by greater harmony than we have ready access to today. Because those teachers had that advantage they were able to perceive and articulate matters in extraordinary depth. The characteristics of western civilization that I have set out earlier in this chapter, including the Tree of Life, are the fruits and ongoing legacies of the synthesis of the left and right hemispheres of those ancient Greeks.

As you are reading the above words you are creating a new experience and the learning of new information and new skills engages the right hemisphere attention more than the left[165]. When you are faced with a difficult and important decision, it is useful to engage new information (like the Tree of Life) because that ensures the right hemisphere will present an array of possible solutions to the problem posed. Subsequently (by a very small margin) the left hemisphere will take the single solution that seems to best fit what it already knows and will seek to latch onto that as the answer to the problem.[166] Remember the context is that we are looking for an outcome worthy of a place in the Kingdom. We are aware that the Pillar of Mercy and the Pillar of Severity must both contribute to the outcome. We are aware that the right hemisphere of the brain and the left hemisphere of the brain will bring a world into being. The world brought into being will be composed of the contextual personal interest of the right hemisphere and the more impersonal affinity of the left hemisphere.[167] It is important to remember the words of Dion Fortune 'the Tree is a method of using the mind, not a system of knowledge'.[168]

The relevant exercise is sometimes described these days as 'brain storming'. The Tree of Life thousands of years ago described the process as a 'lightning strike'. The Tree of Life indicates that the path of the lightning strike travels down and across the Tree of Life in a specific order. The specific order includes the lightning strike moving from The Power to The Glory. This is the direction of brain storming and its temporal hierarchy of attention noted by McGilchrist and described earlier.[169] For my part I see the lightning strike description of the Tree of Life presented in three dimensions, such that a preferable image for me is that of a tornado swirling in a clockwise direction. The movement from The Power to The Glory is part of that tornado swirling. The tornado then swirls back towards the middle Pillar of Equilibrium after having passed through the right hemisphere then the left hemisphere of the brain. The Tree of Life discloses that the tornado (historically the lightning strike) then travels down the middle Pillar of Equilibrium to the sphere known as The Foundation and then down the middle Pillar of Equilibrium to the sphere known as The Kingdom. This movement of creation from the right hemisphere to the left hemisphere then back toward the right hemisphere is noted by McGilchrist in the following manner [170]:

'In summary, the hierarchy of attention, for a number of reasons, implies a grounding role and an ultimately integrating role for the right hemisphere, with whatever the left hemisphere does at the detailed level needing to be founded on, and then returned to, the picture generated by the right. This is an instance of the right -> left -> right progression which will be a theme of this book. And it lies at the very foundation of experience: attention, where the world actually comes into being.'

The Tree of Life suggests that a slightly more accurate description would be that the world that comes into being arises as the progression moves back toward the right but never gets to the right. That is because there is a new creation which is neither right nor left but rather is the product of transformation or subsumption of both (in the middle Pillar of Equilibrium). In fact McGilchrist appears to also reach that conclusion later in his book when he writes[171]:

'I have expressed this reintegration in terms of a "return" to the right hemisphere. This risks suggesting that the achievements of the left hemisphere's interventions are lost or nullified... Instead, the pattern I would adopt to explain the way in which the process occurs in the bihemispheric apprehension of the world is that of Hegel's *Aufhebung*... In this sense the earlier stage is "lifted up" into the subsequent stage both in the sense that it is "taken up into" or "subsumed" into the succeeding stage, and in the sense that it remains present in, but transformed by, a "higher" level of the process.'

And:

'In terms of the thesis of this book, then, the process begins in the realm of the right hemisphere, gets input from the left hemisphere, and finally reaches a synthesis of right with left.'[172]

Atheism, the middle pillar and the corpus callosum

The Tree of Life shows, in diagrammatic form, that life cannot be analysed successfully by recourse to either the pillar of severity or the pillar of mercy. What is needed is the synthesis of both pillars that occurs in the middle pillar of equilibrium. McGilchrist comes to the same conclusion using the language and the structure of the left and right hemisphere of the brain. McGilchrist states 'Ultimately the principle of division, that of the left hemisphere, and the principle of union, that of the right hemisphere, need to be unified: in Hegel's terms, the thesis and antithesis must be enabled to achieve a synthesis on a higher level.'[173]

As noted before, the Tree of Life is to be used as a way of thinking and not as a repository of information that can be substituted for thinking. Or putting that another way, the Tree of Life is used 'to train the mind not inform it.' The application of that approach to the classic perennial existential questions such as 'who am I and what am I doing here' means that such questions are not pursued successfully by recourse solely to the left hemisphere/ pillar of severity. In other words, the left brain appears to be incapable of answering the perennial questions. To attempt to answer the perennial questions using the logic of the left hemisphere is illogical, based on current brain science described by McGilchrist and based on the Tree of Life.

One problem with a left hemisphere dominant approach is that the left hemisphere has an inherent inability to report on right hemisphere perceptions. That is because the left hemisphere reports in left hemisphere terms which do not lend themselves readily to right hemisphere perceptions. That problem can be illustrated by the useful (albeit inadequate) metaphor of what happens when a joke is explained by a process of analytical reasoning. That is, the process of analytical reasoning emasculates the essential jokiness of the joke by the very process of analytical reasoning. The process is apparent by identifying the jokiness in the classic – "Why did the chicken cross the road? To get to the other side." The analysis includes the proposition that the humour resides in the unexpectedly obvious answer. And that is humorous because obvious answers are not generally funny. The juxtaposition, arising from including an obvious answer in a joke, is funny because that is not where one would expect an obvious answer. By the end of the analysis the humour has dried up. As McGilchrist has written 'the left hemisphere world is, by comparison, a virtual, bloodless affair.'[174]

The problem inherent in providing an analytical explanation of a joke is equally problematic when using a left hemisphere approach to the perennial questions. It seems to me that likely provides an explanation for the difference in approach between post modern nihilism on the one hand and 'western civilisation' (as I have described it in chapter 1) when it comes to their respective approaches to the perennial (and other) questions. A cognate difference in approach may also arise between atheism on the one hand and religious belief on the other hand.

The Tree of Life and the modern science of the divided brain, support the proposition that a less than optimal result will arise when the perennial questions are addressed by the left hemisphere/pillar of severity, or by the right hemisphere/pillar of mercy, rather than by a synthesis of both pillars.

A left hemisphere/pillar of severity approach to the perennial questions will lack the necessary reintegration that arises from the process of reasoning moving from right hemisphere to left hemisphere and then back towards the right hemisphere. This is the Hegelian 'thesis, antithesis, synthesis' on a higher level, that McGilchrist recognised. The narrowness apparent in a predominantly left hemisphere approach seems apparent in the analysis of the perennial questions by well known atheist writers such as Richard Dawkins. A predominantly right hemisphere approach brings a different type of problem. However for present purposes I want to explore more deeply the proposition that atheism is the product of a left hemisphere dominant approach to the perennial questions and that atheism is therefore a suboptimal outcome. By suboptimal outcome I mean an outcome that is less true than the outcome that might be produced by the Tree of Life's approach. By the Tree of Life's approach I am referring to that manner of thinking in which the analysis commences in the right hemisphere/pillar of mercy then travels along a path to the left hemisphere/ pillar of severity and then travels along a path to the corpus callosum / pillar of equilibrium.

The proposition that I have described above, in relation to atheism being the product of a left hemisphere dominant approach to the perennial questions, appears to be consistent with the approach taken by McGilchrist. I say that for the following reasons.

First, the atheistic perspective that 'there is no god' may well be true when considered in context. What I mean by that is that such a perspective is highly likely to be soundly based, when based on a particular experience and perspective of life. In other words, using the language of the Tree of Life, the Kingdom when viewed from the perspective of the left brain / the Pillar of Severity, includes components of the Kingdom but not the whole Kingdom. Accordingly, the left hemisphere's examination of the left hemisphere results in a partial picture of the Kingdom and one in which god is not perceived. Another way of expressing this is that the product produced by the left hemisphere / Pillar of Severity is a form. The absence of input from the right brain / Pillar of Mercy (and from the upper regions of the Pillar of Equilibrium) results in the production of a form which does not contain that which, on the other pillars, produces a god.

In my view this is consistent with the experience and conclusion reached by Dr Jill Bolte Taylor in her New York Times best selling book 'My Stroke of Insight - a brain scientist's personal journey'[175]. Jill has a doctorate in neuroanatomy and was working in postdoctoral reseach at Harvard Medical School in the Department of Neuroscience when she experienced a stroke in the left hemisphere of her brain. Jill writes 'Within four brief hours, through the eyes of a curious brain anatomist (neuroanatomist). I watched my mind completely deteriorate in its ability to process information.'[176] Jill writes[177] that 'our left hemisphere looks at a flower and names different parts making up the whole – the petal, stem... It (left hemisphere) excels in academics, and by doing so it manifests a sense of authority over the details it masters. Via our left hemisphere language centers, our mind speaks to us constantly, a phenomenon I refer to as "brain chatter".'

Jill recounts[178] how 'As blood swept over the higher thinking centers of my left cerebral cortex, I began losing my skills of higher cognition – one precious ability at a time.' And 'In the absence of my left hemisphere's analytical judgment, I was completely entranced by the feelings of tranquility, safety, blessedness, euphoria and omniscience.'[179]

As the left hemisphere shut down further, Jill describes[180] 'in the absence of sight, sound, touch, smell, taste and fear, I felt my spirit surrender its attachment to this body and I was released from the pain.'

'My left hemisphere had been trained to perceive myself as a solid, separate from others. Now released from that restrictive circuitry, my right hemisphere relished in its attachment to the eternal flow. I was no longer isolated and alone. My soul was as big as the universe and frolicked with glee in a boundless sea.'[181]

'It was impossible for me to distinguish the physical boundaries between objects because everything radiated with similar energy… In this state of mind, I could not perceive three-dimensionally. Nothing stood out as being closer or farther away… In addition, color did not register to my brain as color. I simply couldn't distinguish it.'[182]

'My stroke of insight is that at the core of my right hemisphere consciousness is a character that is directly connected to my feeling of deep inner peace. It is completely committed to the expression of peace, love, joy and compassion in the world.'[183] And, 'If I had to pick one output (action) word for my right mind, I would have to choose "compassion".'[184]

The correlation between Jill's description and experience of the right hemisphere/Pillar of Mercy and the compassion aspect of the Pillar of Mercy, provides a further demonstration of the prescience of the Tree of Life created many thousands of years prior to split brain neuroscientific discoveries.

Jill writes[185] 'My right mind … thinks out of the box. It is not limited by the rules and regulations established by my left mind that created that box… It appreciates that chaos is the first step in the creative process… It is tuned in to the subtle messages my cells communicate via gut feelings, and it learns through touch and experience.'

Jill concludes[186] 'Based upon my experience with losing my left mind, I whole-heartedly believe that the feeling of deep inner peace is neurological circuitry located in our right brain.' Perhaps this is one of the reasons why a meditator like Sam Harris, who would appear to function predominantly from and with the intellectual honesty of a left hemisphere perspective, is attracted to the right hemisphere perspectives, described by Jill, that arise sometimes from meditation.

Jill writes[187] 'I appreciate that for many of us, if our left mind cannot smell it, taste it, hear it, see it or touch it, then we are skeptical as to whether or not it exists. Our right brain is capable of detecting energy beyond the limitations of our left mind because of the way it is designed.'

This conclusion, based on Jill's experience with her hemispheres, provides support for my view that atheism is likely to be the product of predominant left hemisphere activity. In other words, because god cannot be smelt, tasted, heard, seen or touched by the left hemisphere, the left hemisphere must therefore conclude that there can be no god. Similarly, based on Jill's experience with her hemispheres, it appears that right hemisphere perception will provide a basis for experiencing a wholeness and a unity that might be characterised as god.

The Tree of Life suggests that the optimal life experience in The Kingdom will involve, ideally, an awareness that the right hemisphere/pillar of mercy perceives a spirit undivided, and the left hemisphere/pillar of severity perceives that spirit as having taken on a confined form, so that he/she can interact with other confined forms in The Kingdom.

McGilchrist has stated [188] '...I believe it to be profoundly true that the inner structure of our intellect reflects the structure of the universe'. This is probably what Dion Fortune meant when she wrote[189] that the Tree of Life demonstrates 'as above so below'.

The Foundation

The symbolism of The Foundation contains two seemingly incongruous sets of symbols. On the one hand there is Shaddai the Lord of Great Strength. On the other hand there is the Archangel Gabriel associated with Moon symbolism. Dion Fortune suggests the apparent incongruity can be reconciled and that the reconciliation arises from consideration of the words of the Yetziratic[190] Text which says of The Foundation that it 'purifies the Emanations. It proves and corrects the designing of their representations, and disposes of the unity with which they are designed without diminution or division.'[191]

Dion Fortune suggests[192] that 'We get the concept, then, of the fluidic waters of chaos being finally gathered up and organized by means of the "representations" that were "designed" in (The Glory); this final "proving", correcting, and "disposing of the unity" of these "representations" or formative images resulting in the organisation of the "Machinery of the Universe"... If we liken the kingdom of earth to a great ship, then (The Foundation) would be the engine-room.'

Another way of considering the values inherent in The Foundation is to recall the analysis of McGilchrist which describes one of our thoughts originating in the unbridled fluidic depths of the chaos of our right hemisphere and moving instanteously into the bridled and formative territory of our ordered left hemisphere, before moving instanteously back towards a middle ground. The middle ground is the 'engine-room' which then provides the powering for our actions.

The apparent incongruity of the symbolism of, on the one hand, the Herculean strong man and on the other hand the Archangel Gabriel and the watery lunar moon, provides in fact an apt description of those values inherent in The Foundation. The symbolism describes the process identified thousands of years later by McGilchrist.

So let us explore the values demonstrated by the deeds of the gods and goddesses embedded in the symbol and archetype of the strength of Heracles (aka Hercules) the strong man and Artemis the moon goddess.

Heracles' life teaches us how super strength is needed to battle the existential angst that arises from being fearful about not being as strong as others or not being as clever or virile or as good as others. Heracles' life also teaches us about the cultivation of strength by appropriate self-acceptance and self-honesty.

Heracles

A very full version of the tales of Heracles is set out in the Penguin Classics book 'The Greek Myths'[193].

Once upon a time there was a boy who earned the right to become an immortal god and his name was Heracles. Heracles was the son of the god Zeus. Zeus' wife was the goddess Hera. Hera, however, was not Heracles' mother. Heracles' mother was the mortal woman named Alcmene. Zeus had, to use the Ancient Greek metaphor, jumped the fence and ploughed the paddock of Alcmene by disguising himself as Alcmene's husband.

That is the short summary of how Heracles became Zeus' son. But there are important details that need to be told in order to understand the deep values of Heracles' life.

As Zeus grew older he felt existential angst growing in his heart, in his head and in his gut. As the existential angst grew inside of him, Zeus felt his connection with his divine immortality slipping away from him. Zeus began to suffer more and more from this loss of connection with his divine immortality. Zeus knew that in order to reconnect fully with his divine immortality he needed to create a strong champion. Zeus knew that he himself could not resolve his own suffering. Zeus knew that all of the other gods and goddesses and mortal humans were not able to resolve their own sufferings. Zeus knew that a champion with super strength and super faith was needed to demonstrate by example how to reconnect with divinity. The champion would show every god, goddess and mortal human how to reconnect with divinity by using their own faith and their own strength.

Zeus knew that such a champion had to be half human and half god, so that both humans and gods could relate to the champion. Zeus knew that he had to select the human female mother to be, very, very carefully. Zeus selected a beautiful young woman named Alcmene. Alcmene was the pious and beautiful daughter of King Electryon. Alcmene was promised to the brave human warrior prince named Amphitryon. However Alcmene had told Amphitryon that he could not plough her paddock, as the Greek metaphor goes, until he had avenged the deaths of her eight brothers in a war in a far off land. Amphitryon journeyed to war and fought valiantly avenging the deaths of Alcmene's eight brothers. He then started on his long journey home. The journey home would take many days. Zeus saw all this from his palace on Mount Olympus.

Zeus had great respect for Alcmene so rather than descending from Olympus and ploughing her paddock without her consent, Zeus decided to disguise himself and impersonate her husband the brave prince Amphitryon.

Zeus, disguised as Amphitryon, returned home to a victory party prepared for Amphitryon by princess Alcmene. At the end of the victory party, princess Alcmene took the man, who she thought was her proud and excited warrior prince husband, to her bed chamber. But it was Zeus in disguise who went with Alcmene to her bed chamber.

Alcmene sported gladly and lustily all night long with her supposed husband, as Zeus, disguised as Amphitryon recounted stories of the wild battles in which revenge was extracted for the murder of Alcmene's eight brothers. Zeus knew that the procreation of the great champion was an undertaking that could not be hurried, so Zeus had Hermes bend time and space in order to spread magically one night into three nights.

The next day an exhausted but happy princess Alcmene was confused and startled when the real prince Amphitryon returned home from the war and claimed his nuptial pleasures and began recounting at length his war stories to Alcmene. Neither Alcmene or Amphitryon knew what was happening. They were both very confused when Alcmene said to the real Amphitryon 'Why are you telling me the battle stories again, you told me them all last night. And aren't you tired from all the ploughing you did last night?'. Alcmene and Amphitryon both thought that the other had temporarily gone mad!

Alcmene became pregnant with twins sired by different fathers, Heracles from Zeus and Iphicles from her husband Amphitryon. Medically this is known as heteropaternal superfecundation.

When Alcmene was just about to give birth to the twin boys, Zeus boasted about what he had done. Zeus' long suffering but very jealous wife Hera flew into a violent rage. Hera felt the very ground underneath her had been yanked away by Zeus and his profligate ways. To make matters worse Zeus told Hera that he was going to give the name Heracles, which meant glory of Hera, to the future baby boy. Zeus also said that Heracles would have the right to rule as King of the noble House of Perseus. Hera projected all her hatred for Zeus onto the soon to be born baby Heracles. Hera devised a cunning plan. On the day before Heracles' birth, Hera made Zeus promise an unbreakable oath that any prince born into the House of Perseus before nightfall that day would become King. Zeus made that unbreakable oath thinking that the only baby due that night was Heracles. Hera knew that a nearby Queen named Nicippe was 7 months pregnant. Hera cast magic spells which caused Queen Nicippe to go into labour immediately. Hera then went to the birthing chamber of Alcmene. Hera sat outside the birthing chamber and crossed her fingers and her legs, which magically prevented Alcmene from giving birth. Hera sat crossed in that manner until after Queen Nicippe had given birth to a very premature young baby prince. Alcmene gave birth to Heracles and Iphicles a few hours later. In that way Heracles lost his inheritance. Heracles's security, as a ruler and a leader, was yanked out from underneath him. Zeus' security, of a super champion to lead the gods, goddesses and mortals back to divinity, was yanked out from underneath Zeus.

Zeus felt overcome by his growing existential angst. Zeus feared that all of humanity, as well as all gods and goddesses, would also become afflicted by existential angst. Zeus feared that everyone would lose their connection to divinity unless they were shown by Heracles how to use divine faith and divine strength to overcome the fear and suffering produced by existential angst.

Zeus knew that existential angst could be overcome by divine faith and divine strength. Zeus knew that self-doubt caused existential angst to grow and that it was incredibly hard for humans and gods and goddesses to be free at all times from self-doubt. Zeus felt regularly that he was a failure as a god and that he was not good enough to be a god. On many days Zeus had specific fears about not being as strong as other gods, or as clever or as virile. On many other days Zeus didn't have a specific fear but rather Zeus had a very general fear of the transience and futility of his continued existence.

Zeus knew that Heracles and his strength could provide the antidote to the existential angst that Zeus and all of humanity and all the gods and goddesses were suffering.

Zeus knew that Heracles would need super strength to battle existential angst. Particularly now that Heracles had had his inheritance yanked out from under him by Hera's wicked delayed birth ploy. Zeus came up with a cunning plan. Zeus disguised baby Heracles and asked Hera to act as a wet nurse for this 'unknown' baby. Hera nursed the disguised baby Heracles and Heracles drank the divine breast milk of Hera. Hera was unaware the baby was Heracles. Heracles, by drinking Hera's divine milk, acquired supernatural strength with every mouthful. As Heracles gulped more and more divine milk, Heracles became stronger and stronger and sucked harder and harder on Hera. Heracles sucked so strongly on Hera that Hera had to push the baby Heracles away to avoid being sucked inside out. As Heracles' mouth came loose from Hera's breast, Hera's milk continued to spray out and with such force from Heracles sucking that Hera's milk sprayed across the heavens to form the Milky Way.

Heracles now had supernatural strength and he started to use it. One day when Heracles and his twin brother Iphicles were about eight months old, Hera who was still deeply resentful of Heracles, sent two giant azure-scaled serpents into the boys' nursery with strict orders to kill Heracles. The giant serpents glided over the marble floors with flames shooting from their eyes and poison dripping from their sinister fangs. Iphicles was distraught with fear. By contrast, Heracles grabbed a serpent in each hand and proceed to strangle them. Heracles' mother Alcmene and foster father Amphitryon rushed in and found Heracles bouncing joyfully in his cot, still strangling the serpents like they were toys. Heracles then threw the bodies of the dead serpents out of his cot and onto the marble floor. Heracles was starting to experience and understand his divine strength.

When Heracles was a young man he learned the musical instrument called the lyre from Eumolpus and from Linus he learned literature. One time Eumolpus was away and Linus gave the lyre lesson to Heracles. Linus beat Heracles physically for refusing to depart from the lyre style Heracles had been taught by Eumolpus. Heracles retaliated by killing Linus with a blow of the lyre. Heracles was tried for murder but secured an acquittal by quoting the law of justified forcible resistance. Heracles' foster father Amphitryon sought to avoid further problems and sent Heracles away to tend cattle on a mountain. While tending cattle Heracles was visited by two entities named Vice and Virtue. They offered Heracles the choice between a severe but glorious life on the one hand, and on the other hand a pleasant and easy life. Heracles chose the former. Zeus looked down from Olympus and was pleased. Zeus' plan to save humanity and the gods and goddesses was starting to take place.

Some years later, Heracles married Megara the daughter of King Creon. Hera still resented Heracles and afflicted Heracles with temporary insanity. In a fit of insanity Heracles killed the children he had fathered with Megara. When his insanity subsided Heracles sought guidance from the Oracle of Delphi who directed Heracles to serve King Eurystheus for ten years. Eurytheus set Heracles ten labours and then tricked Heracles into doing two more. The agreed arrangement was that if Heracles performed the twelve impossible labours he would be forgiven and would become an immortal god. This was part of Zeus' divine plan to teach humans, gods and goddesses about existential angst and how to overcome it by using divine faith and divine strength.

The first labour for Heracles was to kill and flay the Nemean lion, an enormous beast with a pelt impervious to iron, bronze and stone. The Nemean lion had been killing villagers and herds of cattle. Heracles shot his deadly arrows at the lion. However the arrows rebounded harmlessly and the lion yawned scornfully. Heracles then used his sword, which buckled hopelessly. Heracles then used his club to bash the lion who suffered a mere ringing in his ears as the club smashed into pieces. The lion wandered, happily and unperturbed, back into its cave lair.

Heracles felt weak and inept. Heracles started to doubt himself and wondered whether he really had the strength to carry on and do what was needed. Heracles felt cowardly and ruminated resentfully about how Hera had yanked his rulership inheritance away from under him all those years ago. Heracles' negative thoughts about himself tied him up in a cowardly bind. Heracles lost faith in himself and in his divine nature and with that loss of faith there was a loss of Heracles' divine strength. Heracles felt vulnerable physically. Heracles looked at the Nemean lion and saw a strong and magnificent warrior. Heracles felt deficient and weak and cowardly. The more Heracles looked at the Nemean lion the more Heracles saw how strong and brave and magnificent and physically imposing the Nemean lion was. Heracles looked at the Nemean lion and saw it growing with every breath, whereas Heracles felt he was diminishing and becoming more fearful and cowardly with every breath. Heracles felt the need to be hyper vigilant because he was caught up in a fight for his very survival. Heracles could hear the Nemean lion pacing around inside the cave. Heracles felt that at any moment he would be attacked and killed by the Nemean lion. In that moment Heracles felt uncertain about everything. The only thing that Heracles was certain about was that if he let his guard down the Nemean lion was going to tear him into pieces and eat him.

Heracles ruminated cowardly about the strength and aggression of the Nemean lion and how dangerous and hateful the Nemean lion was. Heracles compared himself and his cowardly fearful inadequacy and fragility, with the strength of the Nemean lion. Heracles felt fear like he had never felt it before in his life. His belly felt gripped and knotted in fear. His heart felt a lack of courage, a lack of strength, a lack of fortitude. His mind was full of doubt. Heracles questioned his impulses. Heracles said to himself 'I want to kill the Nemean lion. I want to complete my first labour.' But then immediately Heracles said to himself 'Do I really want that. What about just going away and leaving the lion alone. Why don't I just protect myself and survive.' Heracles was wracked with self doubt. Heracles no longer had an inner sense of certainty that he was strong enough to survive the battle with the Nemean lion. Heracles wondered 'Have I made the right decision taking on these labours.' Heracles was suffering very deeply from this picking apart of his impulses by inner questioning. Heracles looked at the Nemean lion and saw a beast that was just concerned about its own welfare. Heracles looked at the Nemean lion and saw a beast that was self seeking and self serving and threatening to Heracles' very existence. Heracles felt like he was a little rabbit, scared and frozen. Heracles felt himself twitching, stopping and starting. Heracles tried to speak but found he could only stutter. Heracles felt his genitals growing smaller and smaller and smaller. Heracles sat down outside the cave of the Nemean lion and whimpered in utter desolation.

Zeus looked down from Oympus and saw the pitiful tragedy unfolding. Zeus too was feeling self doubt. Zeus felt that he himself must be inadequate if his son was weak and cowardly. Zeus decided he must do something, for the very future of humanity and the gods and goddesses depended on Heracles demonstrating his divine faith and his divine strength. Zeus summoned his messenger the god Hermes. Zeus put on a brave and kingly face and told Hermes in no uncertain terms that Hermes must find a way to make Heracles believe in himself and in his divine origins and in his divine strength.

Hermes was a very clever and eloquent young messenger god. Hermes decided he would make Heracles go to sleep and during the sleep Hermes would inspire Heracles in a dream using dream symbols.

Heracles felt his eyes growing heavy and then suddenly Heracles felt he was on the seashore. This was confusing because the cave of the Nemean lion was no where near the ocean. Heracles thought in his dream that maybe that was something to do with climate change and rising sea levels. Now firmly in his dream world Heracles looked into the ocean and saw his reflection on the water. As he gazed harder and harder at his reflection on the water he saw a mighty divine god with bulging muscles. The water on which this projection was occurring turned into a wave. The little wave started getting bigger and bigger and bigger and the image of Heracles projected onto the face of the wave grew bigger and bigger. The wave turned into the size of a massive tidal wave. The wave was hundreds and hundreds of metres high and on the face of the mountainous wave was projected the image of the divine god Heracles with his enormous bulging muscles the size of mountains. As Heracles stared at this dream wave he felt the ocean all around him dragging him out towards the wave. He was powerless to stop himself being sucked out to sea towards the massive wave. Heracles was drawn up the face of the mountainous wave and was perched right at the top of the wave as it began to break. Heracles looked down from the top of the wave and it was like looking down from the clouds he had been lifted so high. As the wave started to break Heracles felt he had a choice to either be driven down under the sea by the wave where he would surely drown in the turbulent ocean depths or he could exercise his divine strength to connect with his divinity and land safely on the distant beach. Heracles chose to access his true nature and in that moment Heracles knew that there was a part of him that would never die and that the image of himself projected onto the huge wave was a projection and a mirroring of himself by himself. Heracles knew that the strong and powerful wave was not something outside himself but was his projection of himself onto the massive wave. Heracles knew that the massive wave with the image of Heracles with massive bulging muscles reflected on the mountainous wave face was something Heracles was creating. In that instant Heracles knew that he was dreaming and was projecting his inner strength onto the mountainous wave. In a flash of insight, Heracles knew exactly what he was, namely a divine god with divine strength. Heracles knew what he had to do.

Heracles sprang immediately to his feet and shook off his dream. Heracles netted one entrance to the cave, so the Nemean lion could not escape then entered by the other entrance. Heracles knew that his weapons were useless and that he would have to wrestle with the lion. As Heracles approached the Nemean lion he said to it 'I will tell you what is going to happen. I will put my left hand out and you will bite it and chew on my fingers. But as you are chewing on my fingers I will put my right arm around your neck and I will choke you to death.' Heracles slowly lifted his left hand and moved it towards the lion's mouth.

As Heracles sat on the body of the now dead Nemean lion, Heracles marvelled at the lustre and strength of the pelt of the Nemean lion. Heracles thought to himself that the pelt of the Nemean lion would make very fine armour which he could use to complete the rest of his labours. Heracles did not know how he could flay the lion because of the imperviousness of its pelt. Heracles thought of a cunning plan. He could use the lion's razor sharp claws as a skinning tool. Heracles made the invulnerable pelt into armour and used the head of the Nemean lion as a helmet.

Zeus looked down from Olympus and was pleased, very pleased. Zeus knew that soon enough all humans and all gods and goddesses would learn of Heracles divine strength and of his divine faith in himself as a son of Zeus. Zeus knew that in that manner, Heracles and Zeus and all humans and all gods and all goddesses could rid themselves of their existential angst.

As stated above, Heracles' life teaches us how super strength is needed to battle the existential angst that arises from being fearful about not being as strong as others or not being as clever or virile or as good as others. Heracles' life also teaches us about the cultivation of strength by appropriate self-acceptance and self-honesty.

Heracles continued to display his divine strength as an immortal son of Zeus as he labored against dangerous and powerful adversaries for many, many years in full bodied physical confrontation. Heracles' labors demonstrate very different values to that of safe spaces, trigger warnings and avoiding offense.

The goddess Artemis

Artemis' virtue is prudence. Artemis is the goddess associated with the 2nd Path on the Tree of Life, the Path known as The Foundation. Prudence is the ability to prepare carefully, wisely and thoroughly for the future. The story of Artemis shows how prudence can be used.

Once upon a time there was a goddess named Artemis. When Artemis was three years old she was seated on the knee of her father Zeus and he asked her what presents she would like. It became apparent immediately that Artemis had given this some prior consideration. Artemis was very prudent. Artemis stated that she sought eternal virginity, a bow and arrow, a saffron hunting tunic with a red hem reaching to her knees, the ability to bring light, sixty ocean nymphs of the same age as Artemis to serve as maids of honour, twenty river nymphs to tend to Artemis' collection of knee high leather hunting boots and to feed her hounds, all the mountains in the world and one city because she would be living on a mountain most of the time in order to avoid the invocations of women in labour who having heard about her mother Leto's pain-free childbirth had appointed Artemis the patroness of childbirth. The nature and extent of the gifts that Artemis sought shows that Artemis was preparing carefully, wisely and thoroughly for the future. Artemis was being prudent.

When Artemis told Zeus her list of requests, Zeus smiled proudly and provided the presents to her. In addition Zeus gave Artemis thirty cities and appointed Artemis guardian of roads and harbours.

Artemis' story shows her virtue of being prudent. Prudence is available to every person by taking steps to prepare carefully, wisely and thoroughly for the future. The story of Artemis shows how the virtue of prudence can be exercised.

Bible story showing the virtue and values of prudence, diligence and independence.

Matthew chapter 25 verses 1 to 13 tells the story of ten young maidens who were tasked with lighting the way to the banqueting house for a bridegroom and his bride. Five of the maidens were prudent and diligent. Five were foolish. The ten young maidens went out to greet the bridegroom and the bride. Five foolish maidens took their lamps but no additional oil for their lamps. The five prudent and diligent maidens took additional oil in vessels along with their lamps. The bridegroom and the bride were delayed. The ten young maidens slept while they were waiting. At midnight there was a cry 'Behold the bridegroom and the bride are coming. Go out to greet them!'. The ten young maidens got up and prepared their lamps. The five foolish young maidens said to the prudent ones 'Give us some of your oil, for our lamps are going out'. The prudent and diligent young maidens answered saying 'Why, there would not be enough for us and for you. Go to those who sell and buy for yourselves.' And while the five foolish young maidens went to buy the oil, the bridegroom and the bride came. The five prudent maidens entered with the bride and the groom into the banqueting house and the door to the banqueting house was locked behind them. Afterwards the five foolish young maidens came and said 'Lord open up to us.' But he answered and said to them 'I do not know you. Be alert, therefore, for you do not know the day nor the hour.'

The story told by Matthew shows the value of prudence, diligence and independence. These are the virtues associated with the Path on the Tree of Life known as The Foundation.

Politics and self doubt

Heracles's reflection about his divine nature, coupled with his self-honesty and self-acceptance as to his strengths and weaknesses enabled him to set aside the envy he had for the Nemean Lion.

I wonder whether the protestors of the extreme political Left and of the extreme political Right are engaged in a similar existential angst driven envy. The envy of the extreme Left being an envy of wealth and an envy of the power of benevolence. The seeking by the extreme Left to share the wealth of others because of self-doubt about his or her ability to create wealth of that magnitude. And whether on the extreme political Right there is a cognate self-doubt about his or her intrinsic worth if subjected to an evaluation by other races, classes or philosophies. In other words, perhaps Professor Ryan was onto something when he suggested that prayer of self-reflection, self-honesty and self-acceptance, rather than politics is the answer to the human conditions. I wonder if Professor Ryan's view might be tweaked by suggesting, consistently with the Tree of Life, that politics produced by self-reflection, self-honesty and self-acceptance may improve the human condition better than by mere prayer alone.

Sal the clinical psychologist says ...

The concept of "Wise Mind" in Dialectical Behaviour Therapy (created by Marsha Linehan) reflects the discussion in this chapter as to the left and right brain and the bridge between the hemispheres performed by the corpus callosum. Wise Mind refers to the wisdom which arises within each person when they access their inner wisdom and prudence. Wise Mind is attained through a synthesis of both "Reasonable Mind" and "Emotion Mind" – that is an "integration of opposites".[194]

"Reasonable Mind" is the extreme of reason. It does not take values or emotions into account and is ruled by facts and logic. Whilst Reasonable Mind can be very beneficial in the world when wanting to get practical things done, such as building a house or organising a meeting, it is dismissive of passion, needs, desires and values, which can be problematic when people are involved.

Interestingly, Linehan states [195]'You cannot overcome Emotion Mind with Reasonable Mind. Nor can you create emotions with reasonableness. You must go within and bring the two together.' Wise Mind has an intuitive quality, in that it is beyond what can be known objectively or through analysis. Generally, when making decisions using Wise Mind, you are free of conflict, as decisions using Wise Mind bring a certain inner peace. Linehan emphasise that Wise Mind depends on an integration of all ways of knowing – 'knowing by observing, knowing by analysing logically, knowing by what we experience in our bodies (kinetic and sensory experiences), knowing by what we do, and knowing by intuition.'[196]

Linehan emphasises that finding Wise Mind can take a lot of practice and involves getting to the heart of a matter, comprehending the whole picture, when before, only parts of the picture were understood. The prudent and wise decision comes from a deep sense of knowing, rather than your current emotional state or thoughts.

Finding the Wise Mind centre within you can be helped by meditative exercises. One such exercise which Linehan describes is 'Imaging being a stone flake on the Lake... Imagine you are by a lake on a warm sunny day. It is a large, clear, very blue lake. The sun is shining warmly on the lake. Imagine that you are a small stone flake from a piece of stone near the lake, and imagine being gently tossed out onto the waters of the lake. Imagine that you are slowly, very slowly floating down in the cool, clear blue waters, gazing at what is around you. And now settling on the clear bottom of the lake, gazing at the clear waters and what is nearby. And when you are ready, open your eyes, come back to the room, trying to maintain your awareness of that clear centre that is within you.'[197]

Summary

- There is a Western tradition of philosophy, psychology, politics and theology.

- Pythagoras, Socrates, Plato and Aristotle form the main part of that lineage which continues to the present day.

- The lineage is called the Western mystery tradition or Western Yoga.

- The Western mystery tradition says that a human being possesses a spiritual dimension known as a soul.

- Ancient Greek conceptions of soul are the primary sources of all Western views of soul, including those of Islam and Judaism. Socrates is credited as the father of the Western conception of soul.

- Democracy and the legal constitutions of the countries of the West are based on the Western mystery tradition and on the idea of an individual possessing a soul.

- The Western mystery tradition is recorded in an image known as the Tree of Life.

- The Tree of Life shows the way the two hemispheres of the human brain operate.

- The Tree of Life showed that way, thousands of years before science made that discovery.

- The scholarly works of Ian McGilchrist and of Jill Bolte-Taylor show the accuracy of the Tree of Life.

- Atheism arises from using predominantly the left hemisphere of the human brain, which the Tree of Life calls the Pillar of Severity.

- Theism arises from using both the left and right hemisphere of the human brain, which the Tree of Life calls the Pillar of Equilibrium.

- The Foundation is the name of the Path situated immediately above the Path known as The Kingdom on the central Pillar of Equilibrium.

- The values and virtues of the Path known as The Foundation are diligence, prudence and independence.

- The Greek God Heracles (aka Hercules) is the god associated with the Path known as The Foundation. The exciting and adventurous labours of Heracles teach us about how super strength is needed to battle the existential angst that arises from being fearful about not being as strong as others or not being as clever or virile or as good as others.

- Heracles' life also teaches us about the cultivation of strength by appropriate self-acceptance and self-honesty as an antidote to envy.

- In the realm of politics, it may be that the envy by the extreme Left of those with vast wealth and of the power of privately funded benevolence, and the seeking by the extreme Left to share the wealth of others, is based on self-doubt about his or her ability to create wealth of that magnitude. Similarly, it may be that on the extreme political Right there is a cognate self-doubt about his or her intrinsic worth if subjected to an evaluation by other races, classes or philosophies.

CHAPTER THREE

PATH 3 – THE GLORY

THE GLORY IS the Path of honesty. In other words, the virtue of the Path known as The Glory is honesty. Jordan Peterson's rule 'tell the truth or at least don't lie'[198] is stating the same virtue. Honesty is a very ancient virtue of Western civilization and of the Western mystery tradition.

Western civilization and our forebears teach us about the importance for us of honesty and the problems for us of deceit. One of the so-called seven deadly sins is called deceit. Dr Liz Greene writes[199] of 'deceit' that 'If left unconscious and unchecked, turns us into liars, cheats and schemers, full of cunning and willing to injure anyone who stands in our way.'

However, Dr Liz Greene also considers[200] that an understanding of deceit 'can become honest pragmatism and a full embrace of the reality of the world in which we must live.'

The Tree of Life uses the Greek God Hermes to teach us about deceit and about honesty. Hermes' life and adventures are, in my view, some of the most hilarious adventure stories ever told. As you will read in this chapter, the stories start with Hermes as a toddler who decides to steal Apollo's cows. Hermes devises a cunning scheme where he puts plaited grass boots on the hooves of the stolen cows so the cows cannot be tracked.

You will read in this chapter how the Greek God Zeus observed these traits in his son Hermes with a mixture of pride and concern, and how Zeus said to Hermes 'You must tell the truth or at least don't lie. You must respect the property rights of others.'

In this way, Hermes' father Zeus was hoping to teach Hermes to transform deceit into an honest pragmatism combined with integrity and compassion. Dr Liz Greene calls[201] that transition a transition from 'deceit' to 'worldly wisdom'.

Hermes' life story shows how Hermes achieves that transition from cunning liar, thief and arch manipulator into a mature person exercising worldly wisdom with integrity.

Archangels

The Tree of Life has, for thousands of years, associated certain Archangels with certain Paths on the Tree of Life. The Archangel associated with the Path known as The Glory is the Archangel Michael. Archangels have been discussed and written about for thousands of years. There is no shortage of brilliant scholars who have explored, in a considered manner, the likely existence of and role of Archangels. Religions and philosophies such as Christianity, Hinduism, Islam, Judaism, Tibetan Buddhism and Zoroastrianism embrace the concept of angels and Archangels. An Archangel leads and supervises angels. The word 'angel' is from the Greek word for 'messenger'. The Bible contains more than three hundred references to angels. In Acts 23: 7-9 the Pharisees champion the argument in favour of angels (and communication with angels) when dealing with dissenting Sadducees. The Apostle Paul was a Pharisee. The Pharisees were regarded highly as expert expositors of Jewish law.

Thomas Aquinas was a scholarly Catholic priest and a Doctor of the Church. He was born in Italy in 1225. He wrote favourably and extensively about Aristotle. One of Saint Thomas' most well known works is the Summa Theologiae. Saint Thomas is regarded widely as one of the greatest philosophers of the Western world. Saint Thomas taught about the existence of angels. He considered that an angel consisted of pure thought or intellect but had the ability to assume a physical body at will, albeit a physical body that was made up of pure thought[202].

The Archangel Michael is an Archangel in Judaism, Christianity and Islam. Jude 1:9 refers expressly to Archangel Michael. The literal translation of the name Michael is 'Who is like God'. Archangel Michael has been depicted traditionally as being an angelic warrior, armed with a shield and a sword or a lance. Archangel Michael's shield bears the Latin inscription 'Quis ut Deus' which means 'Who is like God'. The inscription could be regarded as being Archangel Michael's name, like an athlete's name on the back of her or his outfit. The inscription could be a practical way of seeking to ensure the shield is returned to Archangel Michael if the shield were to go missing. However, the inscription is more likely a clever rebuke and rhetorical question addressed to Lucifer. The relevant context is found in Isaiah 14:14 where Lucifer Morning Star (aka Satan[203]) says 'I will make myself like the Most High.' Archangel Michael's shield inscription 'Who is like

God' alludes to the grandiose aspiration declared by Lucifer. The grandiose aspiration of Lucifer shows the vices of the Path known as The Glory. The vices are falsehood and dishonesty.

The virtues and the vices available to us, as lived experiences, are demonstrated and explained graphically, albeit metaphorically, in the relationship between Archangel Michael and Lucifer (described in Revelation 12:7-9). Archangel Michael and his angels defeated Lucifer and his angels in a war. Lucifer took on the body of a dragon during the war. Lucifer also wore the body of an old serpent 'called the Devil and Satan, which deceiveth the whole world: he was cast out into the earth, and his angels were cast out with him.'[204] The verse shows Archangel Michael is a warrior who engages in war against the vice of falsehood and dishonesty. The Path of The Glory is a path where bold honesty in action is required. It is a path of confrontation where the vanquished are cast out as the result of being fought.

The Bible verse shows Archangel Michael and his angels fought with Lucifer and his angels. This is significant because it shows the value and virtue of fighting for honesty against dishonesty. Angels may need to be fought against. Particularly when they align themselves with a dragon or a serpent.

The Bible verse shows Lucifer and his angels are not killed. Rather they are re-located, cast out of heaven, and 'into the earth'. Revelation 12:12 warns 'woe to the inhabiters of the earth and of the sea, for the devil is come down unto you'. This is important because it suggests that notwithstanding the earthly inhabiters are embodied souls (see chapter one) those souls will experience 'woe... for the devil is come down unto you'. The word 'woe' means great sorrow, suffering and distress. It is descriptive of one immutable part of our human experience as inhabiters of earth. In other words, suffering and sorrow are part and parcel of our lot as inhabiters of the earth. The virtues and values accessible to us to confront suffering and sorrow include diligence, prudence, independence, veracity and truthfulness.

The warrior status of Archangel Michael has been recognised and recorded by painters, sculptors and poets throughout the centuries. The English poet John Milton wrote 'Paradise Lost' in the late 1650s. The poem describes the relationship between Adam and Eve and Satan. Archangel Michael plays an important role wounding Satan with a sword forged by God specially to deal with angels[205]. Milton describes Archangel Michael being sent to the Garden of Eden to visit Adam and Eve after the fall, to show them a vision of life on earth and to tell them about potential redemption through King Messiah. It may be that the reference to redemption through the King is a reference to redemption through Kingly actions in the Kingdom by one's self. Milton was a Hebrew scholar and his familiarity with the Tree of Life is well documented[206].

In the Louvre in Paris, France is the painting 'St Michael Vanquishing Satan' by Raphael the Italian Renaissance artist in about 1518. In the Prado in Madrid, Spain is 'Saint Michael Archangel' by Master of Zafra, painted around 1500, showing Archangel Michael attacking the dragon. There is a large and magnificent bronze statue of Archangel Michael standing on the devil in Saint Michael's church in Hamburg, Germany. The Coptic Cathedral of Archangel Michael in Aswan, Nile Valley, Egypt has a sculpture of Archangel Michael holding a sword in one hand and scales in the other hand. The paintings by Michelangelo on the Sistine Chapel in Rome, Italy includes Archangel Michael holding scales.

This is the judging and evaluating characteristic of Archangel Michael. It is the judging and evaluating aspect of The Glory. Judging and evaluating are part and parcel of the value and virtue of veracity and truthfulness. In other words, in order to be honest and truthful it is necessary to judge and evaluate. The current trend towards non-evaluation and non-judging that occurs in childrens' sports where scores are not kept and where positive reinforcement is favoured over objective evaluation, is a rejection of the value and virtue of veracity and truthfulness. The Tree of Life shows the importance of the value and virtue of veracity and truthfulness. It is timely for that value and virtue to be re-emphasised and for the current trend towards non-evaluation and non-judging to be modified by re-emphasising the virtues of honesty, veracity and truthfulness.

Hermes the Greek god

The Tree of Life associates the delightful and deceitful Greek God Hermes with the Path known as The Glory. As noted above, Dr Liz Greene writes[207] of 'deceit' that 'If left unconscious and unchecked, turns us into liars, cheats and schemers, full of cunning and willing to injure anyone who stands in our way.' Importantly, Dr Greene also considers[208] that an understanding of the roots of deceit 'can become honest pragmatism and a full embrace of the reality of the world in which we must live.'

The fabulous Penguin Classics book 'The Greek Myths'[209] by Robert Graves provides detailed information about Hermes.

Once upon a time there was a God named Hermes. Hermes' father was the god Zeus. Hermes' mother was Maia, the daughter of Atlas. Hermes was born on Mount Cyllene and left home looking for adventure when he was no more than a toddler. Hermes went to Pieria where Apollo, another of Zeus' progeny, was herding cows. Hermes decided to steal the cows.

Hermes devised a cunning plan whereby he used plaited grass to tie bark from a fallen oak tree to the hooves of the cows so that the cows could not be tracked. The ruse succeeded and Apollo searched high and low unsuccessfully for the stolen cows. Apollo decided to offer a reward for information leading to the capture of the cow thief. Silenus, the tutor of Dionysus, heard of the reward, and assembled his band of satyrs (goat- totem tribesmen) to find the cows and claim the reward from Apollo. Silenus and his satyrs searched far and wide, without success.

Then one day when searching near Arcadia they heard music the like of which they had never heard before coming from the mouth of a cave. In the cave was Cyllene the nymph (a nubile woman having grown from the stage of maiden and before growing to the stage of crone). Cyllene told Silenus and his band of satyrs that a gifted boy had recently been born in the cave and the boy had made an ingenious musical instrument from cow-gut and the shell of a tortoise. Cyllene said the boy had used the music to lull his mother to sleep so he could embark on adventures. Silenus noticed two cow hides were stretched and drying outside the cave, so he asked Cyllene 'From whom did the boy get the cow-gut for his musical instrument?'. Cyllene was angry and affronted and said 'Are you insinuating that the boy is a cow thief?'. Angry words hurled back and forth.

Then Apollo arrived. Apollo had deduced, somehow, the identity of the cow thief by observing the suspicious behavior of a long winged bird. Apollo strode into the cave and confronted Maia, the mother of Hermes, saying 'Your boy must return the cows that he has stolen from me.' Maia pointed to the young Hermes who was wearing toddler's clothes and who had his eyes closed pretending to be asleep and said to Apollo 'What an absurd charge you make against the little boy.' However Apollo inspected the cow hides and detected that the hides were from his cows. Apollo picked up Hermes, who was still feigning deep sleep, and took him to Olympus to face a trial for the theft of the herd of cows. Apollo also took the cow hides which were to be the principal evidence for the prosecution.

Zeus thought it unlikely that his new born son was a cow thief and accordingly encouraged Hermes to plead not guilty to the charge. Apollo remained steadfast and eventually

Hermes confessed to the cunning theft but sought to plea bargain by saying to Apollo 'You may have your entire herd of cows, save only for the two cows that I sacrificed to the twelve gods on your behalf.' Apollo asked 'Twelve gods? Who is the twelfth?' Hermes replied 'Me. I am. But I ate no more than my share notwithstanding that I was, and remained, exceedingly hungry. I duly burned the rest in sacrifice.' This was the first flesh sacrifice that had ever taken place. Zeus and Apollo were impressed by the ingenuity of the young Hermes and permitted Hermes to return to his mother Maia at Mount Cyllene.

Upon his return Hermes greeted his mother and went immediately to a sheepskin underneath which he had hidden his unique tortoise shell lyre and tortoise shell plectrum, which he had also invented. Hermes then played an exquisite tune the like of which had never before been heard. Mid way through the intoxicating tune Hermes started singing, making up words in an inspired extemporaneous manner praising Apollo for nobility, intelligence and most of all generosity. When Hermes completed his inspired advocacy, Apollo found himself forgiving Hermes for everything.

Hermes then led the surprised and somewhat infatuated Apollo to Pylus, singing and playing all the way, and there gave him the ten remaining cows, which Hermes had hidden in a cave. Apollo said 'I propose a bargain. I will take the lyre and you shall have the cows.'. Hermes agreed at once. Hermes led the hungry cows out of the cave and while the cows were grazing Hermes cut reeds and made them into a pipe on which he played another extemporaneous composition of mesmerizing magnificence.

Apollo called out 'I propose another bargain. If you give me that pipe I will give you my golden cow herding staff and you shall be the god of all herdsmen and shepherds.' Hermes counter offered saying 'But my pipe is more valuable than your staff. Notwithstanding that fact, I am prepared to do the deal so long as you instruct me in the art of augury.'

Augury was the then popular aristocratic art of omen reading, in particular the deduction of meaning from the manner in which flights of birds were constituted. Hermes replied 'That I cannot do. But if you call upon the Thriae, my old nurses who live on Parnassus, they will instruct you in the art of divining from pebbles.' A bargain was struck. Apollo took the child Hermes back to Olympus and recounted to Zeus all that had happened.

Zeus could not help but be impressed by the nimble nature of Hermes' mind. Zeus said to Hermes, 'You must tell the truth or at least don't lie. You must respect the property rights of third parties. You are an ingenious, eloquent and persuasive godling.'

To which Hermes replied 'If that is a sound opinion, then I would make a useful herald for you, Father. I will take on responsibility for the safety of all divine property, though I cannot promise always to tell the whole truth.'

Zeus smiled knowingly and said 'That would not be expected of you. However your duties will include the negotiation of treaties, the promotion of fair and favourable commercial transactions, and the maintaining of free and effective passage for travelers on roads throughout the world.'

Hermes agreed, whereupon Zeus gave Hermes a pair of winged golden sandals which would transport Hermes with the swiftness of the wind, a round rain hat and a herald's staff with white ribbons, which everyone was ordered to respect.

Hermes was embraced as a welcome member of the Olympian family. Hermes taught them the art of starting a fire by rubbing sticks. The Thriae taught Hermes the art of predicting the future by observing the movement of pebbles in a basin of water. Hermes subsequently invented the game of knucklebones and the art of predicting the future by using knucklebones.

Hermes was also appointed herald by Hades, the god of the underworld and the partner of Persephone. Hermes' duties for Hades included summoning the dying gently and eloquently by laying the golden staff upon their eyes. Subsequently and consequently, the white ribbons on the herald's staff which Hermes had been given by Zeus became mistaken for serpents because of Hermes' heraldic duties for Hades.

Hermes assisted the Three Fates in composing the Alphabet. The Three Fates are also known as the Moerae which means the Triple Moon- goddess - Clotho the Spinner, Lachesis the Measurer and Atropos the One who Cannot be Turned or Avoided. In particular, the Three Fates invented the five vowels and the consonants B and T. Hermes transmogrified those sounds into characters using wedge shapes.

Hermes' ingenuity continued to be profound and practical. He invented a diverse range of human activities and useful information including the arts of boxing and gymnastics, the musical scale, weights and measures, the cultivation of the olive tree and the science of astronomy.

As the god who invented weights and measures, Hermes was an obvious choice for the god of The Glory. Hermes main symbol is the caduceus. The caduceus is in the form of a short staff entwined by two serpents. Originally the staff was entwined by two white ribbons, as described above. The two white ribbons transmogrified into two serpents after Hermes' assumed the dual herald role for both Zeus and Hades. The caduceus is a very old symbol, said to date from 3000 BC. Hermes is associated with Hermes Trismegistus the author of 'The Emerald Tablet of Hermes'. The Emerald Tablet of Hermes is a carving containing a collection of intriguing sentences. The date of its creation is the subject of myths and legends. What we do know for certain is that Isaac Newton has provided a translation of The Emerald Tablet and that translation is stored in King's College Library at Cambridge University in England. The opening words (as translated by Isaac Newtown) are: 'Tis true without lying, certain and most true. That which is below is that which is above, and that which is above is like that which is below to do the miracles of one only thing'. Sometimes the opening words are summarized to the effect 'as above so below' and sometimes 'as above so below but after a fashion'. Dion Fortune when writing about the Tree of Life, has stated[210] 'As above so below, man is a miniature macrocosm. All the factors that go to the makeup of the manifested universe are present in his nature.'

Hermes is associated with Thoth the Egyptian god. Thoth's wife was Ma'at. Thoth is depicted regularly as a man with the head of an Ibis. Thoth is associated with science, the judgment of the dead by using scales and weighing the deceased's heart against a feather, and with the art of writing.

The Islamic tradition claims Hermes Trismegistus to be the builder of the Pyramids of Giza. In the Roman mythology Hermes is regarded as Mercury. The god of financial gain, commerce, eloquence, messages and boundaries. Mercury's temple in Rome was constructed in about 500 BC. Mercury is a complicated character. When Mercury is behaving admirably there are boundaries and propriety and charming eloquence soundly and scientifically based, that is the god of science and books. However, there is another aspect to Mercury which arises when Mercury is behaving badly. When Mercury is behaving badly his aspect as the god of thieves and cunning rogues arises, which is the obverse of the supreme virtue of truthfulness.

The characteristics of Hermes and Mercury provide an illustration of the manner in which Western civilization deals with the values associated with the Path on the Tree of Life known as The Glory. Consistent with that approach, Dion Fortune has described The Glory as involving 'the rational mind imposing inhibitions on the dynamic animal nature of the soul'.[211]

You have seen earlier in this chapter how Hermes learned to use his extremely fine rational mind to impose useful and mature inhibitions on his deceitful dynamic animal nature and thereby turn deceit into an honest pragmatism combined with integrity and compassion. Dr Liz Greene calls[212] that transition a transition from 'deceit' to 'worldly wisdom'. You read about Hermes achieving the transition from cunning liar, thief and arch manipulator into a mature person exercising worldly wisdom with integrity.

Yetziratic texts and symbols

The values of each Path on the Tree of Life are described in a verse known as the Yetziratic text. The Yetziratic texts are often dense and relatively incomprehensible. The Yetziratic text for The Glory is 'The Mean of the Primordial'. Dion Fortune explains[213] that the values behind 'The Mean of the Primordial' are the same values expressed in the representation of Archangel Michael holding in his hands a pair of balances, symbolic of equilibrium.

Dion Fortune provides[214] the following commentary in relation to the values of Archangel Michael:

'The serpent upon which the great Archangel treads is primitive force, the phallic serpent of the Freudians; and this glyph teaches us that it is the restrictive "prudence" of (The Glory) which "shortens" primitive force and prevents it from overflowing its boundaries. The Fall, be it remembered, is represented on the Tree by the Great Serpent with seven heads which overpasses the bounds set for it... It is very interesting to observe the manner in which the symbols weave in and out of each other, and reinforce and interpret each other's significance...and yield their fruits to Qabalistic contemplation.'

As noted before, the values of each Path on the Tree of Life are demonstrated by an accompanying 'Order of Angels". For completeness it is noted that the Order of Angels functioning in The Glory are called the 'Bene Elohim', which means the Sons of God. The value being expressed is that the Bene Elohim are the humble toiler angels overseen by Archangel Michael, who in turn is giving effect to the plans of God working as the Great Architect of the Universe. The Order of Angels can be used to understand at greater depth the values contained in the Path known as The Glory.

Another value recorded in a symbol associated with the Path on the Tree of Life known as The Glory is that of 'the versicles'. Versicles are mantric phrases. A mantra is a sonorous phrase which is repeated over and over, similar to the manner in which a rosary is used. McGilchrist refers to the well known event that occurred in the mid 1960's in a Benedictine monastery in the south of France when as part of the modernization approach introduced by the Second Vatican Council the monks were required to stop their daily Gregorian chanting. For centuries the monks had been thriving on about four hours sleep each night, apparently supplemented by the regeneration and recouperation that occurred by their daily Gregorian chanting. Shortly after being deprived of the daily Gregorian chanting the monks experienced apathy and ennui, disease and general ill health. Medical intervention was unable to reverse the symptoms. Dr Alfred Tomatis, the highly regarded ear nose and throat specialist, reintroduced daily chanting of versicles and within a few months the monks were returned to their former vitality. The association of versicles with the Path on the Tree of Life known as The Glory arises because versicles are a form of precisely ordered communication which creates an internal resonance in the human body at the same frequency as that of the versicles. In that manner the versicles are capable of bringing about a harmonious balance in the human body. The versicles are also capable of waging war and casting out the internal human malaise. It is apparent from the above description that the values inherent in the versicles reflect consistently the characteristics of Archangel Michael that have been discussed above.

Sam Harris has written extensively[215], and well, about meditation and the tendency of human minds to wander in 'stimulus-independent-thought'. The use of versicles is one way in which our ancestors developed an ability to deal positively with that tendency. Almaas has also noted[216] the use of versicles in Judaism, Islam, Kashmir Shaivism and Tibetan Buddhism. The Pythagorean harmonies taught thousands of years ago in the Western mystery schools are another example of the use of versicles.

If you want to dive very deeply into your musical heritage, the book for you is the masterpiece by W.A. Mathieu 'Harmonic Experience – tonal harmony from its natural origins to its modern experience'. Mathieu explains how Pythagoras discovered musical relationships as a way to explore the harmonies of the universe. This is likely to be the same material that Pythagoras taught in his Western mystery school and which formed part of the syllabus learned, and then taught, by Socrates, Plato and Aristotle during their time as students, then teachers, in those Western mystery schools you read about earlier in this book. Mathieu explains, in his chapter 27, how Pythagoras was the first to recognise the Circle of Fifths. The importance of the Circle of Fifths to modern popular music is well recognized and is demonstrated hilariously in 'The Four Chord Song' by the Axis of Awesome. The chord progression I   V   vi   IV is recognizable immediately to any Western ear. Our 21st century link to Pythagoras and his lineage of Socrates, Plato and Aristotle, via modern popular music and its four chords is quite remarkable.

The values of the Path known as The Glory on the Tree of Life include those values associated with 'the apron'. Traditionally an apron was a characteristic garment of a craftsman, that is a maker of forms. As noted previously, The Glory sits at the bottom of the pillar on the tree of life associated with the creation of forms. The use of aprons remains common even these days in the ceremonial rituals conducted in the Masonic lodges and in the Rosicrucian lodges throughout the world. As Dion Fortune has noted[217], the placement of the apron has the effect of covering and concealing what is called the mundane chakra associated with Path on the Tree of Life known as The Foundation.

As you can see from the front cover of this book, The Glory is located at the bottom of the Pillar of Severity. Rav Philip Berg, who was a well known American rabbi, has written[218] that The Glory 'controls left-brain activity'.

Sal the clinical psychologist says ...

Setting clear personal boundaries is the key to ensuring relationships are mutually respectful, supportive and caring. Boundaries are a measure of self-esteem. They set the limits for acceptable behavior from those around you, determining whether they feel able to put you down, make fun, or take advantage of your good nature.

If you are often made uncomfortable by others' treatment of you, it may be time to reset those boundaries to a more secure level. Weak boundaries leave you vulnerable and likely to be taken for granted or even damaged by others. On the other hand, a healthy self-respect will produce boundaries which show you deserve to be treated well. They also will protect you from exploitative relationships and help you avoid getting too close to people who don't have your best interests at heart.

There are many reasons, but people with weak boundaries usually ignore boundaries due to their belief that they have to be accommodating, helpful, should not say "no", and need to be liked. They are often the subject of emotional manipulation.

People with weak boundaries: (1) over-share personal information, (2) have difficulty saying "no" to the request of others, (3) get over-involved with other's problems, (4) tolerate disrespect and abuse.

What are the signs of healthy boundaries ? You have healthy boundaries if you: (1) value your own opinion, (2) don't compromise your values for other people, (3) appropriately share personal information, (4) are accepting of others when they say "no" to you, (5) you don't take things so personally, (6) you disagree with a friend and are able to maintain your friendship, (7) you realise you are not responsible for the actions of others, (8) you become comfortable in receiving as well as giving, (9) you no longer feel responsible for making a relationship work or making another person happy, (10) you no longer blame yourself for everything that goes wrong in a relationship or a friendship, (11) you generally do precisely what you want to do, rather than depending on the suggestions of others, (12) you can say "no" without experiencing major guilt, (13) you act on feelings when you need to.

What are the signs of weak boundaries ? People with weak boundaries tend to have a low awareness of their own needs.

What is the way forward ? Make an inventory of your needs and beliefs. You may discover that you have put your own needs further back on the shelf than the needs of other people. If you want to assess your own boundaries, I suggest you affirm your needs. It will help if you set 'a line in the sand' as it were. Begin by looking at Maslow's hierarchy of needs. For example, evaluate your need for belonging and acceptance. Examine how well you have satisfied your need to love and be loved, as well as be respected and have self-respect. The question is, to what extent are your boundaries helping or hindering the satisfaction of your needs.

So why is it important to have boundaries ? It's important because healthy personal boundaries help maintain a positive self concept. It is important because you can take better care of yourself and not allow other people to define who you are.

What else can you do to create stronger boundaries ? Trust and believe in yourself. You have to recognise that you are the highest authority on yourself. When you reflect upon yourself, you will know what you need, want and value. You recognise that healthy boundaries allow you to take better care of yourself – emotionally, mentally, physically and spiritually.

Your needs and feelings are as important as other people's needs and feelings. This is often a difficult lesson to learn for two reasons. First, the spiritual lessons in your youth may have expected you to put other people before you. Second, modeling from your parents may have supported the belief that you should care for your fellow man. You probably won't go so far as to believe that your life should be sacrificed, however you may think that whenever possible you should try to put other people first.

Learn to say "No". You may have been a people pleaser who has to learn that a certain amount of 'selfishness' is necessary for healthy personal boundaries. You have a right to personal boundaries. You need to take responsibility for how you allow others to treat you. You can recognise that boundaries are filters that permit what is acceptable in life and what is not acceptable. You boundaries protect and define you. They set clear and decisive limits that others can respect.

Some words for setting stronger boundaries – No. No thank you. I'm not sure, I'll get back to you on that. Thanks but I've got a previous commitment. I'd rather not go into that right now. I can help you with this, but I can't help you with that. That's a tough one but I'm sure you'll be able to figure it out. I hear what you are saying but I see it a little differently. I felt angry when you put me down. I'll need my order delivered on time. I lent you money and I'll need it back. You could be right but this is what I would like.

Summary

- The Tree of Life has been used by Western civilization for thousands of years to train the mind.

- The Path on the Tree of Life, described in this chapter, is known as The Glory.

- The value associated with The Glory is honesty. The implementation of honesty gives rise to order and boundaries.

- The Glory is associated with left-brain processes.

- The values associated with The Glory are personified in the nature and deeds of the delightfully cunning and naughty Greek God named Hermes and of the bold Archangel Michael.

- Hermes' life stories are filled to the brim with the wisdom of western civilization embedded in hilarious adventurous escapades and cunningly creative exploits.

- Hermes' ingenuity was profound and practical. He invented boxing and gymnastics, the musical scale and the science of astronomy.

- The Tree of Life has, for thousands of years, associated certain Archangels with certain Paths on the Tree of Life.

- Archangels have been discussed and written about for thousands of years. There is no shortage of brilliant scholars who have explored, in a considered manner, the likely existence of and role of Archangels.

- Religions and philosophies such as Christianity, Hinduism, Islam, Judaism, Tibetan Buddhism and Zoroastrianism embrace the concept of angels and Archangels.

- The Archangel associated with the Path known as The Glory is the Archangel Michael.

- Archangel Michael embodies the positive characteristics of The Glory with his warrior attitude and actions, his preparedness to engage in war with adversaries and with his preparedness to weigh and judge.

- The current trend towards non-evaluation and non-judging that occurs in childrens' sports, where scores are not kept and where positive reinforcement is favoured over objective evaluation, is a rejection of the virtue of honesty, veracity and truthfulness.

- The Tree of Life shows the importance of the virtue of honesty, veracity and truthfulness. It is timely for that virtue to be re-emphasised and for the current trend towards non-evaluation and non-judging to be modified by re-emphasising the virtue of honesty, veracity and truthfulness.

- The values associated with The Glory provide an antidote to the chaos associated with the values of safe spaces and trigger warnings, non-judgmental, non-threatening, non-confrontational and non-evaluative behavior.

- The Glory and its relationship with The Kingdom is referred to in the Lord's Prayer as 'For yours is The Kingdom, The Power and The Glory'.

CHAPTER FOUR

PATH 4 – THE POWER

THE EROTIC ADVENTURES of the Greek Goddess Aphrodite have been used for eons by our ancestors to teach us about the Path known as The Power.

Dr Liz Greene considers[219] that for us to be psychologically healthy we need to understand deeply our natural human desire for 'inappropriate longing' (aka lust).

In this chapter you will read how Aphrodite has a magical girdle which makes everyone lust for its wearer. This is the 'inappropriate longing' described by Dr Greene.

Aphrodite's lust is recounted in ribald fashion. However, the Tree of Life and in particular the Path known as the Power also teach us about the problems that will arise for us when lust is suppressed inappropriately. The inappropriate scuttling of lust arises in dictatorships. Dictatorships do not nurture longings for fine clothes, fine dwellings, fine cars, fine dining, to name but a few.

The Tree of Life records the appropriateness and the necessity of The Power and its creative juices which fuel the healthy, competitive capitalism of western civilization.

The Power is located on the opposite side of the Tree of Life to The Glory. The Lord's Prayer describes The Power and The Glory combining in The Kingdom. This is a very significant idea. We have seen McGilchrist describe in 21st century scientific terms how an idea will arise in the right hemisphere of the brain then flash to the left hemisphere and then ideally will move back towards the right hemisphere before being acted on. Nearly three thousand years ago the Tree of Life depicted that occurring.

The well-known American rabbi Philip Berg wrote[220] about The Power that it 'is associated with intuitive, involuntary "right-brain" processes. It is the realm of the dreamer, the artist and the masculine fertilizing principle.'

The Power is the Path that sits at the bottom of what the Tree of Life calls the Pillar of Mercy. This is associated with the right hemisphere of the brain. The Glory is the Path that sits at the bottom of what the Tree of Life calls the Pillar of Severity. This is associated with the left hemisphere of the brain. Between those two pillars is what the Tree of Life calls the Pillar of Equilibrium. The mind can be trained to obtain information and input from the Path known as The Power. The mind then supplements that information and input from the Path known as The Glory. The mind then moves that information to the Path known as The Kingdom where the idea can take on a form, be actualized, be materialized, be created.

We have seen already how the values of The Glory include constraint and borders and order. The values of the Power are the antithesis. The values of the Power are unselfishness, chaos, fecund uncontrolled diversity of growth, the art of lovemaking, power and beauty. The vice of The Power is Lust. As noted previously, the antithesis described in the three thousand year old Tree of Life is reflected daily in the 21st Century in the political arena and the politics of the far left (The Power) and the far right (The Glory).

We have explored the manner in which the values associated with The Glory were embodied in the warrior Archangel Michael with his tools of action – sword, lance, shield and weighing scales. We will now explore the manner in which the virtues and vices and values associated with the Power are set out in the Tree of Life.

Aphrodite the goddess

Aphrodite shows the virtue of unselfishness, and the vice of lust. Unselfishness and lust are values. Western civilization has used the tales of Aphrodite to teach values and the consequences of actions based on certain values.

The following description of the nature and deeds of Aphrodite have been assembled from the delightful writings of Robert Graves in his inspired and scholarly Penguin Classics book 'The Greek Myths'.[221]

Once upon a time there was a Goddess named Aphrodite. Aphrodite is the goddess of Desire. Reasonable minds differ as to the identity of Aphrodite's parents. One perspective is that Aphorodite's mother is Dione and Aphrodite's father is Zeus. Another perspective is that Aphrodite sprang self-generated from the sea foam around the genitals of Uranus after Cronus had thrown those genitals into the sea surrounding the island of Cythera.

What is not in dispute is that Aphrodite was first seen buck naked riding a scallop shell as a surfboard on a wave breaking on a beach on the island of Cythera. Aphrodite inspected briefly the island of Cythera and where ever she walked grass and flowers sprang from the soil underneath her footprints. Aphrodite considered the island of Cythera to be too small and moved on to Paphos in Cyprus, which city is still the principal place of her worship. Aphrodite is accompanied always by an entourage of doves and sparrows. Doves and sparrows are known for their profligate lechery.

Aphrodite had been assigned one divine duty and only one divine duty. The duty was to make love. One day Aphrodite tried another divine duty, that of working on a loom. However, working on a loom was one of the divine duties assigned to the goddess Athene. Athene took understandable umbrage. Aphrodite apologized profusely and henceforth never turned her hand to anything other than her divine duty of making love.

Aphrodite has a magic girdle which makes everyone fall in love with its wearer. Aphrodite would seldom lend her magic girdle to the other goddesses because the magic girdle assisted Aphrodite in fulfilling her aforementioned divine duty.

Aphrodite had been married off to Hephaestus the lame Smith-god. Hephaestus had been an ugly and weakly baby and developed into a lame, ugly and weakly man. Hephaestus mother was Hera. In a fit of peak and disgust, Hera had dropped the ugly, weakly baby Hephaestus into the sea from the height of Olympus to rid herself of the embarrassment of having produced such a child.

Hephaestus survived the fall and the drowning and was raised by the gentle goddesses Thetis and Eurynome, who set Hephaestus up with his first anvil and bellows in an underwater grotto. Thetis and Eurynome were the sea-goddesses who had created the universe. In his smithy shed in the underwater grotto, Hephaestus made beautiful jewelry. One day Hephaestus' mother Hera saw a brooch made by Hephaestus whereupon Hera took her weakly son back to Olympus and set him up with the finest anvil and Smithy shed with twenty bellows that worked 24/7. Hera and Hephaestus reconciled to such an extent that when Zeus hung Hera from Heaven by her wrists for rebelling against Zeus, it was Hephaestus who reproached Zeus. Unfortunately for Hephaestus, Zeus responded by throwing Hephaestus from Olympus to the earth. It is reported widely that Hephaestus fell through the air for one full day before landing feet first on the island of Lemnos, breaking both legs immediately and painfully on contact with the soil. From that day forward Hephaestus was lame and could only walk with leg-supports, which he fashioned himself in gold.

Besides being lame and ugly, Hephaestus was ill tempered. But he did have strong arms and shoulders from his work as a smithy and it was said by all that his workmanship was unsurpassed. Hephaestus had a creative artistic and practical streak that caused him one day to make a set of golden mechanical women to work as labourers in his smithy shed. The golden mechanical women were very impressive in that they could talk and carry out very complicated tasks. Hephaestus also made for himself a set of twenty tables. The tables were three-legged tables with golden wheels which travelled under their own will and direction around his workshop and even travelled autonomously to and from meetings with the gods.

Hera and Zeus gave Aphrodite in marriage to Hephaestus. Aphrodite promptly presented Hephaestus with three children named Phobus, Deimus and Harmonia. However the true father of those children was Ares the God of War. Ares was known to be drunken, impetuous and quarrelsome, albeit straight-limbed.

Aphrodite and Ares took advantage of the long hours worked by Hephaestus to have frequent and long sex at Ares' Thracian palace. One such sex session continued long through the night and into the early hours of the morning. Helius, the god 'who sees everything' but who is not particularly observant, and who is roused by the crowing of the cock, which is sacred to him, saw Aphrodite and Ares 'in flagrante delicto' (as the Judges' dysphemism goes). Helius told tales to Hephaestus.

Aphrodite returned home from Thrace smiling and radiating the bliss of torrid extra-marital post-coital nefariousness and declared to Hephaestus that she had been away on business at Corinth. Hephaestus hobbled to his shed and devised a cunning retaliatory plan. Hephaestus hammered out angrily a bronze hunting net. The net was perdurable, indestructible and as fine as gossamer.

Hephaestus affixed surreptitiously the bronze hunting net to the posts and sides of his marriage bed and then said to Aphrodite that he was taking a short holiday on Lemnos, his favourite island.

Aphrodite excused herself from attendance on Lemnos and as soon as her cuckolded spouse was out of sight sent word to Ares who arrived promptly. After a night in flagrante Aphrodite and Ares found themselves entangled in the bronze hunting net, buck naked, captured and without means of escape.

The next day Hephaestus returned from the journey to Lemnos and found Aphrodite and Ares entangled in the bronze hunting net.

Hephaestus called upon the gods and goddesses to attend and witness the dishonour of the naked Aphrodite and Ares entangled in the bronze hunting net in Hephaestus' connubial bed. The gods attended eagerly, not so the goddesses who, it was said, remained in their houses from a sense of delicacy.

Apollo and Hermes, two of the gods who had attended at the behest of Hephaestus, gazed longingly at the nearby naked Aphrodite under the bronze hunting net. Apollo nudged Hermes and asked 'I bet you wouldn't mind trading places with Ares?' Hermes replied 'Too right, even if had to put up with three nets. And even if all the goddesses were looking on.' Apollo and Hermes roared with laughter. Aphrodite heard the repartee and blushed with delight.

Hephaestus announced that Aphrodite would be released upon repayment by Zeus to Hephaestus of the valuable marriage-gifts that Hephaestus had paid to Zeus as the father (or adoptive father) of Aphrodite.

Zeus refused to return the gifts. He declared with the sanctimonious and hypocritical gall of an archetypical philanderer that this was a vulgar dispute.

Poseidon, the sea god, stared longingly at Aphrodite's naked body and devised a cunning plan to take Ares' place. Poseidon pretended to sympathise with Haphaestus and said to him 'I think it unfair that Zeus is not re-imbursing you for the financial expenditure you incurred in providing marriage gifts. I will personally guarantee the repayment by Ares of the financial loss you have suffered.

Hephaestus replied 'Noble Poseidon you make an exceedingly generous offer but if Ares defaults you will have to take his place under the net.' Haphaestus said, with attempted feigned indifference, barely concealing his self-satisfied smugness 'I am ready to pay the debt and marry Aphrodite if that becomes necessary.'

Accordingly, Aphrodite and Ares were released from their capture in the bronze hunting net. Aphrodite travelled to the delightful coastal town Paphos on the island of Cyprusres where her virginity was renewed.

Aphrodite then found Hermes and had sex with him in appreciation for his boldly expressed infatuation when she was captured in the bronze hunting net. Their coupling produced Hermaphroditus who was a double-sexed being.

Aphrodite then found Poseidon and had sex with him in appreciation for his intervention on her behalf. Poseidon fathered two sons, Rhodus and Herophilus with Aphrodite.

Ares defaulted on his financial obligation to pay Hephaestus. However Hephaestus did not pursue his financial rights as he was besotted with Aphrodite and never had any intention of divorcing her.

Aphrodite gave herself to the god Dionysus. Dionysus was a son of Zeus. Dionysus was born with horns crowned with serpents. Jealous goddess Hera arranged for Dionysus to be torn into shreds at birth, and for his shreds to be boiled in a cauldron. Notwithstanding that punishment Dionysus was reconstituted and on Zeus' instructions was transformed by Hermes into a kid goat known as a ram. Dionysus invented wine while he was living on Mount Nysa. The coupling of Aphrodite and Dionysus produced Priapus, an ugly child with enormously large genitals. Priapus' appearance was the consequence of intervention by Hera, who you recall was the mother of Aphrodite's cuckolded husband Hephaestus, and who was punishing Aphrodite for her promiscuity.

Aphrodite's magical girdle caused preoccupation and temptation in Zeus himself, albeit that he was the father, or at least the adoptive father, of Aphrodite. One day Zeus decided to humiliate Aphrodite by making her fall desperately in love with a mortal, the handsome Anchises King of the Dardanians. Aphrodite disguised herself as a Phyrgian princess and, clad in a dazzlingly erotic red robe, seduced Anchises in his herdsman's hut on Mount Ida on a couch spread with the skins of bears and lions while bees buzzed soporifically around them. At dawn Aphrodite revealed her true identity as a goddess and swore Anchises to secrecy.

It was not long at all before Anchises revealed the secret. He had been drinking with his friends and one of them asked 'That maiden with the black hair and blues eyes who has recently moved into the village is the most beautiful maiden I have ever seen. I would rather sleep with her than even Aphrodite herself.' Anchises relied vainly 'Well I have slept with them both and your quandary is misplaced.'

Zeus happened to hear of the boast and caused a thunderbolt to be directed at Anchises. However, Aphrodite diverted the thunderbolt by using her magical girdle to lure the thunderbolt into the ground at the feet of Anchises. The shock took its toll on Anchises who thereupon lost the ability to stand up straight with his shoulders back and accordingly Aphrodite lost her passion for him.

So what values of western civilization do we take from these stories of Aphrodite the goddess of The Power. The magical image of The Power is a beautiful naked woman. Aphrodite clearly fits that bill. The Power's 'correspondence in the microcosm' includes the loins and hips, for equally self evident reasons when one considers the use Aphrodite made of those parts of her body. The Vice of The Power is lust and unchastity and the association with Aphrodite is self-evident. One of the symbols of The Power is the girdle. We have seen the manner in which Aphrodite uses the girdle to fulfill her divine duty, and one time as a weapon to save the egotistically outspoken mortal Anchises from the thunderbolt of scornful Zeus. The extraordinary depth of the chaos of insatiable passion driven by instinctual and emotional forces is apparent in the deeds of Aphrodite. The need for those insatiable forces to be bridled and brought to order somewhat in order for there to be an equilibrium, is also apparent. Dion Fortune describes one value in The Power as being 'the factor in ourselves that is the basis of our instincts, each of which in their unintellectualized essence, gives rise to reflexes, just as an infant's lips will suck anything that is inserted between them.'[222]

Dion Fortune considered[223] that in ancient Greece the worshiping of god and goddesses, like Aphrodite, enabled the worshippers to gain access to 'the great natural forces' that were 'so all-important to the material well-being of the worshippers', and that the recounting of the deeds of Aphrodite by the ancient Greeks stimulated the corresponding factor in their nature, thereby developing it.

Aphrodite's Roman counterpart is the goddess Venus. A Temple to Venus was constructed in about 300 BC in one of the southernmost of Rome's seven hills. A marble sculpture of Aphrodite standing nearly 7 feet high was carved in about 130 BC by Alexandros of Antioch. The sculpture is on permanent display at the Louvre in Paris, France where it is known as Venus de Milo. One of the most famous depictions of Venus is that painted by Sandro Botticelli in the mid 1480's. The original hangs in the Uffizi Gallery in Florence, Italy. The painting shows Venus/Aphrodite surfing a sea shell onto a beach. Venus has inspired artists and musicians as diverse as Wagner, Shocking Blue, Bananarama, Lady Gaga and Bjork.

The stories of Venus include that she was born of the foam from the ocean after Saturn castrated his father Uranus and Uranus' blood spilled into the ocean. Venus was married to Vulcan but had many children from many lovers, including Bacchus with whom she had a son Priapus whose characteristics included an absurdly large penis. Venus not only took gods as lovers but also had children with human lovers including Adonis, Sicilian King Butes and Prince Anchises from Dardania.

It is apparent from the above that Venus like Aphrodite is no mere fertility symbol but is also a symbol of the complexity of love and polarity which extends far beyond the sphere of sex.

Historically Demeter and Persephone are fertility goddesses, whereas Venus/Aphrodite (as representative of the Path on the Tree of Life known as The Power) embody a far deeper and more complicated value of instinctual love and polarity. The Power is best understood by remembering that the nature of The Power in the microcosm of The Dominion is represented by Aphrodite/Venus and all that they value, which is far more than mere fertility.

One symbol of The Power is that of the rose. The association between Venus and the rose many thousands of years ago was curiously precocious, in that science subsequently discovered the orbital path of Venus relative to the earth produces a ratio of 8 to 13 which when depicted in a two dimensional diagram produces a delightful rose shaped pattern, which scientists call the Rose of Venus.

As we have seen, Aphrodite made good use of her magical girdle, one of the symbols of Power. Historically the girdle was a long rope like cord that was tied around the waist like a belt. The ends of the girdle were sometimes tied around a Bible and in that manner a Bible could be carried pocket-like without using one's hands. Accordingly Bibles and Breviary became known as Girdle books. The girdle was often worn upon the loins. This provides another linking between those two values associated with the Path of The Power. Greek and Roman women would often wear two girdles, one tied just under the breasts and the other tied just above the hips, thus forming a puckered interval. Sometimes the girdle would be tied into a knot so as to appear like a rose. The girdle is also, traditionally, a symbol of power. Odysseus wore a girdle which enabled him to swim for three days without rest and Thor's girdle doubled his strength. Heracles' ninth labour involved a quest for the enchanted girdle of Hippolyte the Queen of the Amazons. Ishatar the Babylonian goddess wore a fertility girdle which when removed resulted in barrenness. At one time the girdle became a symbol of chastity and virginity. Some marriage ceremonies involved the husband removing the girdle from the wife. For a time, French law prohibited courtesans from wearing girdles.

So, how is the mind trained by the values residing in the Path known as The Power. One way to demonstrate how the mind can use the values residing in the Path known as The Power and in the Path known as The Glory is to recap what we have explored so far and then apply those values to a practical 21st century political issue, that of immigration and border control.

The Tree of Life demonstrates that in order for the prized state of equilibrium to be achieved there must be a synthesizing of the pillar of mercy and the pillar of severity. Too much of the pillar of mercy leads to an out of control passionate chaos of fecundity described in the deeds of Aphrodite. Too much of the pillar of severity leads to the manipulative weighing and measuring of Hermes and the stamping down and setting and enforcing of boundaries by Archangel Michael, oblivious to the wisdom of the now downtrodden serpent. The political far left and the political far right and their extreme dysfunction at their outer edges was predicted by the Tree of Life. The contentious strain between open national borders and closed national borders was apparent in the Tree of Life thousands of years prior to it becoming an election slogan in the USA, Australia, Britain and an increasing number of electorates throughout the world.

At a personal level and at a political level, the Tree of Life describes helpfully the manner in which the values of the pillar of equilibrium can be sought.

The effect of an overabundance of the sphere of The Power in one's life and in one's politics is apparent from certain characteristics of the sphere. As we have seen the 'vice' of The Power is 'unchastity' and 'lust'. The Tree of Life suggests that too much of The Power will result in the 'vice' of 'unchastity' and 'lust'. This is describing a lack of discrimination, in the worst sense of that word and that concept. Unchastity in males and females results potentially in out of control growth. In nature it is the jungle or the bush reclaiming the ploughed paddocks of wheat or the rice padis. There is an incompatibility between virtue and vice. The 'virtue', another old word, for The Power is 'unselfishness'. The Tree of Life describes the need for there to be a balance between unselfishness and unchastity/lust. In the political arena in relation to immigration and borders, the Tree of Life demonstrates that the virtue of 'unselfishness', that is share everything with everyone, will tip into the vice of 'unchastity' and 'lust' where there is too much unselfishness.

Christianity draws a distinction between passion and lust. Lust is on the list of the seven sins. Buddhism's second noble truth is that suffering is caused by lust. In Hinduism, Lord Krishna describes lust as one of the gates to hell[224].

Accordingly, the Tree of Life notes that in order for the sphere of The Power to be balanced, there needs to be an internal balance between unselfishness on the one hand and lust on the other hand. (Of course, the Tree of Life then requires a further balancing of The Power, on the one hand, with The Glory on the other hand). What that means in terms of the political issue of immigration is that one of the initial inquiries at the level of The Power, is as to whether the nature and extent of immigration is at a level that is unselfish but also does not amount to unchastity or indiscriminate selflessness. Once that assessment and evaluation has occurred it would seem that neither fully open borders nor fully closed borders would represent a balanced exercise of The Power.

The next step in the application of the Tree of Life, to the political issue of border control, requires consideration of the sphere known as The Glory, located on the other side of the Tree of Life, in the pillar known as the Pillar of Severity. Remember we are looking to find the point on the middle pillar (the Pillar of Equilibrium) where there is a balance between The Power and The Glory, so that the Kingdom can come into existence.

The next step requires consideration of the characteristics of the sphere known as The Glory. The virtue is Truthfulness. The vice is falsehood and dishonesty. The Glory is located in the feminine pillar where forms are organized. As Dion Fortune noted it was physicists who told us that light is only rendered visible as blue sky owing to its reflection from the particles of dust in the atmosphere. An absolutely dustless atmosphere produces an absolutely dark atmosphere. And so it is in the metaphysics of the Tree of Life. The Glory can only shine in manifestation when there are forms to manifest it.

The Glory has an ancient 'God-name', it is Elohim Tseva'oth. Intriguingly, Elohim is a feminine noun with a masculine plural. There is high authority[225] for the proposition that the English word 'God' is an inaccurate, inappropriate and insufficient translation for the Hebrew word 'Elohim'. The ramifications of a philosophy which uses and used 'Elohim' (with its inherent feminine and masculine attributes) in lieu of 'God the Father', are breathtaking to say the least.

As we have seen, the relevant Archangel is Michael. Michael is represented as trampling upon a serpent/dragon and piercing it with a sword. As Dion Fortune states[226] 'The serpent upon which the great Archangel treads is primitive force, the phallic serpent of the Freudians; and this glyph teaches us that it is the restrictive "prudence" of (The Glory) which "shortens" primitive force and prevents it from overflowing its boundaries.'

The sphere of The Glory is the sphere of Mercury-Hermes, god of science and books. As Dion Fortune writes[227] 'In this Sphere ... god of science and books, how clearly can we see that the supreme virtue is truthfulness, and that the obverse aspect... is that which reveals Mercury in his other aspect as the god of thieves and cunning rogues.'

As we have seen, The Glory is also characterised by the 'versicles', another old word, describing mantric phrases which work as a form of auto-suggestion in the manner of a rosary. Another characteristic of The Glory is the symbol of the apron. The characteristic garment of the craftsman, that is a maker of forms.

Application of the Tree of Life to a contentious issue

So, let's seek to apply that information to the contentious political issue of border control. We know from McGilchrist that the process of thinking involves a movement from the sphere of The Power into the sphere of The Glory. We know that the vice of the Power is lust, that is too much unselfishness.

In relation to border control, if too much unselfishness is applied, that will result in no control at all at the border. That will result in an acceptance of one and all. The Tree of Life suggests a better outcome will arise where some checking and control is applied to temper the 'one in, all in' approach.

In other words, the thinking process moves into the realm where Michael needs to stand on the serpent of primitive force and exercise control over the unbridled passion of nature before its turns from the acceptable unselfishness to the unacceptable lust. The energy of unselfishness must itself be formed up by restricting the unselfishness before it becomes unchaste. There needs to be a prudence, a checking and inhibiting influence. The prudence is based on rational control. The Venus-like effusive natural wantoness is subjected to the coldness of the intellectual rigour of Mercury in the sphere of The Glory.

In relation to border control, this is the application of science and books. This is the application of precedent in the law. This is the learning of lessons. The statute law is here untempered by the subjectivity of equity and idiosyncratic notions of fairness. The realm of statistics is found in the sphere of The Glory. It is here that one calls in aid prudence informed by the statistics of crime. What do the statistics state about open borders and criminal consequences? This is one of the questions that Michael asks while standing on the serpent. Intellectual integrity is paramount. That much is evident from the vice of this sphere of The Glory. The vice is dishonesty. The intellectual analysis must be based on truthfulness and must not degenerate to dishonesty.

In the sphere of the Glory, the analysis of border control must find its internal balance of intellectual integrity where the virtue of truthfulness must be achieved in locating the appropriate place for form to be imposed on nature, for constraint to be imposed on selflessness/unselfishness, for discrimination to be imposed on indiscrimination. In relation to border controls, once the virtue of truthfulness is achieved by recourse to the application of 'science and books' then it is time to seek to balance the virtue of truthfulness with the virtue of unselfishness in order to find the position on the middle pillar, the Pillar of Equilibrium.

This is the Socratic method, the method learned by Socrates in the school of Pythagoras. This is the method that Plato learned from Socrates and that Plato passed on to Aristotle. This is the method of western civilization. The brief example above demonstrates how the Tree of Life can be applied to the contentious issue of border control.

McGilchrist has written[228] that 'The kind of attention we pay actually alters the world: we are, literally, partners in creation.' The Tree of Life agrees. We are partners in creation. We partner in the creation of what occurs in the realm we experience as The Kingdom. The above analysis demonstrates how we can use the Tree of Life to train the mind so that the attention we pay to finding solutions to issues like border control can be used to create a world (The Kingdom) of optimal outcomes (The Pillar of Equilibrium). The brief example shows how the Tree of Life can be used to train the mind <u>how</u> to think, rather than <u>what</u> to think.

Sal the clinical psychologist says ...

Reactivity. Do we overreact to other people's behaviours, feelings and thoughts?

Often our lives can seem to be a reaction to other people. We are pushed and pulled by their ideas and it can affect our view of ourselves. We feel shame, fear, fury, anger and self-hate and believe that "he made me feel this way". When we feel this, we know we are being reactive.

We find ourselves so distracted and so upset by these thoughts and feelings that they hijack our day or week! Given time, we find that we have not followed our own dreams and goals but are on someone else's agenda or we are aimless.

So, why do we react? Some people have grown up in homes where drama and panic were the norm. Not only was it modelled to us as a child but we may have felt that it was the only way to react.

We may also feel that we must react that way because most people seem to react this way. Or we react because we feel that things shouldn't be that way – we have fixed ideas or make quick judgments without all the facts.

Mindfulness is a wonderful tool to help us be less reactive to others. When we are in the moment, just focusing on that moment, we tend to be much more aware of people's faces, body language, behavior, as well as our reactions to them.

I tell clients that when they feel like they MUST react, that is the time they should take a break. Go for a walk, have a soothing bath, do something to distract themselves – and don't say or do anything until they have had time to process it.

It can help to remember that we don't need to be afraid of people in general – they can make requests or even demands and we can choose not to react. We don't need to give away our power.

We don't have to take things so seriously; a thought is just a thought and a feeling is just a feeling. Just because we think someone meant something by their action or inaction, doesn't necessarily mean it is true. Even if a person did mean to hurt us, hopefully we don't need to take their opinion as a reflection of our self-worth.

Reactivity is lessened when we learn who triggers us and what issues in us are affected by their comments. It may be that our defectiveness schema says to us "I'm not good enough". That results in our feeling shame or a feeling that we must help others, which promotes guilt. Learn to understand what your sore-points are.

It can also help to make yourself comfortable by having a walk, a soothing shower or distracting yourself from the event or feelings. You need to slow down and take care of yourself when you feel reactive.

Often long term therapy such as schema therapy is helpful. This can strengthen the healthy adult side of you. This wise person, which we all have within us, knows the best course of action for us in the circumstances.

Summary

- The Tree of Life has been used by Western civilization for thousands of years to train the mind.

- The Path on the Tree of Life described in this chapter is known as The Power.

- The erotic tales of Aphrodite, the Greek Goddess, set out the wisdom of western civilization in relation to using our great natural forces, that are so all-important to our material well-being.

- Aphrodite embodies the values of The Power with her preparedness to engage in chaotic, passionate, life affirming, unbridled breeding with a large variety of partners.

- The values associated with The Power include the passions of polarity, fecundity, effusive diversity and rampant unencumbered natural ferocity.

- The Power is associated with right-brain processes.

- The Tree of Life demonstrates that in order for the prized state of equilibrium to be achieved there must be a synthesizing of the pillar of mercy and the pillar of severity.

- Too much of the pillar of mercy leads to an out of control passionate chaos of fecundity described in the deeds of Aphrodite. Too much of the pillar of severity leads to the manipulative weighing and measuring of Hermes and the stamping down and setting and enforcing of boundaries by Archangel Michael, oblivious to the wisdom of the now downtrodden serpent.

- The political far left and the political far right and their extreme dysfunction at their outer edges was predicted by the Tree of Life. The contentious strain between open national borders and closed national borders was apparent in the Tree of Life thousands of years prior to it becoming an election slogan in the USA, Australia, Britain and an increasing number of electorates throughout the world.

- The Power and its relationship to The Glory is recognised in the Lord's Prayer.

CHAPTER FIVE

PATH 5 – THE BEAUTY

THE PATH KNOWN as the Beauty is worth exploring really deeply. A great way to dive deeply into the Path known as the Beauty is via the Greek God named Apollo.

Western civilization values individuality and self-expression. These values lie at the heart of the path known as the Beauty. For a variety of reasons, the Beauty and its emphasis on the importance of individual identity and individual values, are not politically correct at present.

Dr Liz Greene has written a book[229] about the Greek God named Apollo and the importance and relevance of Apollo for us in the 21st century. Dr Greene has written[230] that:

'At the moment, individuality is not very fashionable. The word "global" is forever on our lips. Nationalism is nasty, elitism is offensive, political correctness appears to be reaching obscene extremes, and the current "dumbing down" process afflicting the British media has reduced intellectual standards to the lowest common denominator in the name of not offending those who cannot be bothered to aspire. We are not supposed to think in selfish, "What about me?" terms. We are encouraged to think in collective terms, with the accent on "sharing" and "participating", and this is reflected in the kinds of government we have voted into power right across Europe…'.

Apollo and the Path known as The Beauty teach us about the constant cyclical process, for each one of us, of struggle and re-emergence. A process that is never ending for any of us. For ever and ever.

Dr Greene considers[231] that we can gain and maintain psychological health by making sure we do not allow a lack of self-respect to restrict our expression of all that is most individual and creative in us.

The brightly shining Apollo is the antithesis of the cold, grey collective. What is being ignored at the present is the importance for the psychological health of an individual to take steps daily to struggle to shine in the idiosyncratic manner of that particular individual. This is the lesson of Apollo and the Path known as The Beauty, taught to us by our ancestors.

Dr Liz Greene has written[232] that:

'The idea that there is a cosmic harmony – personified by Apollo as cosmocrator, "he who puts the heavenly bodies in order" – seems to have first been structured into a philosophical system by Pythagoras in the 7th century BCE… This harmony was understood to be based on numbers and expressed through music… Plato took up this idea and developed it, drawing on the cosmology of the Orphic cults, which portrayed Orpheus the son of Apollo as the poet-singer who articulated the cosmic order through his music. Order in this context means a sense of proportion, balance and interrelationship.'

In that passage Dr Greene refers to the lineage of the Tree of Life that I wrote about in chapter One, ie Pythagoras through to Plato and their use of Apollo to illustrate harmony and balance. Dr Greene also refers to a sense of proportion and balance, which is a description of the ingredients and characteristics of beauty, and Apollo is the God of the Path on the Tree of Life known as The Beauty.

The Beauty

From time immemorial, people have told stories of Great Redeemers who are always born of God and a virgin mother. In the language of the Tree of Life, the Path known as The Beauty is the place where force and form meet. The Beauty is the Path where those stories of Great Redeemers are collected.

The Beauty is located at the central point of equilibrium of the whole Tree of Life. The value and virtue of The Beauty is humble self expression. The vice of The Beauty is pride.

Pride was called 'Superbia' in Latin[233]. From that Latin word we derive the English words 'superb' and 'superior'. The Tree of Life uses the life and adventures of Apollo the Greek God to teach us about humble self-expression and about the uses and abuses of the human energy source and creative impulse called pride. Dr Liz Greene considers[234] that 'Pride can become self-respect, allowing us to express all that is most individual and creative in us.'

The values and virtues of The Beauty can be accessed in a variety of ways. One way is by consideration of the beautiful and venerated wooden statue of the Madonna and Child in the Santa Maria de Montserrat monastery on the Montserrat Mountain in Catalonia, Spain. The statue depicts Mary with a long thin body and face. Mary is seated in a pose known as the throne of wisdom. Mary has the infant Jesus sitting on her lap. The head of Jesus is resting on Mary's heart. Mary and Jesus are depicted as having very, very dark skin. The sculpture is often called the Black Madonna. Some believe the statue was carved in Jerusalem 'at the beginning of religion'[235]. One of the values of The Beauty is that devotion and adoration arise from the relationship between heart and head. The Black Madonna records this in the relationship of mother and child and by showing the head of the infant Jesus resting on the heart of Mary. The context includes the subsequent sacrifice of Jesus. We are reminded that through sacrifice life is returned to its divine source. There is a reciprocal flow of the divine life force between its source and its manifestations. Sir James George Fraser[236] described sacrifice as a ritual slaying of a god in order to rejuvenate the god.

The Beauty is the Path of the Sun gods. Apollo is the Sun god of Western civilization.

Apollo

Once upon a time, as you remember, the King of the Gods was named Zeus and Zeus was famous for his erotic escapades. Zeus used to plough the paddocks of all the beautiful goddesses whenever he got the chance. And Zeus used to make sure he regularly got the chance. One auspicious night when the full moon and the sun aligned, the breath-takingly beautiful goddess Leto, found her paddock being ploughed by Zeus and inside Leto grew Apollo and his twin sister goddess Artemis, the breathtakingly beautiful moon Goddess of the Foundation.

During Leto's pregnancy the Sun changed its course and travelled very close to the earth for nine months. The Sun was sending special solar radiation to Apollo and to his sister Artemis. The solar radiation went into Leto's womb and made Apollo's hair turn the colour of the blazing sun. The Sun and Apollo grew so close during the pregnancy that they shared each other's thoughts.

Zeus' wife Hera heard on the grapevine that Leto was going to give birth to Zeus' progeny. Hera also heard that Apollo and Artemis were going to be the most beautiful and radiant brother sun and sister moon in the history of creation. Hera vowed to extract revenge by preventing the birth of Apollo. Hera devised two plans to prevent the birth of Apollo.

Plan A was to murder Leto before Leto gave birth. Hera assigned a Dragon named Python to murder Leto. Python was named Python because that was the name of the area where Python worked as a Dragon guard.

Hera's Plan B was very cunning. Because Hera was a very powerful Goddess, Hera declared that Leto was banned from giving birth on terra firma. Terra firma was another name for earth. However the Sun heard about Hera's declaration and the Sun devised an equally cunning response. The Sun searched the whole world and found what he wanted. The Sun found a floating island called Delos and because the island was floating it was not, strictly speaking, terra firma. And because the floating island was not terra firma, Leto could give birth to Apollo on that floating island without being in breach of Hera's declaration.

As soon as the Sun devised that cunning plan, the plan also arose in Apollo's mind because the Sun and Apollo were so indivisibly close, even though Apollo was still in Leto's womb.

Apollo communicated the plan to Leto in a dream that his sister Artermis was able to induce in their mother Leto. Leto followed the guidance in her dream and went to the floating island of Delos to give birth to the twins.

Hera was furious when she heard how she had been outsmarted. Hera told the Dragon / Contract Killer named Python to hurry up and get on with the job and murder Leto and her now new-born son Apollo.

As Apollo grew up, his blazing red blonde hair radiated like the Sun. Apollo and the Sun loved each other so much that at times they were almost indistinguishable. For example on days when the clouds blocked the Sun it was Apollo who shone warmth and provided the divine comfort that the people sought from the Sun. The Sun had always wanted to make music but whenever the Sun got too close to musical instruments the musical instruments would burst into flame. So the Sun gave Apollo all of the musical talent of the universe. In that way the Sun was able to play music through Apollo. It was as though the Sun and Apollo were inextricably linked and that although Apollo had his own body he was in truth one undivided entity with the Sun, somehow. There was a harmony between the Sun and Apollo which reflected this indivisible wholeness that they shared together.

The people looked at Apollo and his mere existence gave them hope that one day they too could merge with the divine Sun in the way that Apollo had merged in his day to day life.

Apollo and Python

Meanwhile the underworld dragon known as Python was stalking Leto and Apollo, with the aim of murdering them both at the request of Hera.

As soon as the Sun heard of the plan for the Python to murder Leto, the plan also became apparent to Apollo because of their shared thoughts.

Apollo spent many years travelling the seven seas and travelling to the depths of the Underworld to find Python and to kill Python before Python could murder Leto. At times people thought that Apollo must have died because he spent so much time in the Underworld.

Eventually Apollo found Python. Python was standing guard at a massive and ancient cave on Mount Parnassus. Apollo was armed with golden arrows. The golden arrows had been made by Hephaestus. You will remember that Hephaestus was the lame and ugly blacksmith who had been given the hand (and body) of the breath takingly beautiful goddess named Aphrodite. Hephaestus made the weapons of battle for all of the Gods.

Python was a formidable foe. Python's celestial Goddess mother was the divine and powerful Gaia. Python had extraordinary powers derived from Gaia. Python could fly vast distances very quickly. Python could shoot fire, poison and sharp icicles from his mouth for hundreds and hundreds of metres. Python had extraordinary eyesight and also had the power of prophecy. Python had leathery skin that was crusty and strong like iron.

Apollo came to the mouth of Python's cave and said calmly to Python 'Here is your chance to kill me. I know all about your bargain with Hera, to murder Leto and me. You will never make good on that bargain because I will slay you first!' Python blinked his hooded leathery eyelids from inside the dark damp cave he was guarding. Python was dazzled by the brightness of the Sun being reflected off Apollo and into the cave.

The battle raged for days and nights, and days and nights. Eventually Apollo was able to shoot one of Hephaestus' golden arrows into Python's sleep deprived eye. The arrow pierced the eye and lodged in Python's brain. Python died instantly.

Apollo knew that Python's death would leave the local villagers without access to Python's highly regarded, and very useful, powers of prophecy. Accordingly, Apollo decided to establish his own oracle at Mount Parnassus in order to serve the local villagers of that region. Apollo knew that oracular powers depended on the co-operation of the underworld. To bring about that co-operation, Apollo created a Pythoness. A Pythoness was a human female made by Apollo from a blend of solar light and Plutonian darkness. In order to make the first Pythoness, Apollo had to travel to the depths of the underworld via the darkest, deepest seas. In order to travel to the depths of the darkest seas, Apollo turned himself into a dolphin. The Greek name for dolphin was delphis. Apollo changed the name of the region from Python to Delphi, in order to commemorate the demise of Python and the establishment of the shrine of the Pythoness at the newly named Delphi. For centuries the fame of the Delphic oracle spread far and wide. An earlier chapter in this book described the importance of the civic role played by succeeding generations of Pythonesses as oracles of Delphi.

Zeus wanted desperately to keep on good terms with Gaia, the mother of the now dead Python. Zeus decided that he had to punish his son Apollo severely for killing Python. Zeus sentenced Apollo to serve as a groom and herdsman slave in exile for one year to King Admetus. During this time Apollo made all the cows bear twins.

Apollo and the satyr named Marsyas

After Apollo had redeemed himself by serving King Admetus, Apollo began to wander the world playing beautiful music. The music played by Apollo was like honeyed nectar to the ears of those people who were fortunate to hear the divinely inspired melodies. Apollo's legend as a musical genius spread throughout the whole world. As soon as Apollo heard the young Hermes playing the tortoise shell lyre, Apollo added that instrument to his repertoire. You will remember in an earlier chapter, how young Hermes stole Apollo's cattle and made lyre strings from the guts of one of the cattle. Apollo loved to play the tortoise shell lyre he had acquired from Hermes. Gods, goddesses and humans came from far and wide to hear Apollo play and sing.

In another part of the world, a much darker part of the world, there live a satyr named Marsyas. Satyrs were part man and part beast. They lived in the forests. They had ears and a tail resembling those of a horse. Marsyas used to impress people was by playing popular musical tunes on the flute. However, appearances were deceiving. Marsyas 'played' the flute because he had been cursed by the goddess Athene. It happened this way. Athene made a flute from stag's bones and played it at a banquet of the gods. Athene saw Hera and Aphrodite laughing silently behind their hands when Athene was playing the flute. This annoyed Athene because all of the other goddesses and gods seemed to be delighted by the music. The next day Athene went into the forest and played the flute while sitting beside a stream. Athene saw her reflection in the stream and saw how ridiculous she looked with puffed up cheeks and a bright red face from blowing so hard. Athene threw down the flute and laid a curse on anyone who picked it up.

Marsyas was, initially at least, the innocent victim of the curse. No sooner had Marsyas picked up the flute, the flute started playing beautiful music by itself. Soon Marsyas' reputation as a flute player spread far and wide. Marsyas became very proud of himself. However, Marsyas did not have the humility to disclose that he was not playing the flute but rather the flute was playing itself. Marsyas became more and more proud as more and more townsfolk began to worship him as the god of music. However, Marsyas was not a god he was a satyr who mimed and pretended to play the flute. The god of music was Apollo. The townsfolk said that even Apollo could not make better music than Marsyas. Marsyas was too proud to contradict them.

Apollo heard townsfolk saying that Marsyas could play the flute better than Apollo, so Apollo challenged Marsyas to a contest. It was to be a very unusual contest in that the winner could inflict whatever punishment he pleased on the loser. The nine Muses were impaneled as the jury to determine the winner. Apollo played beautiful songs. Marsyas' flute played beautiful songs while Marsyas mimed along pretending he was the composer and the musician. The contest was very close. The Muses were unable to decide which music was more beautiful. It looked like there might be a hung jury. Apollo thought of a way to break the deadlock and to teach the arrogant satyr a lesson. Apollo said 'I can turn my instrument upside down and play it and sing at the same time. I challenge you do that with your instrument.' Of course Marsyas was not able to do those things with a flute. Apollo turned his lyre upside down and played it beautifully and started singing along to the music he was composing, singing songs of praise to the Olympian gods.

The nine Muses decided unanimously that Apollo was the clear and outright winner. Apollo decided he would inflict a cruel punishment on the satyr in order to deter other people who might be thinking of becoming proud and casting humility aside. Apollo took Marsyas to a plane-tree near the stream where Marsyas had found the flute and Apollo flayed Marsyas alive, then nailed Marsyas's skin to the plane-tree. In that way Apollo was sending a message to the world discouraging the vice of pride and encouraging the virtue of humility.

Dionysus, Priapus and Cloacina – the stench of superbia

There is a more complicated form of Pride that is useful to explore. In Latin the sin of Pride was described by the word 'superbia'. From the Latin word 'superbia' we derive the English words 'superb' and 'superior'. Religious folks often think of themselves in terms of 'superb' and 'superior', for example a head nun may be called Mother Superior. In the past whenever I have felt spiritually superior I have noticed that I give off a stench that these days I call my stench of spiritual superiority. It is a dreadful stench and I try my best to avoid letting it happen. Because of my own spiritual stench I can smell it readily on other people. I often smell my own spiritual stench mixing with the spiritual stench of others at pious gatherings. Recently I was working as Crown Prosecutor in a criminal trial of an Anglican Dean charged with historical sexual child abuse crimes. The Anglican Dean had a spiritual stench of 'superbia' that rivalled my own spiritual stench and at times was even worse than mine. It was horrible to be in the Courtroom when both of us were in fully superbia stench mode. The Anglican Dean's stench of superbia contributed to him being found guilty. But that story is for another day. What we are looking at here and now in this chapter of the book is spiritual pride.

Dion Fortune suggests[237] that spiritual pride is caused by a spiritual vanity which values spurious refinement and idealism. Ms Fortune has written[238] 'It is because Priapus and Cloacina are not given their due as deities that we are cursed by the Sun-god and cut off from His benign influence for an insult to His subsidiary aspects is an insult to Him.'

So let us explore, briefly, the life and adventures of the Greek God named Priapus.

Once upon a time a young God named Priapus was born to Aphrodite. It came as no surprise to Aphrodite, or to those who knew Aphrodite well, that Aphrodite was uncertain as to whether Priapus' dad was Zeus or Dionysus (who was the son of Zeus – one of many, many sons of Zeus). The better view is that Dionysus was the dad. Priapus was born with a remarkable physical attribute. He was born with a permanently erect penis that was the same length and girth as his legs. Furthermore, as Priapus' legs grew longer and thicker, so did his erect penis continue to grow longer and thicker. The medical term priapism (permanently erect and engorged penis) is derived from Priapus' predicament.

Priapus used to spend his days in the garden. He loved getting his hands dirty in the soil. Being in the garden also enabled Priapus to disguise, to some extent, his huge erect penis by wearing loosely fitting gardener's overalls. Sometimes he would put a hat on the top of his penis so that he looked like a kangaroo carrying a joey in a pouch. Whenever Priapus had the opportunity, he would attempt to plough the paddock, as the Greeks called it, of any young maiden in the vicinity. Priapus loved to use a pruning-knife and would readily prune flowers which he would then cast before maidens as part of his seduction playbook.

As Dion Fortune noted above, the Priapus creative impulses have not been managed well by human beings, particularly those who have taken on celibate clergy roles. The failure of many humans to give Priapus his dues as a deity has resulted in being cut off from the benign influence of the Priapus impules. The failure to celebrate and nurture the Priapus impulses has also resulted in restricted access to the full spectrum of the Sun-god Apollo's creative impulses because Priapus is a subsidiary aspect of the Sun-god Apollo.

Us human beings have also failed to fully embrace the creative impulses of the goddess Cloacina. The goddess Cloacina was the goddess who presided over the sewers in Rome and in particular the Cloaca Maxima which was the main trunk of the sewer system in Rome. Cloacina is derived from the Latin word to cleanse. The excretory openings of certain animals is known as the cloaca. This provides the etymology for the Ribald expression (at least in Australia) of 'the clacker'. Mating by cloaca occurs in some animals and is known as cloacal copulation. Some turtles breathe through their clacker in what is known as cloacal respiration. As Dion Fortune noted above, the Cloacina creative impulses have been undervalued by human beings. That has resulted in humans being cut off from the useful influence of the Cloacina impules to cleanse and get rid of waste byproducts in our life. The waste byproducts in our life are not only external waste items but also internal emotional waste that we have created and which we ought to have flushed out of our system a long time ago. The failure to use effectively the Cloacina clean out impulses has also resulted in restricted access to the full spectrum of the Sun-god Apollo's creative impulses because Cloacina is a subsidiary aspect of the Sun-god Apollo.

As we saw above, there is a relationship between the Apollonian creative impulses found in Priapus and Dionysus, namely Dionysus is the father[239] of Priapus. Accordingly, it is useful to explore the life and adventures of the Greek God Dionysus.

Dionysus

Once upon a time a god was born and he was named Dionysus. Dionysus' father was the amorous Zeus. Zeus disguised himself as a mortal and ploughed the field of a beautiful mortal woman named Semele. Zeus' wife Hera found out that Semele was pregnant with Zeus' male child. When Semele was six months pregnant, the scorned and angry Hera disguised herself as an old friend of Semele and told Semele to ask her disguised lover to reveal his true identity so that Semele would know that the lover was not a monster. Hera knew that if Zeus revealed himself, Semele would be destroyed by Zeus' aura. Semele pleaded with her disguised lover to reveal himself. Zeus refused to reveal himself. Semele refused ongoing access to her paddock. Zeus revealed himself and Semele was obliterated into one thousand pieces by Zeus' aura. Hermes found the six-month year old baby boy who had survived miraculously the obliteration of his mother. Hermes sewed the baby boy into the thigh of Zeus. Zeus carried the baby boy named Dionysus for a further three months until Hermes surreptitiously delivered the baby one night. The name Dionysus means twice born or he of the double door.

The baby Dionysus was exceedingly ugly. He had horns growing from his head and serpents wound around his horns. Hera instructed an army of Titans to kill baby Dionysus. Zeus intervened and had Hermes temporarily turn Dionysus into a ram until Dionysus was old enough to protect himself. When Dionysus grew up he discovered how to make wine from grapes. This made Dionysus very popular. Dionysus gathered together a very merry band of Satyrs and Maenads. Satyrs enjoyed drinking to excess at every opportunity and attempting to plough the paddocks of any nearby women. Maenads were female followers of Dionysus. Maenads wore grape vines in their hair and frolicked semi naked in dance circles. Dionysus and his band of Satyrs and Maenads traveled the world planting vines, making wine and teaching humans the joys of inebriation and intoxicated revelry. Zeus was delighted with the joy Dionysus was teaching to humans. Zeus invited Dionysus to join him in heaven as one of the twelve great ones. Dionysus sits at the right hand of Zeus in a place of honour.

Dionysus looked down from heaven and saw that his mother Semele was living in the underworld with Hades and Persephone. Dionysus and his merry army of satyrs and maenads devised a cunning plan to free Semele. Rather than crossing the River Styx and alerting Hades and Persephone to their arrival, Dionysus travelled to the underworld through the Alcyonian Lake at the city of Lerna. The Alcyonian Lake was said to be bottomless. It was so deep that no human had ever been able to plumb its depths. King Nero had every rope in the kingdom joined together so that the length was miles and miles long, but still the depths of the Alcyonian Lake could not be touched. Swimmers who tried to swim from one side of the Alcyonian Lake to the other side found themselves swept downwards in a vortex from which they could not escape. Dionysus however was able to descend through the depths of the lake. Through the darkness where no light penetrated. Through the immense pressure arising from the depth of the dark waters. Dionysus emerged unscathed in the underworld.

Dionysus brought with him a gift of myrtle for Persephone. Myrtle was the favourite plant of Persephone's mother Demeter. Persephone was homesick for her mother Demeter. Persephone would not be seeing Demeter for the next three months during Persephone's annual exile to the underworld. There was no myrtle growing in the underworld and Persephone cried when she saw the beautiful myrtle. Persephone was so grateful to Dionysus for bringing myrtle to the underworld that Persephone released Semele to her son Dionysus. Semele and Dionysus travelled back through the depths of the Alcyonian Lake and arrived safely at Mount Olympus. Dionysus turned his mother into a goddess and renamed her Thyone to disguise her identity from jealous ghosts. Thyone lived happily at Mount Olympus and supervised the divinely inebriated rites that Dionysus and his followers continued to engage in.

The story of Dionysus shows how natural revelry and divine inebriation are valued highly. The Tree of Life records that The Beauty is not only the Path of the Sacrificed God but also the Path of the Inebriating God, the Giver of Illumination. All religions have a Dionysus aspect. The Christian religion has many saints who have referred to the divine inebriation which arises from the adoration of devotion. The magnificent white marble sculpture 'The Ecstasy of Saint Teresa' by Gian Lorenzo Bernini in the Coranaro Chapel, Santa Maria della Vitttoria in Rome, Italy records and demonstrates the divine inebriation. The Bernini scholar Irving Lavin has written[240] 'the transverberation becomes a point of contact between earth and heaven, between matter and spirit.' The painting by Pompeo Batoni 'The Ecstasy of St Catherine of Siena' records a similar experience. This is an important characteristic of the Path known as The Beauty, when it is recalled that The Beauty is the Path where force and form meet.

Dion Fortune considered[241] that the Dionysus aspect of human life is very poorly understood and the misunderstanding in fact prevents the manifestation of the higher spiritual experiences in our modern culture. Not only that, Dion Fortune considered that the failure to celebrate and nurture the Dionysus creative impulses 'permits the strange aberrations of religious feeling that from time to time give rise to scandal and tragedy in the high places of the more dynamic religious movements'[242].

The imitation of Christ

Another symbol[243] of the Path known as The Beauty is the Child-Christ. The Child-Christ starts as a small, vulnerable baby, laid humbly among sheep and cattle and not even housed in the inn with humans. This symbol is intended to teach us that the meeting of force and form is characterised by humble beginnings followed by incremental experiential learnings which build up a body of transcendental experiences with the effluxion of time. This shows up in 2 Corinthians 3:18 where it is written 'Beholding as in a glass the glory of the Lord, are changed into the same image from glory to glory'. The value here is that devotion to something higher than ourselves evokes our idealism, which while we despair of becoming equal to it, yet it makes us aspire to become like it. This is the value contained in the famous book 'The Imitation of Christ' written in Latin in about 1418. It is said to be the most widely read Christian book after the Bible. The book was written anonymously but its author is thought to be Thomas a Kempis, a German-Dutch priest. There have been more than 2,000 editions of the book since 1418. The most recent edition was published in 2015.

In recent times the value of imitating Christ by taking up one's cross and stepping forward has been advocated by Dr Jordan Peterson[244] in words to the effect 'Pick up your goddamn cross and walk up the hill. You've got a heavy load of suffering to bear and a fair bit of it is going to be unjust. So what are you going to do about it? Accept it voluntarily and try to transform as a consequence.' This is the Path of The Beauty on the Tree of Life. It has been an accepted characteristic of Western civilization for nearly 3000 years and was part of the teachings from before the time of Christ. As we have seen The Beauty incorporates the Western teachings in relation to the Sacrificed God long before Jesus Christ took on that vital role.

The virtue and value of humility shows up as devotion to something greater than oneself. Sacrifice is another way of describing devotion to something greater than oneself. Sacrifice includes the voluntary giving up of something. Sacrifice, also refers to regeneration and redemption.

The Path of The Beauty is the focal point for the Christian religion, whereas the pantheistic faiths such as the Greek and the Egyptian have the Path of The Foundation as their focal point, and the metaphysical approaches such as the Buddhist and the Confucian use the Path known as The Crown as their focal point.

Archangel Raphael

The Path known as The Beauty has an Archangel and his name is Raphael. Raphael is the Archangel of healing. Archangel Raphael shares the healing portfolio with Apollo. Archangel Raphael is described[245] in the Book of Tobit as 'the spirit that standeth in the sun'. This is a reference to Apollo and the earlier sun gods. The Book of Tobit is one of the books that forms part of the Bible in the Catholic and Orthodox churches but is not included in the Protestant bible. In the Book of Tobit, Raphael appears disguised in human form as the travelling companion of a young man named Tobias. They travel together and Archangel Raphael uses his healing powers in many ways. There is a famous statue of Archangel Raphael on the Roman Bridge in Cordoba, Spain. The biblical story, in Tobit, of Tobias is the subject of many paintings. Studying the deeds of Archangel Raphael is another way of deepening your understanding of the values of Western civilization that have been recorded in the Path known as The Beauty.

Apollo and The Beauty in the 21st century

You have read earlier how myth portrays universal truths and fundamental human patterns. Our forebears have used the Path known as The Beauty and the myth of Apollo to teach us about the importance of daily engagement with the struggle to find, live and maintain your authentic self. The myth links Apollo with the Sun in order to demonstrate and emphasise the daily nature of this struggle and quest. It is a constant cyclical process of struggle and re-emergence. Dr Liz Greene puts the point this way - 'The Sun sinks down into the darkness and has to fight the dragon of depression and hopelessness.'[246]

Depression is a by-product of inadequate expression of one's true self. In other words, when the Sun is not shining, depression remains. Dr Liz Greene describes the process:

'There is a particular kind of depression which has to do with feeling empty and unreal... Then life seems utterly pointless... This can lead to many distortions of the personality because of the overwhelming dependency on others' love and affirmation. This psychological dynamic is called narcissism. A narcissistic wound means that there is no sense of independent self. There is a sort of hole in the middle, like a Polo Mint. The only time we feel alive and worthwhile is when someone else is mirroring back to us their belief in us as a worthwhile, lovable person. If they go away, we fall into the hole again... We all suffer from some degree of narcissism. It is very much the malaise of the modern era. But some suffer more than others.'[247]

Reading the above description reminds me of the addictive attraction of the approbation available from social media. The lure of virtue signaling, where the 'likes' confirm I am worthwhile and lovable.

The daily struggle for re-emergence is a reference to the re-emergence of that part of you that shines genuinely, authentically, humbly and is your true inner essence and self. The myth of Marsyas shows how we get our butt kicked eventually when we try to be something which we are not. That is, when we do not let our authentic self shine but rather present an image based on someone else. In Marsyas' case he represented falsely that he played beautiful music. The truth was that the music was from Athene not from him. Life flayed him alive for acting in that way. We need to struggle each and every day to bring our true light from out of our darkness and shine it onto the world. This is why the sun with its daily movement from darkness into light is used as part of the Apollo myth.

We know that human beings need sunlight for our survival. Our forebears sought to put the matter as high as that. In other words, we can only be truly alive when have discovered and are living our authentic shining self. And that requires struggle daily for ever and ever.

Another characteristic[248] of Apollo is that he is the carrier of the Sun but he is not the Sun itself, he is not the light itself. This is an important message. The message here is that we are a vessel for the light of the spirit. The virtue of humility and the vice of pride in the Path known as the Beauty are used to emphasise this relationship of carrier of light not the light itself. Dr Liz Greene describes[249] the point in the following manner:

'A being comes into mortal existence on this plane of reality, and they are carrying something. We have a huge list of words to try to define that something, and we get nowhere with it. We can call it spirit, we can call it God, we can call it the One, we can call it the spark of divinity, we can call it the Self. Or we can merely call it the life-force, a term which is non-spiritual but nevertheless is just as awesome. We can call it anything we like, using religious, psychological or biological terminology. All we seem to understand is that it isn't me or you and yet it is the life-bearing spark that allows each of us to be alive... When we die, it isn't there anymore... There is an animating life-principle which incarnates into, or is carried by, our mortal selves.'

Another characteristic of the Sun is that it makes the fruits of the earth ripen. The message here for us is that our innate potential will blossom and flower when we access and live our authentic self. Marsyas did not live his authentic life and he perished. Dr Liz Greene puts it this way:

'... the seeds with which we begin life. For these seeds to mature, we need the Sun... The feeling of continuity which is so important for self-confidence is lost or has never been present, because we are flung about from one emotional state to another, from one complex to another. That would be how I understand this image of maturing or ripening the fruits of the earth.'[250]

Another characteristic of Apollo is his power of divination and prophecy. Remember how he created the Pythoness to provide oracular advice to the townsfolk of Delphi. The message here for us is that there is an unfolding and purposeful pattern in life that can be discerned if we are prepared to explore deeply. There is also a profound message about mastering and humanizing the prophetic power of the instincts by exploration of the relationship between the individual and the collective.[251]

Another characteristic of Apollo is that he is the god of music. Remember how the Sun could not play music directly, because the Sun burned up the musical instruments by the intense heat of the Sun whenever the Sun got too close to the musical instruments. Instead the Sun played music via Apollo as the musician who could actually physically hold and play the musical instruments. The message here is that we have a creative power which is an expression of the spirit.

I noted earlier the current political incorrectness of the celebration of Apollo. The message of Apollo is that each life shines with a unique purpose and a unique place in the larger order. This message sits very uncomfortably with the current politically correct message of the allegedly superior virtues of collective sharing and losing oneself in the greater whole. Another way of looking at this concept, of the importance of the self, is in terms of integrity and being loyal to oneself, particularly where that internal voice is speaking contrary to the current voice of the collective. Dr Greene describes[252] this as being 'the individual harmony ... We need to learn to hear, and play our own special form of inner music.'

The deep exploration of the myths of Apollo and of the Path known as the Beauty may serve as an antidote to the over identification with the collective. The over identification with the collective occurs at the expense of developing an awareness of the uniqueness of oneself. Dr Greene describes the point in the following manner:

'When we are young, we need someone who says, "I know it's taking you a long time to find your feet. I know you are confused. But I also know you are someone very special. I can see your potential, and I believe that one day you will get there." Ideally, the parents should be able to offer this kind of individual affirmation. It doesn't require a lot. Sadly, they often make things worse by reminding the child how selfish he or she is. A teacher might provide the right support. But in Britain we don't educate our teachers psychologically, and they are often ignorant of their own problems and unable to help their students. Or they are so determined to inculcate their political ideology that they aggravate the difficulty. We hope that a young person in this situation will reach the point where they can say "The world is huge and full of problems, and I can't redeem it. No individual can. But I am going to try to sort out my small corner and make a positive individual contribution. And I intend to enjoy life at the same time."'

There are a number of interesting points made by Dr Greene in the passage above. First, the recognition of your innate Apollo-ness. Second, the recognition that your innate Apollo-ness may well not be nurtured by your parents. Accordingly, you will need to do it yourself. Third, the recognition that your teacher may seek to inculcate a political ideology based on a rejection of Apollo-ness. In other words, your teacher may seek to inculcate a political ideology based on the alleged virtue of selfless collective sharing. Fourth, the suggestion that a good place to focus your action is on your own small corner. This suggestion brings to mind Dr Jordan Peterson's suggestion that you 'Set your house in perfect order before you criticize the world'.[253]

While dealing with the subject of teachers and their capacity to inculcate anti-Apollonian values in their charges, I found it interesting to read the following commentary by Dr Liz Greene:

'Our educational establishment is riddled with people who have become teachers not because they love teaching, but because they have failed to develop their own solar light. They may be terribly destructive towards a child who displays special abilities. This is usually cloaked under the guise of a political ideology. No elitism must be shown, even if it means a talented child is undermined or denied much-deserved encouragement... Envy has recently acquired a politically correct demeanour, and lots of people are being fooled by it.'[254]

The political ideology described above is that which values and promotes participation above competition. It provides the basis for not keeping score at children's football games.

However, this issue is not straightforward. It is true that just beyond the boundaries of a healthy Apollonian attitude to life, there lurks the mire of insensitivity, ruthlessness, megalomania, unacceptable selfishness and brutalizing other people.[255] It is also true however, as pointed out by Dr Liz Greene that 'The word "selfish" is … used in a socio-political context and is often combined with unconscious envy – hence the frequency of word on the lips of those who try to convince us to "do good" by giving them what we have, rather than working for it themselves.'[256]

Another important characteristic of Apollo and of the Path known as the Beauty is that of a spark of ephemeral joy arising from a sense of fulfillment in being ourself. In other words, a conviction of individual purpose gives rise to joy. Dr Greene describes it this way:

'…without that experience of "I"-ness, we need other people to keep feeding us. Without them, we cannot find a reason to keep going. Happiness then keeps eluding us, because it depends on others to provide the illusory centre that we lack within ourselves.'[257]

The absence of a conviction of individual purpose results in a lack of joy, for the reasons identified above by Dr Greene. In my view we see this daily in the joyless indignation expressed by folks on social media who are offended by the actions and opinions of those espousing a non-collective perspective. However, there is a dark aspect to Apollo. Although he is beloved by gods and by humans, he has no wife, no partner and no family. Apollo courted Daphne, however she preferred to become a laurel tree rather than becoming his wife. The message is that the light is not guaranteed a warm welcome. This characteristic of Apollo stands in stark contrast to other gods like Zeus who create ongoing dynasties. The message is that the dark side of solar light is the experience of aloneness and separation from the collective. Dr Liz Greene has identified that aspect in the following manner:

'… we become insensitive to the suffering of the more vulnerable than we are. And perhaps also cut ourselves off from the subtler or higher dimensions of life which might provide solace for the pain of mortal existence.'[258]

Because Apollo is a lonely god, our daily struggle is one we have do ourselves, for ever and ever. Inherent here is the idea of a price being paid, a sacrifice being involved. This message is contained in the image in the Beauty of the baby, who will one day grow up and be sacrificed, resting peacefully on his mother.

Another part of the dark aspect of Apollo is the inevitability of the daily journey into darkness and the daily struggle to move out of the darkness. Dr Liz Greene writes[259] that, for each one of us, the 'question is not "Is there a difficulty?" but rather "What is the nature of the difficulty?" '.

One aspect you might want to explore at some time is the extent to which you dampen your potential brilliance because of your fear of being the subject of envy of others. As noted above, Apollo is a lonely god. Dr Liz Greene puts it this way – 'One learns to hide the light in order to avoid being the recipient of envy.'[260]

The virtues and vices associated with Apollo and with the Path known as The Beauty teach us that it is appropriate to strive for confidence but not arrogance. Dr Liz Greene suggests[261] that you can develop the relevant Apollonian virtues by saying to yourself "I'm human. I have many flaws. But I'm doing the best I can with what I've got. I will keep trying to become more of what I know I can be. But I don't wish I was somebody else."

Sal the clinical psychologist says ...

Values. Values are different from morals. They are not so much those rules that guide how we interact with others (morals) but more those principles that hopefully guide our lives and which we find important. Our values may have nothing to do with other people.

It is important to know your values as they guide your goals, your true purpose in life and can be the basis of what links two people. Usually, your partner and friends have several values in common with you. That is why you tend to talk about different things with different friends. Usually, you are talking about the values that you share with that person.

Values are different from social idealism. The society in which you live may, for example, emphasise that having a stable job and a home is incredibly important. If your top value is freedom however, that will clash with your society's ideals. You know you are following you family or society's values (rather than your own) when you use phrases such as "I should..." or "I really must...". When you are following your own values you feel a sense of energy and peace when thinking of or acting out that ideal.

Two people can do the same activity but do it fueled by two different values. I am in the process of creating a beautiful garden, as beauty is a top value of mine. A work colleague is doing the same thing, but she is ensuring that the garden is full of native trees and plants, as the ecology is a primary value for her.

So how do you know what you value?

Have a look at how you fill your professional or personal space. Is it full of books (about what?), awards (for what?), photos (of what?), beautiful or comfortable objects (what value do these objects have for you?), sports gear, games or souvenirs.

How do you spend your time ? If something is really important to you, you tend to find the time to do it. I spend my time learning, making my space beautiful, talking to family members, being involved with personal growth and doing spiritually inspired things such as meditation, reading, teaching. These are based on my top values. Somehow I don't seem to have money for lots of trips, a desire to play sports or find time to cook as much, as these are not as important to me.

Where are you most organized? It could be your exercise regime, your work, your diet, your cooking, finances, spiritual rituals or home cleaning – depending on your values.

Where do you spend your money? What facts do you remember most – and what do you forget? Usually we remember things that are important to us (top values) and forget those which relate to values we don't hold.

I think some values can change over time, but usually your values have been there for a long time. I have always had a love of beauty and spirituality. I enjoyed learning and personal growth. I realise that my change in career from law to psychology was fueled by a desire to follow my highest values and live them out in a practical way.

Values can be obscured at times by sickness, financial problems or addictions. You may not be able to live out your values when external factors like these over-ride your values. Knowing what your true values are however, can guide you like a beacon to the life you wish to pursue and to your life purpose when you recover.

Summary

- There is a Western tradition of values, ethics, morality, philosophy, psychology, politics and theology.

103

- Pythagoras, Socrates, Plato and Aristotle form the main part of that lineage which continues to the present day. Some call it the Western mystery tradition. Some call it Western yoga.

- The Western tradition considers that a human being possesses a spiritual dimension known as a soul.

- The Western tradition is recorded in an image known as the Tree of Life.

- The Western mystery tradition and its values of soul, ethics and morality provide an antidote to the chaos inherent in nihilism and post-modernism.

- Each path on the Tree of Life has virtues and vices. The virtues and vices represent the values of Western civilization.

- The virtues and vices of the paths on the Tree of Life have been taught for thousands of years in the Ancient Greek goddess and god myths and in the Bible stories.

- Apollo is the god associated with the Path known as The Beauty.

- The myths of Apollo provide very profound, wise and useful messages from our ancestors in relation to the importance of expression of our Self.

- The myths of Apollo include his slaying of the dragon named Python. Apollo's creation of the oracle of Delphi known as the Pythoness. Apollo's musical duel with the fraudster named Marsyas.

- The virtues of Apollo are currently considered politically incorrect by large numbers of folks. I take the opposite view.

- The Path known as The Beauty is the path of devotion to something greater than oneself. Sacrifice is another way of describing devotion to something greater than oneself.

- Dionysus is the god of divine inebriation. Dionysus is a very under-valued god. Priapus and Cloacina are also undervalued gods. Undervaluing the importance of Dionysus, Priapus and Cloacina is a modern malady that leads to psychological problems.

CHAPTER SIX

PATH 6 – THE STRENGTH

BUCKLE UP BECAUSE this is a really exciting path.

This path is all about Courage. The courage to change. Courage is the virtue of this Path. Cruelty, destruction and wrath are the vices of this Path.

Dr Liz Greene considers[262] that wrath 'can become courage and even heroism, as well as the will to take up life's hard challenges with integrity.'

Since the 1960's Western society has become less willing to celebrate the virtuous side of wrath. Countless young people, particularly young men (including me) adopted a pacificist approach to wrath. In the Indian Yoga school I attended, I was taught about the virtue of 'Ahimsa', a Sanskrit word which means non-violence. Mahatma Ghandi was held up, to me and by me, as the noble embodiment of Ahimsa. Fortunately, in my view, the pendulum appears to be self-correcting and swinging back towards a less extreme view of the way to approach our human tendency towards wrath.

Dr Liz Greene has written[263] in very positive terms about the psychological benefits of wrath and anger. Dr Greene considers[264] that 'Wrath is a highly complex issue. Defensive anger is a fundamental instinct in all animal forms of life, and it can be extremely healthy and appropriate … there are moments in history when the only possible way to stem a tide of collective violence has been to respond with violence in order to survive.'

Western civilization recognizes the importance of that approach by incorporating in the criminal justice system a right to legitimate self-defense in the face of violence. That legal right to wrath has been fine tuned in Western democracies for centuries.

You will read in this chapter about the adventures of Greek God Ares. Those mythical adventures contain the wisdom of our elders in relation to the legitimate and illegitimate exercise of wrath. The Tree of Life puts Wrath / Ares at home in The Strength on the Pillar of Severity. The Tree of Life sets out the relationship between Wrath and Deceit. The Tree of Life illustrates that the courage we can achieve by the brave and honest exercise of Wrath will be used by us in achieving and exercising worldly wisdom. In other words, the diagram of the Tree of Life shows how Courage (Wrath) descends into Worldly Wisdom (Deceit) down the Pillar of Severity.

Dr Liz Greene makes the same point when she wrote[265] 'Sigmund Freud once said that the qualifications for being able to descend to the depths of oneself in order to understand one's own psyche are threefold: Courage, Courage and Courage.'

Ares is the war god. Interestingly, one of symbols used by the Tree of Life for this Path, for thousands of years, is the symbol of the Pentagon. In the United States of America, the Pentagon is the name of the building which houses the United States Department of Defense. 'The Pentagon' is the phrase and figure of speech used to describe the leadership provided by the Department of Defense. The construction of the Pentagon began on 11 September 1941. On that day 60 years later, American Airlines Flight 77 was hijacked and flown into the western side of the Pentagon building.

You will read in this chapter how Ares is condemned by many as being bad, unspiritual and unevolved. However, in my view, there is much to be said for men and women harnessing their Ares' Path of Strength in the service of even-handed justice and as an antidote to the humanitarianism of the Pillar of Mercy which has been abused and made ridiculous and has lost touch with actualities. My view is that western civilisation is presently undervaluing and failing to understand the fundamental importance of the Path known as The Strength, and that this absence of understanding of the proper role and use of The Strength is the cause of many of our difficulties in modern life.

Feminism and me

As a student at the University of Sydney in the 1970's I studied feminism and read the works of Betty Friedan, Shulamith Firestone and other second wave feminists. I also read about Mahatma Gandhi and the importance of non-violence. I struggled with reconciling those approaches with the deep joy I experienced when fighting competitively on the taekwondo dojos and battling in the crowded surf breaks in Australia and Indonesia. Having spoken to hundreds and hundreds of men sitting in circles at men's groups over the last fifteen years I discovered I was not Robinson Crusoe in that struggle. My present view is that the problem of evil and force and severity have not been dealt with adequately in modern Western civilisation and that the Tree of Life and in particular the Path known as The Strength provides a useful way of training the mind in this vital area.

My teenage son lamented recently when I told him that for many years my favourite beverage was a soy latte. Soy milk and tofu were my staples, my daily bread. I had signed on to the vegetable eating team. I ate vegetables because I did not want to be involved in the killing of animals. I felt smugly spiritually superior to those who had not discovered the secrets of the vegetables. I experienced some discomfort when I read about carrots emitting sub-audible screams when being cut. But my spiritual superiority had its limits. My soy diet was accompanied by a preparedness to see the best in every person even if the person was a dishonest rogue whose behaviour was appalling.

One time I attended a men's work workshop and we did an activity where we had to stand face to face with another bloke about 30cm away and forcefully say 'no' and keep repeating 'no' to that person. I found it hard to confront another man in that manner.

I found it a confusing time because there was within me a need to give voice to the Ares' virtues. However I was unable to work out how I could simultaneously turn the other cheek and also stand up for myself and others. I looked for role models among my friends. Eventually I found the Ares' virtues turned up when they were needed. I searched out adventure situations like surfing big dangerous waves, sparring in a martial arts gym, galloping horses up and down mountains and on the polocrosse and polo grounds. I found that in those situations an instinctive vitality and physicality reared its head. There was an Ares' virtue lying dormant but able to be accessed readily when needed. Bit by bit the Ares' virtues came up when the adventures were not physical but were in the court room in a battle of wits and words with another barrister.

My view these days is that much of my tolerance in the past was not born of wisdom but of my cowardice in not being prepared to call on the Ares' virtue of strength.

Dion Fortune wrote[266] that 'whenever there is anything that has outlived its usefulness, (the Path known as The Strength) must wield the pruning-knife... Someone has got to cry "Halt" to the aggressor, and "Move on" to those who are blocking the way...We must learn to love and trust the mailed warrior with the sword...There should be room in our ideal for the virtues of the ruler and leader – courage, energy, justice and integrity...the child that is never checked is a spoilt child, the youth who lacks the spur of competition is apt to be a slack youth, for it is only the few who will work for work's sake.' These values triggered many of my generation and the generations that followed. Competition and learning to love the mailed warrior with the sword, were values very different to the values and feelings of wearing 'flowers in your hair' as the 60's songs advocated sweetly.

The life and deeds of Ares demonstrate how vital it is to have ready access to the energies associated with the Path known as The Strength. The life and deeds of Ares also illustrate how complex and misunderstood are those aspects of our human nature.

Ares

Once upon a time there was a Greek God named Ares. Ares is a warrior. We first meet Ares standing on the blood encrusted dry grassy plains of the battlefield in the Trojan war between Greece and Troy. Ares has an impressive physique but that is not the first thing that we notice. The first thing you see is the red lustre in his bronzed skin, his ruddy complexion and the redness running through his cropped blonde-red hair. He is not as muscular as Heracles. Ares is chiselled where Heracles is roundly pumped. Ares has a severity about him that stands him out from the other warriors on the battlefield. There is something else you notice. Ares brings out fear and awe in others, simply by his presence and poise. It is overreaching to describe Ares as exuding evil but it feels that evil is lurking nearby, companion like.

As we look more closely at the battle-field we see that Ares is standing in a war chariot. Ares has the reins in his right hand. He is right handed and is armed with a number of weapons. Ares has a selection of five swords of varying lengths, thicknesses and weights. Ares also has a selection of five thrusting spears and throwing spears, some made from heavy iron and others made from strong light wood. At Ares right hand is a scourge made of leather. Its five thongs are dripping with dark fresh sticky blood. Underneath the sticky trickling blood are layers upon layers of parched flaking dark red blood, mixed with gristles of long dead warriors' flesh, tendons and bone chips. At Ares feet is coiled his deadly chain weapon. The chain is made of the finest grade sharpened light weight iron and is five metres long. It weighs 5kg. Like Ares' scourge, Ares' chain has layer upon layer of built up parched flesh, tendons and bone chips from dead warriors vanquished in battle by Ares.

We can see on the battlefield how Ares commands the respect and awe of his warriors but also the warriors of the opposing forces. This appears to be a characteristic of effective warrior leaders throughout the ages, including Robert E. Lee, as described in General Stanley McChrystal's magnificent book 'Leaders – myth and reality'.[267]

The Trojan army is being led by Diomedes, a great warrior but a mortal man not a God. Diomedes sees Ares coming for him and Diomedes trembles involuntarily. Ares has made a deliberate and open-eyed choice to engage in physical combat with Diomedes. Ares sees Diomedes as an evil warrior. Evil because Diomedes' patience has become weakness and Diomedes' mercy has become a folly which exposes his men to danger. Ares has determined that Diomedes' death will be like a clean cut to an open wound that would otherwise go septic. The clean cut will give the Trojan army a chance to heal, unfestered by the misplaced patience and mercy of Diomedes.

Standing between Ares and Diomedes is a band of approximately 80 Trojan foot soldiers known as Diomedian Hoard. The Hoard has a sinister reputation for merciless violence against the weak. Ares reaches for his Scourge and careers his chariot directly at the most violent looking Hoard Warrior. Ares's Scourge bites into the face of the Hoard Warrior and reduces it to a bloody gelatinous mess. Ares' action halts the advance of the aggressive Hoard. The other members of the Hoard pause, frozen for a moment, and then press forward towards Ares.

Ares has no intention of negotiating with the Hoard. Ares intends to set an example by flaying the Hoard with his Scourge and his Chain. Ares considers that the best way he can protect the warriors under his command against the merciless Hoard is by wielding his Scourge and Chain like a pruning knife cutting the Hoard out of the Trojan army. Ares reflects scornfully on the actions of some of his minor commanders who sought unsuccessfully to restrain the Hoard by a policy of non-resistance. Ares' experience is that non-resistance to evil can never be successful in these frontier conditions. Ares' experience is that non-resistance to evil can only be pursued satisfactorily in a well-policed society, and there was no well-policed society in operation on the plains of the Trojan battlefield.

Zeus looked down from Olympus and saw Ares flaying the Hoard. Zeus decided that the battle had reached a point where the rhythm of the battle needed to be equilibrated. That is, the rhythm of battle now required Ares to be subjected to a counter force, moving the battle back towards a centre of transient stability. Zeus was aware that if Ares was allowed to move too far and too freely, Ares would move into the arena of cruelty and inappropriate destruction. Zeus needed to redirect the battle towards mercy and mildness. Zeus was aware that on the battlefield, as in life, there is a time when the Ares' approach overreaches and moves into the arena of cruelty and misplaced destruction. Zeus considered that point had been reached and that it was time to move against Ares. Zeus was aiming for a rhythm in the course of the battle, not aiming for an unrealistic and unworldly stability, but rather a shift in emphasis away from the pillar of severity, where Ares is located, towards the pillar of equilibrium where Apollo operates.

With that consequence firmly in mind, Zeus brought Ares' sister, the beautiful goddess Athena into the battle on the side of Diomedes. Athena is wearing the battle helmet of Hades which makes her invisible, even to Gods like Ares. Zeus magically transports Athena into Diomedes' chariot just as Diomedes decides to make a strategic retreat to protect his troops from Ares' onslaught. Athena disagrees with that strategy and grabs the reins of Diomede's chariot, putting Diomedes' chariot directly in the path of Ares' thundering chariot. Ares' chariot is about 100 metres away and is bearing down relentlessly on Diomedes' chariot. Athena chooses to provoke Ares even more and makes a stream of fire flare from Diomedes' shield and helmet. Athena's invisibility causes Ares to believe that Diomedes is choosing to be deliberately provocative. Ares takes one of his deadly throwing spears and launches it with all his mighty force directly at Diomedes' heart. The deadly spear punctures Diomede's shield and is just about to pierce his armour when the invisible Athena seizes the spear and snaps it in half. Ares is dumbfounded and fails to see that Diomedes has launched his own spear at Ares. Usually Ares would be able to scornfully stop such a human spear in mid-flight. However, the invisible Athena had helped Diomedes launch the spear and the spear is travelling at supersonic Goddess speed. The spear pierces Ares' body armour and strikes him violently in his stomach. The invisible Athena drives the spear deeper and deeper into Ares' stomach. Ares screams in pain with the voice of ten thousand men and flees the battle for that day, vowing to return tomorrow to continue the battle.

In this battle, as in all his battles, Ares shows the passion of the war god. The nobility and honour of the love to fight. Prowess and honour in battle. Ares is condemned by many as being bad, unspiritual and unevolved. However, he never displays gratuitous cruelty. He lives to serve and his honour is worth more than his life. He is devoted, fearless, honest, loyal and passionate. He is a realist. He does not whimper meekly about the spiritually superior merits of pacifism when confronted by the stark necessity of winning or dying.

Ares displays emotions that humans secretly feel but are generally afraid to identify and certainly reluctant to express. Ares considers war as a brutal necessity. He does not romanticise war. Ares choses to fight with clarity, discipline, nobility and skill. Ares is brave rather than sensitive and indolent. He is disciplined rather than sensuous and self-indulgent. Ares' enemies, who do not express their honourable warrior side, hate him with a cowardly cruelty and malice triggered by their sense of impotence.

Ares' noble battlefield courage is the antithesis of the violence of a football hooligan, a drunken lout, a conscienceless mercenary or a corrupt dictator.

In the 21st century there is much to be said for men and women harnessing their Ares' Path of Strength in the service of even handed justice and as an antidote to the humanitarianism of the Pillar of Mercy which has been abused and made ridiculous and has lost touch with actualities.

David and Golilath

The Bible story[268] of David and Goliath shows the value and virtue of the courage of the armed warrior.

Once upon a time, the Philistines gathered their armies for battle. They were massed at the border of Judah. Saul and the men of Israel were gathered together, and encamped in the valley of Terebinth. They set their army to fight against the Philistines. The Philistines stood on a mountain on one side and Israel stood on a mountain on the other side. A valley was between them. There went out a mighty man, from the camp of the Philistines, named Goliath of Gath, whose height was six cubits and a span. A cubit is 18 inches. A span is 6 inches. So Goliath of Gath was 9 feet six inches tall. He had a helmet of brass upon his head, and he was armed with a coat of mail. The weight of his coat of mail was five thousand shekels of brass. A shekel of brass weighed approximately 10 grams. So the coat of mail weighed approximately 50 kg. He had greaves of brass upon his legs, and a cuirass of mail between his shoulders.

Goliath stood and shouted at the armies of Israel, 'Why have you come out to set your battle in array? Am I not a Philistine, and you the servants of Saul? Choose a man for yourselves, that he may come out against me. If he is able to fight with me and kill me, then we will be your servants; but if I prevail against him and kill him, then you shall be our servants and serve us'.

When Saul and all of Israel heard the words of Goliath, they were dismayed and greatly afraid. Now David was the son of a man named Jesse. Jesse had eight sons. Jesse was very old. The three older sons of Jesse followed Saul to the battle. David was the youngest. David was at home tending his father's sheep.

For forty days, every morning and evening, Goliath presented himself and shouted his challenge.

Meanwhile, back at Jesse's home, Jesse said to David his son, 'Take now for your brothers an ephah of parched wheat and ten loaves of bread, and run to the camp to your brothers. And carry these ten cheeses to the commander of their thousand and inquire into the welfare of your brothers and bring the news of them to me.'

Now Saul and all the men of Israel were in the valley of Terebinth fighting with the Philistines. David rose up early in the morning and left the sheep with the keeper, and took and went as Jesse had commanded him; and he came to the camp in the valley which goes up to the battle array, and the army shouted for the battle. Then Israel and the Philistines put themselves in battle array, army against army. David put off his provisions by the side of the baggage, and ran into the army ranks, and came and saluted his brothers. And while he was talking with them, behold, there came up the champion, the Philistine of Gath, Goliath by name, out of the armies of the Philistines, and spoke the same words; and David heard them. And all the men of Israel, when they saw the mighty man, were afraid and fled from him. And the men of Israel said, 'Have you seen this man who has come up? Surely to defy Israel he has come up; and it shall be that the man who kills him, the king will enrich him with great riches and will give him his daughter and make his father's house free in Israel.' David said to the men who stood by him, 'What shall be done for the man who kills this uncircumcised Philistine and takes away the reproach from Israel? For who is this uncircumcised Philistine that he should defy the armies of the living God?' And the people told him the king's promises, saying, 'So shall it be done to the man who kills him.'

Eliab his eldest brother heard him when he spoke to the men; and Eliab's anger was kindled against David, and he said to him, 'Why have you come down here? And with whom have you left those few sheep in the wilderness? I know your boldness and the evil of your heart; for you have come down to see the battle.' David said, 'What have I done now? Behold, I was just talking.' And he turned from him to the other side, and spoke in the same manner; and the people answered him again as they had done before.

When the words which David spoke were reported to Saul, he sent for him. And David said to Saul, 'Let no man's heart fail because of him; your servant will go and fight with this Philistine. ' Saul said to David, 'You are not able to go against this Philistine to fight with him; for you are but a boy, and he has been a man of war from his youth.' David said to Saul, 'Your servant was tending his father's sheep, and there came a lion and a bear, and took a lamb from the flock. And I went out after the lion and smote him, and delivered it out of his mouth; and he growled at me, and I caught him by his beard, and I smote him and slew him. Your servant slew both the lion and the bear; and this uncircumcised Philistine shall be as one of them, seeing he has defied the armies of the living God.' David said moreover, The Lord who delivered me from the paw of the lion and from the paw of the bear will deliver me out of the hands of the Philistine.'

And Saul said to David, 'Go, and the Lord be with you.' Saul armed David with his own armor and put a helmet of brass upon his head; and armed him with a coat of mail. David girded his sword upon his armor, but he was unwilling to go; for he had not tried them out. So David took them off. And he took his staff in his hand, and chose five smooth stones out of the gravel, and put them into his shepherd's bag, even into his wallet, and his sling was in his hand; and he drew near to the Philistine.

And behold, Goliath came and drew near to David; and his shieldbearer went before him. When the Philistine looked about and saw David, he disdained him; for he was but a youth, and ruddy, and of a fair countenance. The Goliath said to David, 'Am I a dog, that you come to me with a staff?' And Goliath cursed David by his gods. And Goliath said to David, 'Come to me, and I will give your flesh to the fowls of the air and to the beasts of the field.' Then David said to Goliath, 'You come against me with a sword and with a spear and with a shield; but I come against you in the name of the Lord of hosts, the God of the armies of Israel, whom you have defied. This day the Lord will deliver you into my hands; and I will slay you and take your head from you; and I will give the carcasses of the host of the Philistines this day to the wild beasts of the earth and to the fowls of the air, that all the earth may know that there is a God in Israel. And all this assembly shall know that the Lord saves not with sword and spear; for the battle is the Lord's, and he will deliver you into our hands.'

And, behold, when Goliath came and drew near to meet David, David hastened and ran to the battle line to meet Goliath. David put his hand in his bag and took thence a stone, and slung it and struck Goliath in his forehead, and the stone sunk into his forehead; and he fell upon his face to the earth.

So David prevailed over Goliath with a sling and with a stone, and smote Goliath and slew him; but there was no sword in the hand of David. Therefore David ran and stood over Goliath, and took his sword and drew it out of its sheath, and slew him and cut off his head. And when the Philistines saw that their champion was dead, they fled.

The value of courage demonstrated by David in the Old Testament part of the Bible is very different to the emphasis placed by 21st century New Testament Christianity on the values and virtues of meekness and mildness. David demonstrates how one can be dynamic and forceful but also a very controlled person with an even temper and patience under provocation. In this manner David is like a professional boxer who knows that if he gets angry and starts fighting instead of boxing, the odds are against him. As Dion Fortune has described[269] '...characteristic virtues... well known on the sports field, which is the play-aspect of the god of War, that a loss of temper gives the game away.'

The Strength as shown on the Tree of Life

Dion Fortune dives deeply into spiritual philosophy when she suggests that there is a certain type of courage which does not fear the dissolution that arises from the exercise of the Ares' Strength because that type of courage knows that 'spiritual principles are indestructible, and so long as the archetypes persist, anything can be rebuilt. (The Path known as The Strength) is only destructive to that which is temporal; it is the servant of that which is eternal; for when by the acid activity of (the Path known as The Strength) all that is impermanent has been eaten away, the eternal and incorporeal realities shine forth in all their glory, every line revealed.' [270]

Dion Fortune has expressed the view that the great weakness of Christianity lies in the fact that it ignores rhythm and seeks to balance God with Devil. In other words, that the dualism is antagnostic rather than equilibrating. Fortune suggests that in such circumstances there can never be a functional third in which power is in equilibrium. Fortune suggests the great weakness of Christianity is that God is considered to be the same yesterday, today and forever and does not evolve with creation, but rather indulged in one special creative act and then rested on His laurels. Fortune suggests that the whole of human experience, the whole of human knowledge is against the likelihood of such a concept being true.[271]

Fortune considers[272] that the great weakness of Christianity, described above, results in the view that because a thing is good then its opposite is evil. It is Fortune's view that there should be room in our ideal for the virtues of the ruler and the leader – courage, energy, justice and integrity. Fortune considers that Christianity has nothing to tell us about those dynamic virtues and that consequently those who get the world's work done cannot follow the Christian ideal of meekness, mercy and love. That is because those values have limitations when applied to real world actualities. Fortune considers that the result is the ridiculous spectacle of a civilisation, committed to a one-sided ideal, being forced to keep its ideals and its honour in separate compartments.

The psychology of the Path known as The Strength

Dr Liz Greene has written[273] extensively about the Ares' virtues and vices and their relevance to life in Western civilisation in the 21st century. Greene describes the Path known as The Strength as involving 'the fighting principle'. The necessity for a fighting principle is obvious, says Greene[274], since there is a big world out there in which sooner or later one will meet conflict or challenges to one's individuality, one's values, and even one's physical and psychological survival. Greene says[275] that the capacity to "know what we want and do what we have to do to get it" is dependent on an individual being able to express, in a conscious way, the virtues of the Path known as The Strength.

Greene suggests that an extremely common result of a disconnection from the Path known as The Strength is a chronic state of depression. A chronic state of depression is different fundamentally from a period of depression which arises from perfectly understandable external causes such as separation or loss, as we all experience one time or another. Chronic depression has deeper roots, and Greene suggests that all too often the taproot is a profound sense of impotence, frustration and rage, generated by the feeling that one has no capacity for choice, nor power over one's own life. This kind of chronic depression is experienced as a state of apathy and deadness, where nothing is worth bothering with, not even anger, because it is assumed that nothing will change anyhow no matter what one does or says. Greene says that many people dissociate from this kind of deep depression, and consciously gear themselves up to keep the surface of life functioning, finding escape routes such as compulsive work, large doses of television, sex, alcohol or tranquillisers. There is illness or tiredness or inability to sleep properly.

I found it very interesting that Greene suggests[276] that sometimes 'the escape route from this dark tangle is provided by a philosophy or ideology of nonattachment, which can find its way into politics as well as into religion. This approach labels personal desire as selfish, and thereby condemns the principle (of the Path known as The Strength) dooming it to the underworld where it must function as covert rage and envy. I have found that those who are most angrily vocal in their condemnation of individual striving usually have' an unsatisfactory relationship with the Path known as The Strength. I dealt earlier with the Yoga of the East's reliance on nonattachment as a fundamental pillar of its approach to life. I expressed the view that this is a reason why the Yoga of the West provides a more healthy psychological path for those of us born and living in the West, than the popular and better known path of the Yoga of the East. The Yoga of the East has another stated virtue that of 'Ahimsa' or non-violence. It seems to me that this is another 'escape route' from an inability to access and express a healthy Ares' approach to the Path known as The Strength. That provides another reason, for those of us living in the West, to reject those particular values of the Yoga of the East.

You may recall how earlier in this book, in chapter 1, I suggested that the hard left wing approach to the virtues of nihilism was misplaced. It seems to me that Greene's explanation about the inability to cleanly express courageous anger, as part of the Path known as The Strength, explains the allure of the hard left social justice approach to the condemnation of the individual and the striving of the individual. Greene provides[277] the following colourful description of such conduct, 'One can almost smell the god Ares clanking around in the basement in such situations, furious and frustrated and beating his sword against the locked door.' The hard left SJW protests on campus against the providing of a platform for Jordan Peterson and for Ben Shapiro are probably explicable as a fanaticism arising in this manner. Greene suggests[278] that 'Fanaticism is also often the product of a blocked (Path known as The Strength) because the more uneasy we feel at that sound of banging and shouting coming from behind the locked door, the more blindly emotional and even violent we become in our efforts to convert others to our conscious viewpoint. I have never found an honestly expressed (Path known as The Strength) to be fanatical; one pursues one's own goals and other people are left alone to get on with theirs.' I agree completely.

Greene suggests that Russell Crowe's character Maximus in the Ridley Scott film 'Gladiator' shows the Ares' virtues. Maximus' nemesis is Commodus. Commodus' actions show the Ares' vices of cruelty and destruction. Viewing the Maximus film is a good way to see the Ares' values in action. Greene considers that the Ares' values are survival in the face of dangers, a competitive instinct and an urge to build something concrete in the world.

Greene considers that Ares' actions provide a very useful demonstration of the importance of expressing anger in a clean, honest way. Greene is concerned that Christianity and Walt Disney have demonised the Ares' values and have made it difficult for us to come to terms with our own inner warrior. Greene, who holds a doctorate in psychology and is a qualified Jungian analyst, considers that the absence of a practical application of the Ares' values by people in western civilisation in the 21st century is often linked with depression. Greene's view is that when people live in a society where individual expression is stifled and the capacity to make things happen is restricted, rage will build up and, unless expressed, violent eruptions could follow, or more often, individuals end up medicating themselves, tranquilising their rage with Prozac. Greene considers that the courageous expression of anger is often the beginning of the healing process for severely depressed people. Greene's view is that rather than tranquilising rage with Prozac, the courageous expression of anger can be the antidote to depression for many people. Greene, goes so far as to suggest that the courageous expression of anger has also resulted in the healing of physical symptoms such as headaches, chronic pain and skin rashes. Greene's view is that a good approach is to work through the rage with someone who can contain it without condemning it. [279]

Sal the clinical psychologist says ...

Anger. Anger can make people frightened and defensive. Some families send messages to their children, either openly or subtly, that anger is not permissible.

It can be incredibly difficult to deal with this built up anger when we do not have a way of releasing it. Anger leaks out in other ways – we start to feel resentful, pull small smirks and frowns, break things, do sneaky things to get back at people and punish them. Finally, if unresolved, we move into full rage.

There are myths about anger which are interesting to consider. Some people feel that nice people don't get angry and that anger is a waste of time or of precious energy, so why bother? However, we can't always control the emotion of anger, and everyone feels anger during their lives. It is not so much that anger is problematic because we feel it, but rather the way we respond to it can make a difference to the outcome.

Anger does have a purpose, which is to inform us that a right has been violated and it can motivate us to take action. It is worthwhile to consider whether the thing that made you angry is worthwhile resolving?

Another myth surrounding anger is that if someone feels angry with us, we made them feel that way and we are responsible for resolving their anger. No one can MAKE you feel a particular way. Of course realistically, certain actions on your part will make it more likely that people will be angry with you. We need to take responsibility for those actions but we also need to acknowledge that the other person owns their anger.

Conversely, some people believe that if someone made us feel angry, it is the responsibility of that other person to make us feel better. We can try to resolve matters with another person to lessen the chances of future fights. However, we may never get that apology or the person may never change their behavior. We may need to radically accept that this is the way that person is and find a way to manage the emotions they elicit from us, or choose not to and walk away.

Anger is a feeling that is better acknowledged than repressed. My clients deal with it by acknowledging the feeling and what provoked it. They often journal these feelings, which gives them insight and cools them down. Other people walk away from fights, and use cold water, intense exercise or paced breathing to calm themselves. Once calm, then try to resolve the matter, often with family systems therapy or couples counselling.

Meditation also helps to create that pause button between feeling an emotion and acting upon it, which helps incredibly if anger is a go-to emotion for you.

Summary

- There is a Western tradition of values, ethics, morality, philosophy, psychology, politics and theology.

- Pythagoras, Socrates, Plato and Aristotle form the main part of that lineage which continues to the present day. Some call it the Western mystery tradition. Some call it Western yoga.

- The seminal value of the Western mystery tradition/Western yoga is meaningful engagement in life and family and commerce.

- The Western mystery tradition has the ideal that a human being possesses a spiritual dimension known as a soul.

- The Western mystery tradition is recorded in an image known as the Tree of Life.

- The Western mystery tradition and its values of soul, ethics and morality provide an antidote to the chaos inherent in nihilism and post-modernism.

- Each path on the Tree of Life has virtues and vices. The virtues and vices represent the values of Western civilization.

- The virtues and vices of the paths on the Tree of Life have been taught for thousands of years in the Ancient Greek goddess and god myths and in the Bible stories.

- The Path known as The Strength is the path of courage and the courageous exercise of anger, particularly when directed to a righteous cause that is greater than oneself.

- Ares is the God associated with the Path known as The Strength. Ares' courage is demonstrated in the tales of his battles. Ares is a warrior but a considered clinical courageous warrior.

- Ares is a very under-valued and misunderstood God. Undervaluing the importance of Ares is a modern malady that leads to psychological problems, in particular depression.

- The Bible story of David and Goliath also demonstrates the value of courage.

CHAPTER SEVEN

PATH 7 – THE MERCY

THIS IS THE last Path that we will be looking at in detail.

On this Path we learn about Aspiration.

The lesson from our wise ancestors is that we all have a need to aspire which arises from a natural and healthy innate sense of dissatisfaction. But we need to be very careful to ensure that our dissatisfaction and aspirations do not turn into gluttony.

The importance of the lesson is undervalued and is widely misunderstood today. For example, the movements today seeking to enhance the self-esteem of children by not keeping score in games or by ensuring an equality of outcome irrespective of competence, represent a failure to understand the complex relationship between dissatisfaction, aspiration and gluttony.

On the Path known as the Mercy we learn from the life of the Greek God Zeus. Those lessons include the proposition that wonderful things can be created on Earth by using the Aspiration which arises from our urge towards Gluttony. The soundly based distaste for Gluttony does not mean that Aspiration is to be chided and replaced by equal opportunity outcomes of scoreless draws. Such an approach castrates (or spays) the creative juices of Aspiration.

You will read about Zeus' insatiable appetite for more lovers, more power, more popularity, more food and drink. You also read about how, at times, Zeus was able to act as a merciful, wise and prudent ruler. At those times Zeus was a visionary, benevolent planner. Zeus formulated prudent plans for the expansion of the kingdom, including the layout of harbours, wharves, warehouses, railways, hospitals, court houses, jails, banks, industrial areas, residential areas, recreation areas, environmental protection areas and agricultural areas.

The stories of Zeus teach us that when Zeus was responding to his dissatisfaction in a mature and appropriate manner, he was able to use his strengths and his resources to create abundance for himself and for others. The stories of Zeus teach us that dissatisfaction can be used to produce and power aspiration.

The Tree of Life teaches that aspiration is a wonderful virtue to be celebrated and cultivated. However, the Tree of Life also teaches that the dissatisfaction that motivates aspiration can over-reach and produce gluttony. Importantly, aspiration will not lead inevitably to gluttony. This is one of the lessons our wise ancestors have sought to teach us by the Zeus stories and by the Tree of Life. The lesson is that aspiration is to be celebrated and cultivated and also to be watched very carefully to ensure that moral integrity is exercised so there is no misplacement and conversion of dissatisfaction into gluttony.

Zeus

Once upon a time there was a god named Zeus. Zeus' parents were the goddess Rhea and the god Kronos. Kronos' father Uranus prophesied that one of Kronos' sons would dethrone him. Kronos sought to get around the prophesy by eating his children every year. Rhea tried to safeguard Zeus by giving birth to Zeus secretly in the middle of the night on Mount Lycaeum in Arcadia where no creature casts a shadow. Rhea then bathed Zeus in the River Neda and gave Zeus to Mother Earth to protect and raise him.

Meanwhile cunning mother Rhea wrapped a baby sized stone in swaddling clothes. Kronos ate the swaddling clothed stone believing it was his baby son Zeus.

Mother Earth carried Zeus to Crete and told him to hide in the cave of Dicte to be nursed by the nymph Adrasteia and her sister Io. Zeus obeyed his mother's directions. Zeus was fed goat's milk and honey. Also in the cave was Pan, the goat god, who was then only a baby, but who became a lifelong friend of Zeus.

Zeus had a golden cradle which was hung in a tree so that Kronos was unable to find him in heaven, on earth or in the sea. The Curetes stood guard over the baby Zeus. The Curetes clashed their spears against their shields and shouted to drown out the noise of the wailing of the baby Zeus so that Kronos would not be alerted to the existence and whereabouts of the baby Zeus.

Kronos eventually found out about Zeus and sought to murder him. Zeus escaped capture and death by transforming himself into a serpent and transforming his nurses into bears.

Zeus evaded Kronos for many years by living in caves and spending time with the shepherds of Ida. Zeus became dissatisfied with his life of living in caves. Zeus aspired to greater things. Zeus sought out Metis the Titaness for advice. Metis advised Zeus to take vengeance against his father Kronos. Metis advised Zeus to visit his mother Rhea and ask Rhea to appoint Zeus as the cup-bearer to Kronos, so that Zeus could engage in a cunning plan of vengeance. Zeus obediently followed the advice of Metis. Zeus was motivated by a deep dissatisfaction with his life and a feeling that he wanted to achieve great things with his life.

Zeus' mother Rhea agreed to help Zeus have vengeance against Kronos. Rhea arranged for Zeus to be appointed cup-bearer to Kronos. Kronos did not realise that his new cup-bearer was none other than his son Zeus. Metis had advised Zeus to put an emetic potion into Kronos' night-time drink. Rhea provided the emetic potion and Zeus mixed the emetic potion into Kronos' honeyed night-time drink. Kronos drank deeply. The honeyed emetic did its work and Kronos vomited up the stone covered in the swaddling clothes. Kronos then vomited up Zeus' elder brothers and sisters.

Zeus' elder brothers and sisters emerged unharmed and in gratitude asked Zeus to lead them in a battle against Kronos and the Titans. The battle was fought for year after year. In the tenth year, Zeus' grandmother, Mother Earth, told Zeus to make allies with the Cyclopes and the Hundred-handed ones, who Kronos had banished to the underworld. Zeus tracked down the goaloress of the Underworld, killed her and took her keys. Zeus then released the Cyclopes and the Hundred-handed Ones and provided them with divine food and drink. The Cyclopes were very thankful for their release and gave Zeus power to unleash thunderbolts, which Zeus could use as a weapon. The Cyclopes armed Zeus' brother Hades with a helmet of darkness which could make Hades invisible when he was wearing the helmet. The Cyclopes armed Zeus' brother Poseidon with a Trident, which was a superb and fearsome weapon that struck fear into the hearts of all who saw it.

Zeus and his brothers Hades and Poseidon held a counsel of war and devised a bold, cunning and dangerous plan to bring the war to an end by attacking their father Kronos in his bed chamber.

Hades entered unseen into Kronos' bed chamber by using the helmet of darkness and invisibility he had been given by the Cyclopes. While Hades was in Kronos' bed chamber,

Poseidon used the mighty Trident to threaten and distract Kronos. At the same moment, Zeus' childhood friend and ally, named Pan, emitted an horrendous cry which created fear, anxiety and wildly unthinking behavior in Atlas and his Titan army, who were supporting Kronos. Pan's cry was thereafter known as inducing 'panic' and creating 'pandemonium'. In the ensuing panic and pandemonium, the invisible Hades stole all of Kronos' weapons. While Kronos was unarmed and distracted, Zeus struck down Kronos and Atlas with thunderbolts. The Hundred-handed Ones, who Zeus had broken out of prison in the Underworld, pelted rocks at the Titan army and soon Kronos, Atlas and the entire Titan army were defeated and banished to the Underworld, guarded there by the Hundred-handed Ones. Atlas, as the war-leader of the Titans, was singled out for a heavy punishment. Atlas was ordered to carry the sky on his shoulders.

Soon after leading the mighty victory, Zeus married the beautiful and wise Goddess named Hera and together they became co-sovereigns of the Council of Gods. For many, many years Zeus ruled as an excellent King. He sat royally on his throne and formulated prudent plans for his kingdom. He discovered inland plains and rivers and designed wharfs and warehouses, railway lines, hospitals. Zeus' imagination mapped out the main streets and determined wisely to stake corner lots so that Zeus could prosper along with the prosperity of the new settlement.

For many, many years, Zeus ruled as a wise, benevolent, merciful ruler, seated upon his magnificent throne, holding a scepter and orb, ruling and guiding his subjects with stability and generosity. Zeus took action regularly and steadily so as to ensure his vision of prosperity for all was carried out and came to fruition.

Famous paintings of Zeus show that in his left hand he holds a scepter, which denotes a firmness. In his right hand he holds a crook. The crook is a wooden staff about two metres long, with a semicircular hook at one end, used by a shepherd to tend sheep. The crook was a symbol of Zeus' role as a shepherd for his people. As a shepherd Zeus was required to keep his people safe and sound.

After many, many years of wise and bountiful ruling, Zeus started to get bored and dissatisfied.

Zeus started eating and drinking far too much. Zeus felt a void of dissatisfied emptiness inside of himself. Zeus binged on roast chickens and potatoes and black ale every day and soon became a glutton. At times Zeus was unable to stand up and get off his throne because of the vast amount of roast chickens, potatoes and black ale he had consumed.

Zeus found he was bored and dissatisfied by his beautiful Goddess wife Hera. Zeus pretended to act virtuously, like a devoted and loyal husband, but behind his wife Hera's still gorgeous back he would plough the paddocks day and night, as the Ancient Greek metaphor goes, of goddess after goddess, and then mortal maid after mortal maid, and then mortal maiden after mortal maiden. The more Zeus felt dissatisfied with his life, the more he tried to fill that dissatisfaction with wine, women, food and song. Zeus wanted more lovers, more food, more drink and then he started to want more power and more popularity.

But the more Zeus consumed and desired, the more his dissatisfaction with his life increased. Zeus became a tyrant and a hypocrite as well as a glutton. Zeus would ask the other gods to eat frugally because, Zeus said, it was good for the soul. Then Zeus would eat secretly throughout the night until there was no food left in the palace kitchens and the cooks would have to take food from the kitchens of the poor peasants. Zeus became a hypocritical, tyrannical glutton.

When Zeus heard that peasants were complaining about having to give him their meagre supplies of food and ale, Zeus imprisoned the peasants. Then Zeus imprisoned their children and cousins, uncles, aunts.

Finally, Zeus' gluttony became so intolerable that Hera, Poseidon, Apollo, and all the other Olympians, except Hestia, could no longer abide it. The Olympians surrounded Zeus as he slumped intoxicated on his throne. The Olympians bound him with rawhide thongs, knotted into a hundred knots, so that he could not move. Zeus threatened the Olympians with instant death, but they had placed his thunderbolts out of reach and laughed insultingly at him.

While the Olympians were celebrating their victory, and scheming jealously as to who was to be Zeus' successor, Thetis the Nereid, foreseeing a civil war on Olympus, hurried in search of the hundred-handed Briareus, who swiftly untied the thongs that bound Zeus, using every hand at once, and released Zeus from his hide bound throne.

Zeus screamed with delight upon being released and because it was Hera who had led the conspiracy against him, Zeus hung her up from the sky with a golden bracelet on each wrist and an anvil fastened to each ankle. The other Olympians were vexed beyond words, but dared attempt no rescue for all her piteous cries. In the end Zeus undertook to free Hera if the Olympians swore never more to rebel against him; and this each in turn did, albeit grudgingly.

As Zeus grew older and wiser, he reflected on his earlier, happier days, when he was planning and building useful, fun things like towns and cities. Zeus remembered that he felt happy and satisfied when he was planning and building useful things. Zeus started planning more towns and more cities and more buildings. True it was that he would design and build magnificent places that he named after himself, like Zeus Tower, Zeus Plaza, Zeus International Golf Links and Zeus Park, but nevertheless such buildings and places were truly magnificent and very useful. Day after day, plan after plan, tower after tower, the dissatisfaction disappeared slowly. Zeus' consumption of wine, women and song decreased. Zeus' dissatisfaction decreased. Zeus' aspired to build taller Zeus Towers but he also aspired to build, and did build, taller hospitals and schools and bigger parks and gardens. Goddess Hera found it in her heart to forgive Zeus and together they presided for the rest of their days over a glorious epoch in Olympian history.

The psychology of The Mercy

The Path on the Tree of Life known as The Mercy and the life of Zeus teaches us about the virtues and vices of this Path – obedience, bigotry, hypocrisy, tyranny and gluttony. First and foremost is the vice of Gluttony. Gluttony is not restricted to over eating and over drinking. Gluttony includes overconsumption and inordinate desire. Dissatisfaction is another way of describing inordinate desire. The psychologist Dr Liz Greene has stated[280] that Gluttony is not all bad because it can be a gateway to Aspiration. What Dr Greene is describing is the powerful creative drive called Aspiration that arises from feelings of dissatisfaction. We can see how this played out in the life of Zeus. Remember how Zeus desired to dethrone his father Kronos. Zeus's aspiration was fueled by that desire. Zeus lived in caves for many years while formulating his plan to get Kronos to vomit up Zeus' siblings so that Zeus could use his siblings to dethrone their father Kronos. This demonstrates how a Vice can have a Virtue within it. For example, Gluttony produces feelings of inordinate desire and feelings of dissatisfaction. Those feelings of inordinate desire and dissatisfaction fuel aspiration. On the Tree of Life we can see how the feelings that arise from Gluttony will move across the Tree of Life to the Path of The Strength where they can fuel the actions that take place on the Path of The Strength.

We can see from the life of Zeus how the Virtue of Obedience played out. Remember how Zeus obediently hid in the cave of Dicte as directed by his mother. Remember how Zeus obediently acted as the cup-bearer to Kronos so Zeus could get close enough to Kronos to drug Kronos with the emetic.

It is really important to recognize that at a personal level, diving deeply into your inner life, into your deepest feelings and your deepest thoughts, there is a delightfully complex relationship between you and Obedience to your inner Self. The obedience is to your siren call of your aspiration, fueled by your gluttony, fed by your dissatisfaction. The motivation of gluttony fed dissatisfaction can provide personal rocket fuel for the creation of wonderful, magnificent relationships and the creation of wonderful, magnificent things. Obedience is very complicated. Deliciously and delightfully complicated.

Our forebears have taught us about the delicious, delightful and dreadful depths of the human creative impulse of Obedience and the related Aspiration, Dissatisfaction and Gluttony, by using the most complex and perplexing story in Western civilisation, namely the Bible story of Job.

JOB[281] – The BIBLE story about obedience

As I have mentioned earlier in this book, my favourite translation of the Bible is the one by George Mamishisho Lamsa. The translation is from the original Aramaic. The translation includes nuances that seem to me to be more accurate and more logical and more likely to have been intended by the original writers. I have relied heavily on the HarperOne Kindle Edition. The infelicities in expression and omissions are mine alone.

Once upon a time there was a man named Job. Job had seven sons and three daughters. Job had worked hard and had invested wisely for many years. Job was very successful. Job and his sons feasted in the house of each other on the appointed days and they would invite their three sisters to eat and drink with them. When the days of their feasting were over, Job rose up early the next morning and prayed.

One day God was visited by his sons and daughters. One of God's sons was named Satan.

God said to Satan, 'What have you been up to?' Satan said, 'I've been on the earth walking around.' Then God said to Satan, 'Have you seen my servant Job? There is no-one else like him on the earth. Job is an innocent and upright man, one who reveres God, and turns away from evil'

Satan said, 'Does Job revere God for nought? Thou hast rested thy hand of protection upon him and upon his house and upon his children and upon everything that he has everywhere; thou hast blessed the work of his hands, and his substance is increased in the land. But put forth thy hand now, and destroy all that he has, and he will curse thee to thy face.'

God said to Satan, 'Behold, all that Job has is in your power; only upon himself you shall not put forth your hand.' So Satan left the gathering intent on smiting Job's goods and chattels and getting Job to curse God.

Sometime later a messenger came to Job, and said to him, 'The oxen were plowing, and the asses feeding beside them. Robbers raided them, and carried them away, and they have slain the servants with the edge of the sword, and I only have escaped to inform you.' While that messenger was speaking, there came another, and said to Job, 'The fire of God is fallen from heaven, and has burned up the sheep and the shepherds, and consumed them; and I only have escaped to inform you.' While he was speaking, there came another, and said to Job, 'The Chaldeans divided themselves into three bands, and raided the camels, and carried them away, and slew the servants with the edge of the sword; and I only have escaped to inform you.' While that messenger was speaking, another messenger arrived and said to Job, 'Your sons and your daughters were eating and drinking wine in their oldest brother's house and behold, there came a great wind from the wilderness, and smote the four corners of the house, and it fell upon them and they are all dead; and I only have escaped to inform you.'

Job was utterly distraught. He went into mourning, shaved his head, and fell down on the ground and worshipped. Job said, 'Naked I came out of my mother's womb, and naked shall I return. God gave, and God has taken away. Blessed be the name of God.'

In all these disasters, Job did not sin, nor did he blaspheme against God.

Some short time later, the sons of God visited God. God said to Satan, 'My servant Job still reveres me. He still holds fast to his integrity, although you provoked me against him, to destroy him without cause.'

Satan said, 'Skin for skin, yea, all that a man has will he give for his life, to save it. But put forth thy hand now, and touch his flesh or his bone, and he will curse thee to thy face.' God said to Satan, 'Behold, he is delivered into your hands; only spare his life.'

So Satan went forth and smote Job with cancer from the sole of his foot to his brain. Job sat down in ashes. Then his wife said to him, 'Do you still hold fast your integrity?

Curse God, and die.' But Job said to her, 'You speak as one of the foolish women speaks. We have indeed received God's blessings, now shall we not also receive his afflictions?'

In all these misfortunes Job did not sin, nor did he blaspheme against God.

Job's three closest friends heard of all this misfortune. They set a time of meeting to console and comfort him. When they saw Job he was so riddled with cancer that they did not recognize him. They wept and threw dust upon their heads toward the heaven. They sat down with Job on the ground for seven days and seven nights, and none spoke a word to him; for they saw that his affliction was very great.

After seven days and seven nights, Job spoke and said, 'Let the day perish wherein I was born... my moanings are poured out like water. For the thing which I greatly feared is come upon me, and that which I was afraid of has befallen me. I am not at ease, neither am I calm, nor am I at rest; and yet misfortune came.'

Then Job's close friend Eliphaz the Temanite answered and said: '..a spirit passed before my face ... I heard a gentle voice, saying, "Shall mortal man be declared more righteous than God? Shall he be more pure than his Maker?"'

Then Bildad the Shuhite said, '...Does God pervert justice? Or does the Almighty pervert right? ... If you were innocent and upright, surely then he would be attentive to you, and would make the habitation of your righteousness prosperous....'

Job answered and said,'... God has condemned me, and spread his net over me...He has destroyed me on every side, and I am no more; and my hope has he removed like a piece of tree. He has also kindled his wrath against me, and he counts me as his enemy...'

Then Eliphaz said to Job, 'So do you consider that are you equal in wisdom with God ? ...'

Job continued '...I have not turned aside my steps from the way, and my heart has not followed after my eyes, and I have acquired nothing unjustly; But when I sowed, then I ate, and when I planted, then I cultivated and gathered the crops...If God is present, let him answer me, and let him write the sentence in a book. Surely I would take it upon my shoulder, and make it a crown to me.'

The words of Job are ended.

So, these three men who wanted to condemn Job ceased answering him, because he was found righteous in their eyes.

Then Elihu was angry. His wrath also kindled against his three friends, because they had found no answer to Job so that they might condemn him. Now Elihu had waited to correct Job with words, because the other men were older than he. When Elihu saw that these three were unable to answer Job, then he was incensed.

'Hear my speech, O Job ... I have heard the voice of your words, saying, I am blameless without transgressions, I am righteous; and there is no iniquity in me, and I am far removed from wickedness... Truly, God does not commit iniquity, neither does God pervert justice. ... and he who is innocent will not be condemned justly;...Therefore he knows them by their works, and he overturns them in the night...'

Then the Lord answered Job out of the whirlwind, and said '... I will question you, and you shall answer me. Where were you when I laid the foundations of the earth? ... ...Have you entered into the depths of the sea? ... Where is the dwelling place of light, and where is the place of darkness?... Do you remember when you were born, and do you know if you will live many days?...... Can you send forth the lightnings ? ... Who has given prey for the lion? Or filled the appetite of the young lions? ...Will the unicorn be willing to serve you, or will he spend the night at your crib? Can you bind the yoke on the neck of the unicorn? ...'

Then Job answered the Lord, and said, ' Behold, I am unworthy; what shall I answer thee? ... I will proceed no further.'

Then the Lord answered Job out of the whirlwind, and said,' ...Have you an arm like God? Or can you thunder with a voice like him? ... Behold, Job, you now are set free from your afflictions. So your God will also remove your bitterness...Whatever is under the whole heaven is mine.'

Then Job answered the Lord and said, 'I know that thou canst do all these things... I will keep silent, and repent in dust and ashes.'

And it came to pass, after the Lord had spoken these words to Job, the Lord said to Eliphaz the Temanite, 'My wrath is kindled against you, and against your two friends; for you have not spoken in my presence that which is right, as my servant Job has...'

And the Lord restored to Job all that he had lost... the Lord gave Job twice as much as he had before. After this Job lived one hundred and forty years ...So Job died, being old and contented and full of days. There endeth the story of Job.

Hmn ... what to make of that? I will limit myself to seven matters. First, Satan is one of God's sons and a very close son. That is consistent with the approach taken by the Tree of Life to 'evil'. I will explore that in the next chapter. Not only is Satan one of God's sons, Satan's relationship with God is sufficiently close for Satan to be able to get God to act in an egotistical, tyrannical manner. This occurs when Satan gets permission from God for Satan to destroy Job's health and Job's valued possessions built up over a lifetime of steady work by Job. Not only does Satan get God to allow Satan to destroy Job in that way, but Job has done nothing to warrant his destruction. In fact, it is the very reason that Job has done nothing to warrant his destruction, that singles Job out for his abuse by God and by Satan. It gets worse, because Job's destruction is allowed by God in order that God can show Satan that God is so worthy of praise that Job will not turn on God, even when Job has been destroyed. What we see here is a powerful message from our forebears that we are not living in a benign cocoon. Rather, one of the characteristics of the scenery into which we have been born is that the scenery is capable of destroying us no matter how kind, faithful and righteous we are. I suspect our forebears who lived through invasions, pillages, plagues and the great depression did not need to be reminded of that, however the boomers and post boomers will likely be unsettled by the warning about the capacity of the scenery to become very sinister at the drop of a celestial hat.

Second, God can act out of pride if need be. We see that when God allows Satan to toy with Job. God wants to show Satan that God is sufficiently superb to warrant and justify adoration by Job, notwithstanding God's role in Job's unwarranted and unjustified downfall. The Latin word 'superbia' means Pride. Our word 'superb' is derived from the Latin word 'superbia'. God is here being motivated, in part at least, by pride. Because pride is one of the seven sins, the message to us is that God can sin, and will sin if need be. That is consistent with the approach taken in the Tree of Life to sin. I will explore that in the next chapter. Our forebears are sending us the dreadful message that part of the set-up into which we have been born, includes the presence of something akin to a celestial manager and script writer who shares one of our creative impulses, that of Pride. Further, God can and will act out of pride if need be.

Third, because God can act out of pride at whim, and thereby wreak havoc on a healthy, wealthy, comfortable human life, the times when God is not so acting are times to be enjoyed and savoured and used prosperously, industriously and gratefully. That is because those bucolic days can end at the wanton drop of the proverbial celestial hat. This heads up from our predecessors feels uncomfortable and disarming initially. But really is no more threatening than being aware that a disease is counting down within us, capable of killing or maiming us at any moment. The Tree of Life suggests that hay can be made and ought to be made while the sun is shining, because there will come a day when the sun does not shine for us any longer. Until that day, the Tree of Life shows us how to think. Importantly the Tree of Life does not tell us or purport to tell us what to think.

Fourth, the Tree of Life says 'as above, so below, but after a fashion'. What that means for present purposes is that the story of Job shows that because God can act out of pride and because a human can learn about herself or himself by reflecting on actions taken and not taken, then God can learn about God by experiencing the interaction with Job. In summary, God can learn about God via Job. True it is that this is a very anthropomorphic perspective on God. However, the Tree of Life is an unashamed champion of anthropomorphism or theomorphism.

Fifth, Satan walks on the Earth according to the Bible story of Job. That does not mean that Satan can be seen by us. Although equally it does not mean that he can't be seen by us. If knowledge of the Job story was more widespread, it might result in better behavior, for example in traffic when merging, due to the possibility that the other driver was Satan.

Sixth, if God can act out of pride, can God also act out of one or more of the remaining six sins? In the next chapter I explore what the Tree of Life teaches us about the uses and abuses of the creative impulses known as the seven sins. However for present purposes, is the story of Job consistent with a creator who acts out of envy or deceit or wrath? Lust and gluttony seem far-fetched.

Seventh, I cannot leave the story of Job without marveling at the fabulous questions attributed to God when God says to Job 'I will question you, and you shall answer me. Where were you when I laid the foundations of the earth? ... Can you send forth the lightnings? ... Will the unicorn be willing to serve you, or will he spend the night at your crib?'. I have heard some very difficult questions asked of witnesses in cross-examination over very many years. For a variety of reasons, the questions asked by God of Job are every bit as difficult.

Sal the clinical psychologist says ...

Detachment. Removing ourselves from unhealthy obsessions about people.

Being over-involved with other people's lives can keep us from living our own life. We find ourselves constantly thinking about them, trying to 'fix' their problems and unable to enjoy ourselves in our own free time. When we over-worry and over-control others, we lose touch with who we are and what we want in our lives. I often see people, usually in their 50's, who have spent their lives helping others in a co-dependent way. Their energy is depleted and they bitterly ask me "why don't they care about me after all I have done for them! I have no career and no hobbies. What now?"

There is an alternative to this fear, anxiety and sadness. The alternative is to detach.

This doesn't mean that you coldly cut other off (although that was my first reaction when I heard the term). It is also not a way to get out of our true responsibilities in life or a Pollyanna like attitude that everything will be fine.

As set out in the Al-Anon brochure, detachment is done mentally, emotionally and sometimes physically, in love. It is a way of us disentangling ourselves from problems which we can't solve. The idea is that people are responsible for themselves and we develop a policy of tending to our own problems and keeping our hands off other's issues. In allowing people to face their own difficulties, they may fail, and we allow them to do this, knowing it is not our responsibility to save them. We implement boundaries in life, knowing the wisdom in the proverb, "good fences make for good neighbours".

This can be incredibly hard with people with people that you love. Clients talk of lending money to people, helping friend's addictions and work failures, but the real difficulty comes with adult children. Certaintly, when children are younger it is our responsibility to help them. But this includes letting them 'fail' and pick themselves up from the situation in order to learn resilience and to change their attitudes. Ultimately we can't control other people's behaviour. We accept what we cannot change. We guide our children when young, but as adults we do not co-dependently exist in their lives, thereby enabling their inability to face the consequences of their actions or inactions.

I have felt sadness when I can see a client's behavior will probably cause disaster in the future. However, I detach with love and remember the proverb "The river travels at its own speed." I have also known that at times I have intellectually known that I could do things to improve my life, but did not feel ready at that moment to implement them. So I also understand my clients' reluctance and even willful resistance to change, as I recognised my own.

The benefits of detachment include a deep serenity and an ability to give and receive love in a positive way that leaves you energised and not drained. We can live our lives without excessive guilt or over-responsibility to others. When we detach, this can give the other person the motivation to begin to worry about themselves – and they often find their own solutions to their problems.

Detachment can help you live a joyful life even with heavy burdens such as a disabled child, a spouse with an addiction or a teenager who is hell-bent on destruction. Detachment can become a habit that can replace the obsessive worrying and controlling behaviours.

When will you know you have successfully detached? When you have an inner security, and your primary focus is on yourself, not in a selfish way, but in a balanced and positive way that makes your life joyful.

Summary

- There is a Western tradition of values, ethics, morality, philosophy, psychology, politics and theology.

- Pythagoras, Socrates, Plato and Aristotle form the main part of that lineage which continues to the present day and is known as the Western tradition.

- The Western tradition is recorded in an image known as the Tree of Life.

- The Tree of Life is used to train the mind, not to inform it.

- The Mercy is the name of the sphere/path located on the Pillar of Mercy directly above the Path known as The Power.

- Each path on the Tree of Life has virtues and vices. The virtues and vices represent the values of Western civilization.

- The virtues and vices of the paths on the Tree of Life have been taught for thousands of years in the Ancient Greek goddess and god myths and in the Bible stories.

- Zeus is the God associated with the Path known as The Mercy. The tales of Zeus have been studied by humans since at least 1,500BC.

- Our forebears have used the tales of Zeus to teach us about aspiration which arises from a natural and healthy innate sense of dissatisfaction.

- The lesson from our wise ancestors is that we need to be very careful to ensure that our dissatisfaction and aspirations do not turn into gluttony.

- The importance of the lesson is undervalued and is widely misunderstood today. For example, the movements today seeking to enhance the self-esteem of children by not keeping score in games or by ensuring an equality of outcome irrespective of competence, represent a failure to understand the complex relationship between dissatisfaction, aspiration and gluttony.

- The Bible story of Job is used by our forebears to teach us about the way things are.

CHAPTER EIGHT

EVIL AND THE SEVEN SINS

THE TREE OF Life has a view about Evil. In summary, the Tree of Life considers that Evil is misplaced behavior[282].

There are three misplacements – proportional, spatial and temporal[283]. Proportional misplacement arises when there is an inappropriate excess or an inappropriate lack[284]. Spatial misplacement arises when an action is misplaced in space, that is if the action occurs in the wrong place[285]. Temporal misplacement arises when an action is out of date or before its time[286].

I will give an example of these by looking at the Seven Sins of seven Greek Gods. This will show how the Seven Sins are recorded in the Tree of Life to teach us about Evil. Dr Liz Greene makes the same point when she writes[287] 'The Seven Sins have always been a powerful metaphor for the ways in which humans "go wrong" in life.'

SLOTH (aka depression[288])

You read earlier about the Path known as The Kingdom and the Goddess Demeter and her tribulations and adventures. You recall how Demeter fell into a slothful slump of depression and apathy when her daughter Persephone was abducted to the Underworld. The Tree of Life uses Demeter to teach us lessons about the detriments and the benefits of Sloth.

The Path known as The Kingdom is where Demeter resides and where the wisdom about the evil / sin of Sloth is recorded. For thousands of years the evil / sin of Sloth was described by the Latin word Tristitia[289], which means profound, debilitating sadness. Another Latin word for this evil / sin was Acedia[290] which means Apathy.

The evil / sin of Sloth arises where there is a proportional misplacement of Sloth. That is, where there is an extreme misplacement of too much sloth or too little sloth. You can imagine a pendulum[291] on the Tree of Life suspended above the Central Pillar of Equilibrium and hanging down to The Kingdom. Imagine that pendulum swinging to an extreme of utter sadness towards The Power. This is where Demeter found herself, bereft of inspiration and unable to function and participate in life in a practical day to day way in The Kingdom.

The evil / sin of Sloth can arise equally when there is an extreme misplacement of too little sadness. The too little sadness is often accompanied by an extreme misplacement of what might be termed anti-sloth. We have all seen this where a person forgoes sleep and companionship in a myopic driven-ness to avoid feeling appropriate sadness and appropriate apathy. Those are examples of the evil / sin on Sloth arising from proportional misplacement.

The evil / sin of Sloth can also arise from temporal misplacement. We saw that when Demeter stayed too long in apathetic sadness longing for her abducted daughter Persephone. The evil / sin of Sloth could equally have arisen by temporal misplacement of spending too little time experiencing feelings of loss and separation and thereby missing out on the consequential and beneficial deepening of the heart and the love which arises from the human experience of loss of love and separation from a loved one.

The evil / sin of Sloth can also arise from spatial misplacement. The pendulum over-reaches and debilitating sadness is felt in the wrong place. For example if Demeter had felt debilitating sadness in the company of anyone who had lost a daughter that would be misplaced. I remember a kindly old Judge contacting me after my client farmers lost their legal case against a Bank and were being evicted from their centuries old family farm. The Judge said to me words to the effect 'If you bleed for everyone you will bleed to death and that won't do anyone any good.' The message to me was get up off the canvas, heal my wounds and fight another day.

Dr Liz Greene considers that an understanding of the roots of the evil / sin of Sloth 'can yield a profound understanding of our deepest emotional needs, our most cherished longings and our share in the cyclical nature of life.' [292]

Envy (aka self-doubt)

The evil /sin here is self-doubt according to Dr Liz Greene[293]. You will recall reading about Heracles earlier in this book. Heracles' life shows how super strength is needed to battle the existential angst that arises from being fearful about not being as strong as others or not being as clever or virile or as good as others. In other words, the evil / sin of Envy arises in us from self-doubt and evaluative comparison[294].

Dr Liz Greene makes that point when she wrote[295] 'Envy … might be better described as Self-doubt because it involves the perception that others have more or are better than oneself.'

As you read earlier, evil / sin arises from misplaced behavior. The misplacement can be proportional, spatial or temporal or any one or more of them. Dr Liz Greene considers[296] that the evil / sin of Envy arises where self-honesty and self-acceptance are lacking. Dr Liz Greene suggests that the sin of Envy is best understood and worked with in terms of Authenticity[297]. Dr Greene also considers[298] that 'Envy can become an appreciation of the worth and talent of others and a spur to develop our own individual gifts.' I agree. This is apparent from the way in which the Tree of Life uses Heracles to teach us about the cultivation of strength by appropriate self-acceptance and self-honesty.

You have read earlier in this book about the first labour of Heracles. Remember how Heracles had to kill and flay the Nemean Lion. Heracles shot his deadly arrows at the Lion but the arrows rebounded harmlessly as the Lion yawned. Heracles used his sword which buckled hopelessly. Heracles then used his mighty club which broke into pieces, whereupon Heracles felt weak and inept. Heracles felt envious as he looked upon the strength, bravery and physical magnificence of the Nemean Lion.

Remember reading about how Heracles then had a dream in which he recalled his divine nature and saw his physical reflection in the face of a huge ocean wave. And how in his reflection he saw his massive muscles and knew that he could access his strength to wrestle the Lion, which he then did. The story of Heracles reminds me of something you read earlier in this book when the political scholar Professor Alan Ryan wrote words to the effect that 'perhaps it is prayer rather than politics that provides the answer to human problems'. In other words, it was Heracles's reflection about his divine nature coupled with his self honesty and self acceptance as to his strengths and weaknesses that enabled him to set aside the evil / sin of Envy he had for the Nemean Lion.

I wonder whether the protestors of the extreme political Left and of the extreme political Right are engaged in a similar Envy. The Envy of the extreme Left being an Envy of wealth and an Envy of the power of benevolence. The seeking by the extreme Left to share the wealth of others because of self doubt about his or her ability to create wealth of that magnitude. And whether on the extreme political Right there is a cognate self doubt about his or her intrinsic worth if subjected to an evaluation by other races, classes or philosophies. In other words, perhaps Professor Ryan was onto something when he suggested that prayer of self reflection, self honesty and self acceptance, rather than politics is the answer to the human conditions. For the sake of completeness, I wonder if Professor Ryan's view might be supplemented usefully by suggesting, consistently with the Tree of Life, that perhaps politics produced by self reflection, self honesty and self acceptance may improve the human condition, rather than mere prayer alone.

Lust (aka inappropriate longing)[299]

The Greek Goddess Aphrodite showed us time and time again how lust created chaos in her life and in the lives of those around here.

Dr Liz Greene considers[300] that the evil / sin of Lust, needs to be understood in terms of 'inappropriate longing'. I agree.

You will remember that we saw earlier in this book how Aphrodite has a magical girdle which makes everyone fall in love with its wearer. The inherent lack of discrimination arising from the profligacy of the magical girdle illustrates the 'inappropriate longing' described by Dr Liz Greene.

The Tree of Life illustrates that the evil / sin of Lust arises on the over-reach, when the pendulum swings too far one way or another. For example, the 'inappropriate longing' arising from Aphrodite's magical girdle is 'inappropriate' when unfettered by time, place and frequency. In other words, the evil / sin of Lust arises from misplacement of longing such that the longing becomes inappropriate.

Aphrodite's time / place / frequency Lust is recounted in ribald fashion, time and again, in the tales of Aphrodite, as you read earlier in this book. However, it must be remembered that the evil / sin of Lust also arises from the misplacement of longing. There is a misplacement of longing when desire is castrated or spayed. The evil / sin of Lust can also arise from the inappropriate scuttling of longing.

The evil / sin of inappropriately scuttling longings arises in dictatorships. Dictatorships do not nurture longings for fine clothes, fine dwellings, fine cars, fine dining, to name but a few.

The Tree of Life records the appropriateness and the necessity of The Power and its creative juices which fuel healthy, competitive capitalism.

Deceit

Dr Liz Greene writes[301] of 'Deceit' that 'If left unconscious and unchecked, turns us into liars, cheats and schemers, full of cunning and willing to injure anyone who stands in our way.'

However, Dr Liz Greene also considers[302] that an understanding of the roots of the evil / sin of Deceit 'can become honest pragmatism and a full embrace of the reality of the world in which we must live.'

The Tree of Life uses the Greek God Hermes to teach us about the roots of the evil / sin of Deceit. You will remember reading earlier in this book about the life and adventures of Hermes. We first met Hermes when he was a toddler who decides to steal Apollo's cows. Hermes devises a cunning scheme where he puts plaited grass boots on the hooves of the stolen cows so the cows cannot be tracked.

Remember how Apollo tracked down Hermes, who thereupon cunningly manipulated and deceived Apollo by singing a song, the words to which Hermes made up on the spot, praising Apollo for his nobility, intelligence and most of all his generosity. Hermes' devious scheme charmed Apollo, who generously agreed to forgive Hermes for everything.

Remember how the Greek God Zeus observed these traits, in his son Hermes, with a mixture of pride and concern, and how Zeus said to Hermes 'You must tell the truth or at least don't lie[303]. You must respect the property rights of others.'

In this way, Hermes' father Zeus was hoping to teach Hermes to tweak Deceit into an honest pragmatism combined with integrity and compassion. Dr Liz Greene calls[304] that transition a transition from 'Deceit' to 'Worldly Wisdom'.

Hermes' life story shows how Hermes achieves that transition from cunning liar, thief and arch manipulator into a mature person exercising worldly wisdom with integrity.

The evil / sin of Deceit can also operate very close to home. I know that from personal experience. For many years I tended to hide my real views, about many issues, from other people, in order to avoid being excluded and isolated. It was my fear of 'cancel culture' before that was even a named thing. In that way I was exercising a kind of dishonesty which caused me to betray my individual values. It seems to me that much of the political correctness and its tendency/aim to avoid the triggering of people, is a consequence of a Hermes' like Deceit in operation at a very personal level. Hermes' life shows us that the antidote to the political correctness and the trigger warnings is a willingness to deal with verbal confrontations cleanly and openly with a willingness to allow others to see you, rather than using cunningly plaited grass boots to disguise my/your true foot prints.

Wrath

Remember how you read about the Greek God Ares, earlier in this book. Ares' life is used by the Tree of Life to teach us about the wonderful side of Wrath.

Dr Liz Greene considers[305] that the evil / sin of Wrath 'can become courage and even heroism, as well as the will to take up life's hard challenges with integrity.'

As I wrote earlier, since the 1960's Western society has become less willing to celebrate the virtuous side of the evil / sin of Wrath. Countless young people, particularly young men (including me) adopted a pacificist approach to wrath. In the Indian Yoga school I attended, I was taught about the virtue of 'Ahimsa', a Sanskrit word which means non-violence. Mahatma Ghandi was held up, to me and by me, as the noble embodiment of Ahimsa. Fortunately (in my view) the pendulum appears to be self-correcting and swinging back towards a less extreme view of the way to approach our human tendency towards Wrath.

Dr Liz Greene has written[306] in very positive terms about the psychological benefits of wrath and anger. Dr Greene considers[307] that 'Wrath is a highly complex issue. Defensive anger is a fundamental instinct in all animal forms of life, and it can be extremely healthy and appropriate … there are moments in history when the only possible way to stem a tide of collective violence has been to respond with violence in order to survive.'

Western civilization recognizes the importance of that approach by incorporating in the criminal justice system a right to legitimate self defense in the face of violence. That legal right to Wrath has been fine tuned in Western democracies for centuries in a way that reflects completely the Tree of Life's approach that evil / sin is misplaced behavior.

What I mean by that is, the criminal justice system says Wrath is an evil / sin and is unlawful when it is misplaced proportionally, spatially or temporally. For example, for Wrath to be lawful self-defense, the Wrath must be proportional to the attack. Accordingly, the criminal justice systems of Western civilization do not allow a machine gun to be used to resist a home invasion by a clearly unarmed intruder.

The criminal justice systems of Western civilization also reflect the Tree of Life by requiring Wrath to not be misplaced spatially. For example, a home invader cannot lawfully be tracked down to another location in another city and have Wrath inflicted on him or her at that spatially misplaced venue. The infliction of Wrath by you, on a home invader at your home, can be lawful, whereas the infliction of the same wrath on the same home invader is unlawful when carried out at an unrelated location. This illustrates how the evil / sin of Wrath is accepted by the criminal law of Western justice systems to arise from spatial misplacement.

The criminal justice systems of Western civilization also reflect the Tree of Life's approach to evil whereby the criminal law requires the Wrath to not be misplaced temporally. As I wrote at the beginning of this chapter, evil is misplaced behavior, according to the Tree of Life. There are three misplacements, namely, proportional, spatial and temporal. The criminal justice systems of Western civilization judge Wrath to be acceptable and thus not criminal when the Wrathful behaviour is not misplaced temporally. In other words, the law allows you to inflict Wrath on a home invader at your home at that moment but will not allow you to detain the invader and inflict Wrath over the next few days. This demonstrates that Wrath must not be misplaced temporally in order for Wrath to be lawful under the criminal justice systems of Western civilization.

The stories about the adventures of Greek God Ares, set out earlier in this book, contain the wisdom of our elders in relation to the legitimate and illegitimate exercise of Wrath. The Tree of Life puts Wrath / Ares at home in The Strength on the Pillar of Severity. The Tree of Life sets out the relationship between Wrath and Deceit. The Tree of Life illustrates that the courage we can achieve by the brave and honest exercise of Wrath will be used by us in achieving and exercising worldly wisdom. In other words, the diagram of the Tree of Life shows how Courage (Wrath) descends into Worldly Wisdom (Deceit) down the Pillar of Severity.

Dr Liz Greene makes the same point when she wrote[308] 'Sigmund Freud once said that the qualifications for being able to descend to the depths of oneself in order to understand one's own psyche are threefold: Courage, Courage and Courage.'

Gluttony

Dr Liz Greene considers[309] that the evil / sin of Gluttony refers to our misplaced behavior in response to 'Dissatisfaction'.

The Tree of Life uses the Greek God Zeus to teach us about the complexities of the evil / sin of Gluttony. You read earlier in this book about the adventures of Zeus. You read about Zeus' insatiable appetite for more lovers, more power, more popularity, more food and drink. You also read about how, at times, Zeus was able to act as a merciful, wise and prudent ruler. At those times Zeus was a visionary, benevolent planner. Zeus formulated prudent plans for the expansion of the kingdom, including the layout of harbours, wharves, warehouses, railways, hospitals, court houses, jails, banks, industrial areas, residential areas, recreation areas, environmental protection areas and agricultural areas.

The stories of the God Zeus teach us that when Zeus was responding to his Dissatisfaction in a mature and appropriate manner, he was able to use his strengths and his resources to create abundance for himself and for others. The stories of Zeus teach us that Dissatisfaction can be used to produce and power Aspiration.

The Tree of Life teaches that Aspiration is a wonderful virtue to be celebrated and cultivated. However, the Tree of Life also teaches that the dissatisfaction that motivates aspiration can over-reach and produce the evil / sin of Gluttony.

Importantly, Aspiration will not lead inevitably to the evil / sin of Gluttony. This is one of the lessons our predecessors have sought to teach us by the Zeus stories and by the Tree of Life. The lesson is that Aspiration is to be celebrated and cultivated and also to be watched very carefully to ensure that moral integrity is exercised so there is no misplacement and conversion of Dissatisfaction into Gluttony.

The importance of that lesson is undervalued and is widely misunderstood today. For example, the movements today seeking to enhance the self esteem of children by not keeping score in games or by ensuring an equality of outcome irrespective of competence, represent a failure to understand the lessons of Zeus and the structure of the Tree of Life.

True it is that us humans are powered by a dissatisfaction that produces Gluttony unless managed with moral integrity. However, the lessons of Zeus and the Tree of Life teach us that wonderful things can be created on Earth by using the Aspiration which arises from our urge towards Gluttony. The soundly based distaste for Gluttony does not mean that Aspiration is to be chided and replaced by equal opportunity outcomes of scoreless draws. Such an approach castrates and spays the creative juices of appropriate Aspiration.

Pride

The sin of Pride was called 'Superbia' in Latin[310]. From that Latin word we derive the English words 'superb' and 'superior'.

Our forebears have used the life and adventures of Apollo the Greek God to teach us about the uses and abuses of the human energy source and creative impulse called pride. Dr Liz Greene considers[311] that 'Pride can become self-respect, allowing us to express all that is most individual and creative in us.'

You will recall how the life of the God Apollo was characterized by Apollo's life and death battle with the satyr named Marsyas. Our predecessors have used an unusual story telling approach when dealing with Apollo. You will remember how our predecessors taught us about the evils of Gluttony by having Zeus act out Gluttony, and how the evil of Deceit was demonstrated by Hermes acting deceitfully. In contrast, when it comes to Apollo, the evil of Pride is demonstrated by the actions of the satyr Marsyas juxtaposed against the actions of Apollo.

Specifically, you read earlier how Marsyas acquired an unearned reputation as a prodigious flute player by pretending to play a flute that actually played by itself. Marsyas found that he could impress people by pretending to be a virtuoso flautist, whereas in reality he could not play the flute at all. In contrast to Marsyas' inauthentic façade, Apollo was an authentic musician who was able to competently play the flute to express his authentic self.

You will recall how Marsyas travelled from town to town, pretending to play his flute. In some towns the most popular form of music was sad and slow. Marsyas said to those townsfolk that was his favourite music and he ingratiated himself by pretending to play and pretending to love the sad and slow tunes. In that manner, Marsyas would impress those townsfolk and win over their admiration and approval. Marsyas would then move on to a different town and those new townsfolk would tell him how they loved fast and happy tunes. Marsyas would seek to impress them by saying to them that he only ever played fast and happy tunes because he only loved fast and happy tunes. Marsyas would then pretend to play the flute, which dutifully maintained the inauthentic façade by playing fast and happy tunes, to the delight of those townsfolk. And so on, Marsyas toured the countryside, moving from town to town, being feted as a long lost member of that township because of his alleged heartfelt affinity for their particular type of music.

In that manner, Marsyas was displaying the worst form of Pride. Marsyas was not superb as a flute player. Marsyas was not superior to other flute players. Marsyas could not play the flute. Marsyas was a chameleon of the worst caliber. Marsyas had no authentic love for a particular type of music. Marsyas had not applied himself so as to discover the music he authentically enjoyed. Rather, Marsyas adopted the opinions of others as his own, notwithstanding that those opinions changed inconsistently every few days as he changed towns.

In contrast, Apollo could play well and more importantly, played what he felt. When townsfolk asked Apollo to play them something that he enjoyed, Apollo did not ask them what they enjoyed and then play what they wanted to hear under the pretense that was what he enjoyed. Rather, when Apollo was asked to play something he enjoyed, he had the courage to risk being unpopular by playing what the townsfolk may not have wanted to hear.

Apollo's courage to express his authentically held views stands in stark contrast to Marsyas' inauthentic populist façade.

Dr Liz Greene considers[312] that the evil / sin of Pride arises when we allow a lack of self-respect to restrict our expression of all that is most individual and creative in us.

A modern day Marsyas can be seen re-Tweeting posts that he or she thinks will earn approbation from the townsfolk wanting to hear their favourite tune.

The antidote to the evil / sin of Pride is loyalty to your inner Self. Thereby rejecting a Marsyas like performance recital, miming the favoured tunes of others, as a way of compensating for a lack of a deeply explored inner Self.

Evil

The Tree of Life says that if the questions are asked 'What is evil ? Why does evil exist?' The Tree of Life answers 'Evil is misplaced behavior. Evil exists because it is part of the Tree of Life.'

The Tree of Life can (and does[313]) provide more information about the manner in which evil is part of the Tree of Life. The Tree of Life uses the word 'Qliphoth' to describe the deeper characteristics of evil and the role of evil. Mercifully, such depth is beyond the scope of this book.

CHAPTER NINE

THE LORD'S PRAYER - AS A METHOD OF MEDITATION

MATTHEW CHAPTER 6 VERSES 9 TO 13

THE TRANSLATION IS by George Mamishisho Lamsa. In my view this very scholarly translation is the most accurate translation available at present.

> *Our Father in heaven, hallowed be thy name*
> *Thy Kingdom come, Thy will be done, as in heaven so on earth.*
> *Give us bread for our needs from day to day.*
> *And forgive us our offences, as we have forgiven our offenders.*
> *And do not let us enter into temptation, but deliver us from wrong, wickedness and error.*
> *For thine is the Kingdom and the Power and the Glory for ever and ever.*
> *Amen.*

The context in which the prayer occurs, includes the statement that prayer is not be carried out 'like the hypocrites' who stand at the street corners so that they can be seen to be praying. Rather 'enter into your inner chambers, and lock your door, and prayer to your Father who is in secret'. Also 'do not repeat your words like the pagans, for they think that because of much talking they will be heard'. Rather 'pray in this manner'.

Our Father in heaven, hallowed be thy name.

There is a certainty here. The prayer does not say 'If there is heaven and if there is a Father'.

The value that is recorded is that there is a heaven and there is a Father in heaven.

The prayer then states that the name of the Father in heaven is hallowed.

Hallowed is a very deep and rich word. Synonyms for Hallowed include respected, admired, venerated, inspired by.

The name is not spelled out. This reflects the oral tradition where hallowed names and sounds were passed from mouth to ear in a time honoured ceremonial manner. The power of sound is becoming well understood these days. From glass shattering operatic singing to inaudible dog whistles, from the 'minor fall, the major lift'[314], the ability of sound/name to transmit a vibration that has consequences is undoubted.

A hierarchy is also established. The person speaking the prayer is recognizing that there is a Father who is in heaven and that the Father's name is hallowed.

This records the importance for a human being of being in a relationship of veneration. In other words there is a Father who deserves the status of hallowhood. And we do not have a reasonable basis for such a claim about ourselves. The acknowledgment of subservience to one's better is well recognised these days as being therapeutically sound. A healthy grown up ego has the capacity to recognise a hierarchy in which it is below, way below where it might be one day.

I think the translation could be improved by changing the first sentence to 'Our Mother and Father in heaven, hallowed be thy name.' The original sentence is to the effect 'God in heaven, hallowed be thy name.' In the original Aramaic the word God does not need to be translated as masculine singular. Rather the word God can just as readily be translated as 'Mother and Father' or even 'Mothers and Fathers'. The Tree of Life provides support for the proposition that the 'formula' for God depicted in the Tree of Life is a formula where female and male share equally in the process of creation. Accordingly the first sentence of the Lord's Prayer, in my view, is properly stated as 'Our Mother and Father in Heaven, hallowed be thy name.'

It is self evident that the phrase 'thy' (in 'thy will be done') accommodates reference to the plural 'Our Mother and Father' just as readily as 'thy' accommodates the singular masculine 'Our Father'.

Thy Kingdom come, Thy will be done, as in heaven so on earth.

The value stated here is that there is a relationship between earth and heaven. We know from the first verse that heaven is where God is. We know from the first verse that the God in heaven is worthy of being hallowed. The will of such God is 'done' on earth. And the will is done on earth 'as in heaven'. This records the ideal 'as above, so below' from the Golden Tablet of Hermes. That is that the earth and heaven share characteristics. One of the shared characteristics is that earth is a place where the will of the Father can be done. That is, it is possible for the will of God to be done on earth. The aspiration in the prayer is that the will of the Father 'be done' on earth. That is, the will has not yet been done. Rather the hope is that the will 'be done'. This is a reference to a future possibility, a hope. The Kingdom has not yet come, neither on heaven or on earth. That is, there is an ongoing creation of a Kingdom, of the hallowed God, in heaven and on earth.

There is an equating of 'Thy will' with 'Thy Kingdom come'. That is, there is a possibility that the Kingdom on earth may be a place where the will of God, with the hallowed name, is done. But that time has not yet occurred.

Give us bread for our needs from day to day.

The reference is to 'our needs from day to day'. 'Needs' can be contrasted with toys, jewels and fantasies. That is, what we are asking for is that we get our needs met. Not our fantasies but rather our needs. Further, the relevant needs are our needs 'from day to day'. Not our needs for ever and ever. Not our needs for the next ten years. Rather, our needs 'from day to day'. There is a practicality in having a focal point of 'day to day'. The time span 'day to day' is manageable, generally speaking. The reference is to 'bread'. This is a recognition that our other needs like air and water have already been supplied. What is needed is 'bread'. Bread is eaten and provides an energy source for metabolism. Bread is a metaphor. What is being sought from the Father is that which we need from day to day. The story of the grain goddess Demeter and her daughter Persephone reminds us that there will be a time when nothing grows. A time when Persephone is in the underworld with Hades. That is, during such times we need the Father to give us bread because we will otherwise have unmet needs. I remember going on a surfing trip about forty years ago to a remote island in the Solomon Islands. We took some US dollars along with surfboard wax. We were dropped on the island by a villager in a dug-out canoe. He spoke virtually no English, but enough to communicate that he would come back for us in about one week. It soon became apparent there were no cafes and no hotels, no homestays. In fact there were no shops. We did not starve, mostly because the island dwellers fed us and showed us what vegetation we could eat. One of the lessons I learned was that sometimes

I need help for my 'needs from day to day'. Everyone has found and will find herself, or himself, in the position where their needs cannot be met autonomously.

And forgive us our offences, as we have forgiven our offenders.

This verse follows immediately the verse about 'our needs from day to day'. Myriad other topics could have followed on. The verse could have dealt with murder or other gods. But what followed on was 'offences'. In other words, 'offences' are very important. Notice that the verse does not say 'if we ever happen to offend'. Rather, the verse says 'forgive us our offences', that is, I will commit an offence and you will commit an offence. Offences will occur. The verse asks the Father with the hallowed name to forgive my offence. What follows is curious and slightly concerning. The prayer, which you will remember is the one and only prayer (ie 'pray in this manner'), asks for forgiveness 'as we have forgiven our offenders'. There are at least two things being communicated here. The first and the most important matter is that I need to forgive a person who has offended me. That is, you will offend me sometime and I will forgive you for that offending. The second matter is that I am asking the Father to forgive me in the same manner (ie 'as') I have forgiven other people. That is, if I forgive someone on the condition that the person does something for me, like publishes an apology in a newspaper, then that is the process I am advocating. The lesson is that I need to forgive in the same manner as I want to be forgiven. There is also a timing component in the words 'as we have forgiven'. That is, I get to go first. I forgive my offender and then I get to ask the Father to forgive me for my offending. The verse also implies that there is nothing for which the Father will not forgive me. That is each and every one of my offences can be the subject matter of my prayer for the Father to forgive me for my offending. It is not just offences where I have offended the Father. This means that if I offend you then I need to ask the Father to forgive me for my offence against you. This means that offences are not just interpersonal. If I offend you then I am offending in a manner that needs forgiveness from the Father. The verse requires us to forgive a person who offends us. The verse does not require us to seek forgiveness from that person.

And do not let us enter into temptation, but deliver us from wrong, wickedness and error.

One common and standard mistranslation states 'lead us not into temptation'. The current Pope is now correcting that error in translation. The error in translation existed for a couple of hundred years and has led people to wonder why we would ask the Father not 'to lead us into temptation'. Why would the Father lead us into temptation?

The original translation does not suffer from that mistake. The correct translation asks the Father to not let us enter/fall into temptation. The verse recognises that we will be tempted by temptation. And also that we can and will enter into temptation. Temptation is described negatively. A good choice is to not enter into temptation. A poor choice is to enter into temptation. There is a hierarchy of value established. Entering into temptation is on the bottom of the list of values. Above it is the choice of not entering into temptation. Temptations are endless. Drug abuse, alcohol abuse, being resentful for too long, being unnecessarily violent. The verse asks the Father to provide assistance to us. The assistance is to not let us enter into temptation. In practice that assistance shows up in our deep feelings about the choice we are about to make. We get a gut feeling as to what the good choice is. The gut feeling is a subtle assistance. The ultimate choice to enter into temptation or not is up to us. That is the way temptation is set up. The prayer then asks for assistance from the Father to 'deliver us from wrong, wickedness and error'. The verse is equating 'wrong, wickedness and error' with 'temptation'. That is, temptation can be identified because its result is error or wickedness or 'wrong'. The prayer asks the Father to 'deliver us'. This acknowledges we do not have to act out 'wrong, wickedness and error'. We can avoid acting that way. One way in which we are delivered from acting that way is by the feelings in our gut telling us that what we are about to do is 'wrong wickedness and error'. Deliver is an old world. It has two parts. The 'livered' part refers to the liver in the gut. The gut feeling. Livered also refers to the way something shows up in the world. Its appearance. How the talk is walked. The livery of a horse or an airline or a football team is the outfit being worn or the fit out. The presentation, the acting out. The 'de' in delivery gives the meaning of assisting in the putting on of the presentation. Deliver us from wrong wickedness and error is asking the Father to assist in providing the gut feeling that goes with us acting out wrong, wickedness and error.

For thine is the Kingdom and the Power and the Glory for ever and ever. Amen.

This verse acknowledges that The Kingdom is the Father's dominion. As we saw in chapter one, The Kingdom is the earth. The Kingdom is a Path on the Tree of Life. The verse acknowledges what we see on the Tree of Life, that is The Power and The Glory form two points of a triangle. The third point on the triangle is The Kingdom. The three points work together. The way The Power and The Glory and The Kingdom work together is described in the early chapters in this book. The verse says that relationship of chaos (Power), order (Glory) and the earth (Kingdom/Dominion) is fixed 'for ever and ever'. The prayer then ends with the word 'Amen'. Amen is a versicle. A very, very old word describing an even older sound that human beings have made 'for ever and ever'.

The sound is made up of sounds that came before sentences. The sounds in 'Amen' have been used by humans to acknowledge the presently ineffable mystery of life and death. The sound is written 'Aum' by cultures which hear the sound that way. The sound is written 'Amin' by other cultures that hear the sound that way. The sound is the same. The different spelling is like the way the city in India known now as Kolkata used to be known as Calcutta. The meaning of the sound Amen, Aum, Amin is the same. For ever and ever, humans have been making that sound in the context of the mystery of life and death. The prayer ends with that sound. The preface to the prayer says 'pray in this manner'. The making of that sound 'Amen' is part of the tradition of prayer. My experience is that the repetition of the sound 'Amen' creates a gateway towards the presently ineffable mysteries of life and death.

CHAPTER TEN

FOR EVER AND EVER

WHAT, IF ANYTHING, does the Tree of Life say about the origin of the universe?

The study of the origin of the universe is called 'cosmology'.

The Tree of Life uses the image of Three Veils to train the mind about cosmology. Remember, as described earlier in this book, the images in the Tree of Life are symbolic, the images are not descriptive. The images are designed to train the mind, not to inform the mind.

The Tree of Life has the image of Three Veils sitting at the very top of the Tree of Life. The image of Three Veils is used to train the mind how to inquire into the origin of the universe. The Tree of Life shows that immediately beneath the Three Veils there is the very first Path on the Tree of Life. That first Path has the name, in English, The Crown.

The Crown sits above the head. This image suggests The Crown is beyond the head. Another name given to the Path known as The Crown is the Concealed of the Concealed. Another name is the Head which is not. Another name is the Inscrutable Height. By the use of such names and by the use of the image of a Crown which sits on the top of a head, our mind is being trained to consider an existence beyond our present existence. And to stretch our mind to consider an existence prior to existence. And to stretch our mind to consider a prior non-existence. The Three Veils can be so regarded.

The image of the Crown sitting above the head is designed to train the mind to explore a realm that is beyond thought, a realm that is beyond the head. A realm which precedes thought. In other words, a realm separate from our head and thus separate from our state of consciousness.

The Three Veils suggest there is a realm beyond which the mind cannot see clearly. The Three Veils suggest there is a limitation on human perception beyond the Three Veils.

The image does not suggest there is nothing beyond the Three Veils, in fact quite to the contrary, the image suggests rather that what is beyond the Veils is shrouded from clear perception.

The Tree of Life has Three Veils. Not one veil, not two veils, but three veils. Each Veil is different. Each Veil has a different name.

Consistent with the image of a Veil as preventing clear perception of what is beyond the Veil, the names of the Veils verge on the un-thinkable. That is hardly surprising given that the mind is being taught there is a realm beyond the Veils that is beyond thinking but which exists nonetheless.

The name, in English, is the Limitless Light, for the Veil closest to the Path known as the Crown. In other words, the image is that there is a Crown which sits above a head, and sitting above the Crown there is a Veil named Limitless Light.

The image of this part of the Tree of Life therefore includes a Veil named Limitless Light which somehow contributes to the bringing into existence of The Crown, which sits on top of, above and beyond a human head.

If we then look at more of the Tree of Life we see that far below The Crown there is the Path known as The Kingdom. Of course, the ruler of The Kingdom wears a Crown on top of her or his head. This is an important image. Thus, the Tree of Life displays two Crowns. One Crown is the Crown immediately below the Veil of Limitless Light. The other Crown is the Crown sitting on top of the ruler in The Kingdom.

In other words, within the Path known as the Crown there is a further Kingdom. A useful image is that of Russian Dolls stacked one inside another. The Tree of Life records that Russian Doll relationship as The Crown is The Kingdom of The Veils.

Another way of describing the relationship of The Path known as The Crown and The Path known as The Kingdom, is that there is a Tree of Life inside a Tree of Life. You might find it useful to visualise this as a hologram where The Path known as The Crown contains the whole of a smaller Tree of Life, and that the smaller Tree of Life contains another Kingdom and another Crown. This is another example of "As above, so below."

The Tree of Life shows that sitting above The Veil named The Limitless Light there is another Veil. That Veil is named The Limitless.

Accordingly, the image is that The Veil named The Limitless precedes The Veil named the Limitless Light.

In other words, the image that the Tree of Life wants our minds to explore is that Limitless Light is produced by The Limitless.

The next Veil is named Negativity. The image of the Tree of Life is therefore that the Veil named Negativity produces the Veil named The Limitless, which in turn produces the Veil named The Limitless Light, which in turn produces The Path known as The Crown. And within The Crown there is an entire mini-Tree of Life containing its own mini-The Crown stretching down to its own mini-The Kingdom.

The Tree of Life uses the image of a ruler wearing a crown but we only see the face of the ruler in profile and the side of the face that we see is the right side of the face. In this manner the Tree of Life is suggesting that the way to use the mind in this region of the Tree of Life is to use the right side of the brain. The earlier chapters dealing with the right hemisphere of the human brain and the experiences of Jill Bolte-Taylor and Ian McGilchrist demonstrate why the right side of the brain is better equipped for exploring the imagery in this region of the Tree of Life. Remember how Bolte-Taylor opined that 'I appreciate that for many of us, if our left mind cannot smell it, taste it, hear it, see it or touch it, then we are skeptical as to whether or not it exists. Our right brain is capable of detecting energy beyond the limitations of our left mind because of the way it is designed.'[315] Bolte-Taylor is describing a method for us of 'detecting' information in the realms of, and beyond, The Three Veils, by using the capacity of our 'right brain … (which does not have) the limitations of our left mind because of the way it is designed.' The description by Bolte-Taylor is putting in words what we see on the Tree of Life where the right side of the face on The Crown receives impressions from, and beyond, the Three Veils.

The above material sets out the way the Tree of Life instructs us to use our mind to explore the origins of existence. This is a further example of the approach taken by the Tree of Life to teach us how to think, not what to think. In other words, the Tree of Life is not saying the Big Bang theory is the way the universe came into existence. Rather, the Tree of Life says you have a mind and here are images you can use as tools to use your mind to explore cosmology.

Another image used by the Tree of Life to explore cosmology is that of Metatron the Arch-Angel. Remember how reference was made earlier in this book, in chapter three, to the scholarly writings of Thomas Aquinas in 1225 concerning angels and archangels. Thomas Aquinas is considered one of the greatest philosophers of the Western world. Thomas Aquinas concluded that angels exist and that such angels, whilst consisting of pure thought or intellect nevertheless have the ability to assume a physical body at will, albeit a physical body that was made up of pure thought. The reason I remind you of that, and remind myself of that, is that when a scholar of the intellectual caliber of Thomas Aquinas expresses such a conclusion, it is appropriate to examine the possibility that his opinion may contain some useful information, even if such information does not accord with your current thinking and your life experiences to date.

And so with that in my mind, what do we know of Metatron? The short answer is we know very little. The Editors of Encyclopaedia Britanica state[316] that Metatron is 'the greatest of angels in Jewish myths and legends. Metatron is not a figure of the Hebrew Bible, but his name appears briefly in several passages of the Talmud.' Dion Fortune considered[317] that Metatron 'was responsible for the glyph of the Tree of Life's being given to man'. However, Fortune provides no authority for that proposition.

For completeness I note that the Path known as The Crown, that I have been describing above, sits towards the top of the Tree of Life. You can see this on the front cover of this book. Below The Crown and on its right (as you look at the Tree of Life) is the Path known as The Wisdom. The Path known as The Understanding sits opposite. The relationship between The Crown, The Wisdom and The Understanding is beyond the scholarship of this humble book. A very useful entry point for exploration of this part of the Tree of Life is found in chapter 7 of Dion Fortune's book[318].

ENDNOTES

[1] Alan Ryan 'On Politics: A History of Political thought from Herodotus to the Present', published by the Penguin Group, Allen Lane, 2012 at pages 34, 299,300,301; Gregory Vlastos, 'Socrates: Ironist and Moral Philosopher', Cambridge University Press, 1991, page 106 footnote 91; Julia Annas, 'Plato', Oxford University Press, 2003, chapter two; Arthur Fairbanks, 'Pythagoras and the Pythagoreans', 1898, London, K.Paul Trench Trubner & Co. Ltd, chapter 9 pages 132 to 144, particularly 'Simplicii in Aristotellis physicarum libros qua ores' editit H.Diels, Berlin 1882, and Simplicius "Commentary on Aristotle's De caelo'; Osho, 'Meditation – the first and last freedom', 1988, Rebel Publishing House Germany, page 168; Dion Fortune, 'Mystical Qabalah', Weisner Books revised edition published in 2000, first published in 1935 by Williams and Norgate Ltd London, chapter 1 paragraphs 3, 6 to 15; Charles H. Khan, 'Pythagoras and the Pythagoreans', 2001, Hackett, pages 1,5 and 6; Mysterium Coniunctionis: An Inquiry into the Separation and Synthesis of Psychic Opposites in Alchemy: Volume 10 (Collected Works of C.G. Jung) at footnote 118 referring to Scholem 'Major Trends in Jewish Mysticism' at page 76 and following; 'The Greek Qabalah' by Kieren Barry, published by Samuel Weiser Inc, 1999 at locations 109, 450, 458, 469, 488, 522 and 1228 of 5935. Interested readers may wish to explore the connections said to exist between the Pythagoreans and the earlier mystery schools of Pharaoh Tutmoses III who ruled Egypt from 1500 BC to 1447BC and Pharaoh Amenhotep IV who changed his name to Akhnaton.

[2] The photograph is of a print 60" x 40" known as a giclée. Copies of Patricia's beautiful painting are available via the website that bears her name.

[3] There is a delightfully complicated system of metaphysical mathematics called 'Gematria'. The numbering system I have used in this book for the spheres and the paths does not use the approach of Gematria. The reason I have taken that approach is because I am simplifying the material. In my opinion, the additional precision that arises from Gematria does not provide sufficient return on the investment of time required to explore Gematria. Further, Gematria has been described as a 'tangled jungle … very susceptible to abuse'. See Mystical Qabalah op cit, chapter 28 location 4887 of 6417.

[4] 623 BC per the United Nations Educational, Scientific and Cultural Organisation [UNESCO], Decision 40COM 7B.42 – Lumbini, the Birthplace of the Lord Buddha, referring to the history set out on page 1 of UNESCO World Heritage List No. 666 rev, which included 'The Shakya Prince Siddharta Gautama, better known as the Lord Buddha, was born to Queen Mayadevi, wife of King Suddodhana, ruler of Kapilavastu, in 623 BC at the famous gardens of Lumbini, while she was on a journey from her husband's capital of Tilaurakot to her family home in Devadaha.'

[5] 551 BC per Encyclopaedia Britannica, 'Confucius Chinese Philosopher' written by Professor Roger T. Ames, University of Hawaii, Manoa and 'Thinking Through Confucius' with David L. Hall.

[6] 570 per Encyclopaedia Britannica, 'Muhammad Prophet of Islaam' per Associate Professor Nicolai Sinai University of Oxford 'The Qur'an: A Historical-Critical Introduction' and Professor William Montgomery Watt University of Edinburgh 'Muhammad: Prophet and Statesman'.

[7] Mystical Qabalah by Dion Fortune, ibid, chapter 1 paragraph 13 'In the system of Pythagoras we see an adaptation of the Qabalistic principles to Greek mysticism.'

[8] Alan Ryan 'On Politics: A History of Political thought from Herodotus to the Present', published by the Penguin Group, Allen Lane, 2012 at pages 299, 300, 301.

[9] The delightfully and shamelessly provocative Ben Shapiro has come to the same conclusion in his bold and terse tome 'The right side of history: how reason and moral purpose made the west great', 2019, Harper Collins.

[10] Mystical Qabalah, ibid, page 8.

[11] Allan B. Ullam 'Lenin and the Bolsheviks', 1969, London: Fontana at page 104; David Shub 'Lenin: a biography' 1948 New York; Michael Prawdin 'The unmentionable Nechaev: a key to Bolshevism', 1961 London, George Allen and Unwin; Robert Payne 'Zero: the story of terrorism', 1951, London: Wingate at page 42.

[12] Sergey Nechayev 'Catechism of a Revolutionary' opening lines, per Professor Paul Avrich at Queens College and the Graduate School the City University of New York, author of 'The Haymarket Tragedy', 1986, Princeton: Princeton University Press page 171.

[13] Negayev, S 'The Revolutionary Catechism', ibid, paragraphs 23 to 25.

[14] Dr Jordan Peterson '12 Rules for Life: An Antidote to Chaos', 2018, Allen Lane part of Penguin Random House, at page xxvii and xxvii, 'Aleksandr Solzhenitsyn, the great documenter of the slave-labour-camp horrors of the latter (Soviet Union), once wrote that the "pitiful ideology" holding that "human beings are created for happiness" was an ideology "done in by the first blow of the work assigneer's cudgel." In a crisis, the inevitable suffering that life entails can rapidly make a mockery of the idea that happiness is the proper pursuit of the individual.'

[15] Act 2 scene 2 lines 221 and following.

[16] Swami Satyananda Saraswati, 'Sannyasa Tantra',1976, Bihar School of Yoga, Monghyr, Bihar, India, pages 45 to 57.

[17] The Yoga Sutras of Patanjali comprise 196 verses. Sutra 15 states 'When an individual becomes free of cravings for the sense objects he has experienced as well as those of which he has heard, that state of consciousness is vairagya.'

[18] Copyright 2018 FitnessHealth101.com All Rights Reserved, Friday 20 July 2018.

[19] Dion Fortune "The Mystical Qabalah', ibid, chapter 2 paragraph 7.

[20] Dion Fortune "The Mystical Qabalah', ibid, chapter 1 paragraph 2.

[21] A similar perspective has been stated by Gareth Knight, 'If the object of created life is for the human spirit to express itself within the worlds of form, through a process of personal spiritual evolution, it is hardly likely to be achieved by turning away from natural life. Thus the Path of the Hearth Fire as she (Dion Fortune) called it, involving the responsibilities of family life, was a sound and effective part of any initiate's training.' This is from the Introduction written by Gareth Knight to Dion Fortune's book 'Applied Magic' published by Red Wheel/Weiser.

[22] Negayev, S 'The Revolutionary Catechism', ibid paragraph 8.

[23] Dr Jordan Peterson '12 Rules for Life', ibid at Rule 11 'Do not bother children when they are skateboarding' 'Danger and Mastery'.

[24] The school is known as the Servants of the Light (or SOL). Its website is servantsofthelight.org. It describes itself, accurately, as providing practical training in the western esoteric tradition. The first degree course, which I completed by many years of daily part time study, is demanding and time consuming, frustratingly slow and laboured at times but does provide practical training in the western esoteric tradition. As at mid 2018 SOL is not admitting new students. However, that is

likely to change when its new director of studies Dr Steven Critchley takes over fully from Dolores Ashcroft-Nowicki who served as director of studies from 1976 to June 2018.

[25] In that regard a poem attributed to Kabir states 'Why put on the robes of the monk and live aloof from the world in lonely pride? Behold, my heart dances in the delight of a hundred arts and the Creator is well pleased.'

[26] Dr Jordan Peterson '12 Rules for Life: An Antidote to Chaos', 2018, Allen Lane part of Penguin Random House, at page xxxiii from the Overture. See also pages 80, 86, 92,115,162, 187,201,203, 243, 340, 358 for Dr Peterson's analysis of nihilism and the manner in which its symptoms can be addressed by practical actions.

[27] A.H. Almaas, 'The Inner Journey Home', Shambala Boston and London 2012, locations 8164 and 8204 of 13861 – Appendix A – Western Concepts of Soul.

[28] CG Jung suggested that 'The Kingdom' could also be called 'The Dominion'. See 'Mysterium Coniunctionis: An inquiry into the separation and synthesis of psychic opposites in alchemy: Volume 10 Collected Works of C.G. Jung' page 41 footnote 14.

[29] Matthew chapter 6 verse 13.

[30] Mystical Qabalah by Dion Fortune, ibid, chapter 1 paragraph 12 '...the closing chapter of the Lord's prayer is pure Qabalism. Malkuth the Kingdom, Hod the Glory, Netzach the Power, form the basala triangle of the Tree of Life with Yesod the Foundation or Receptacle of Influences, as the central point. Whoever formulated that prayer knew his Qabalah.'

[31] Ibid at xxvii.

[32] It is sufficient to say, for present purposes, that of the 32 paths, ten of the paths are spheres. Emphatically ten, as stated in the book 'Sefer Yetzirah' to the effect ' ten and not nine, ten and not eleven.'

[33] Alan Ryan 'On Politics: A History of Political thought from Herodotus to the Present', published by the Penguin Group, Allen Lane, 2012 at pages 34, 299,300,301; Gregory Vlastos, 'Socrates: Ironist and Moral Philosopher', Cambridge University Press, 1991, page 106 footnote 91; Julia Annas, 'Plato', Oxford University Press, 2003, chapter two; Arthur Fairbanks, 'Pythagoras and the Pythagoreans', 1898, London, K.Paul Trench Trubner & Co. Ltd, chapter 9 pages 132 to 144, particularly 'Simplicii in Aristotellis physicarum libros qua ores' editit H.Diels, Berlin 1882, and Simplicius "Commentary on Aristotle's De caelo'; Osho, 'Meditation – the first and last freedom', 1988, Rebel Publishing House Germany, page 168; Dion Fortune, 'Mystical Qabalah', Weisner Books revised edition published in 2000, first published in 1935 by Williams and Norgate Ltd London, chapter 1 paragraphs 3, 6 to 15; Charles H. Khan, 'Pythagoras and the Pythagoreans', 2001, Hackett, pages 1,5 and 6; Mysterium Coniunctionis: An Inquiry into the Separation and Synthesis of Psychic Opposites in Alchemy: Volume 10 (Collected Works of C.G. Jung) at footnote 118 referring to Scholem 'Major Trends in Jewish Mysticism' at page 76 and following; 'The Greek Qabalah' by Kieren Barry, published by Samuel Weiser Inc, 1999 at locations 109, 450, 458, 469, 488, 522 and 1228 of 5935; 'From the Origins to Socrates' by Giovanni Reale, translated by John R. Catan, published by the State University of New York Press, 1987, pages 9,13,14,17,59,67,68 ,71,203,293,294.

[34] Dion Fortune 'The Mystical Qabalah', ibid, chapter 1 paragraphs 6 to 15.

[35] Two volume set, Liveright; 1 edition (2012)

[36] Mary Beard author of 'The Roman Triumph' quoted on the Amazon web site.

[37] Anthony W. Marx, President of the New York Public Library, quoted on the Amazon web site.

[38] Steven Lukes, author of 'Power: Radical View', quoted on the Amazon web site.

[39] Alan Ryan, 'On Politics: A History of Political thought from Herodotus to the Present' published by the Penguin Group, Allen Lane 2012, at page xxiii.

[40] Jordan Peterson, '12 Rules', ibid, Coda at page 364.

[41] Ryan, op cit, page 69.

[42] On Politics, ibid, at page xxiii.

[43] On Politics, ibid, at page 31.

[44] On Politics, ibid, at page 29.

[45] Cambridge University Press 1991.

[46] Gregory Vlastos, 'Socrates: Ironist and Moral Philosopher', op cit, page 106 footnote 91.

[47] Charles H. Khan, 'Pythagoras and the Pythagoreans', Hackett, 2001, pages viii and ix.

[48] Ibid page 1.

[49] Ibid pages 5 and 6.

[50] Osho, 'Meditation – the first and last freedom', 1988, Rebel Publishing House Germany, page 168.

[51] Moshe Idel writing in the Introduction to the Bison Book edition of Reuchlin's 'On the Art of the Kabbalah', 1993, Abaris Books Inc., University of Nebraska Press, page xii, quoting Pico della Mirandola.

[52] Johann Reuchlinn, 'On the art of the Kabbalah', 1517, republished 1993, Bison Book edition, University of Nebraska Press, page 39.

[53] Ibid page 8.

[54] Johann Reuchlinn, 'On the art of the Kabbalah', 1517, republished 1993, Bison Book edition, University of Nebraska Press, page 131.

[55] Johann Reuchlinn, 'On the art of the Kabbalah', 1517, republished 1993, Bison Book edition, University of Nebraska Press, page xiii in the introduction by Moshe Idel.

[56] Vlastos, ibid, page 242 and following.

[57] Vlastos, ibid, page 251.

[58] On Politics, ibid, at page 34.

[59] Ryan, ibid, at page 59.

[60] Vlastos, ibid, page 239.

[61] Vlastos, ibid, page 240.

[62] Vlastos, ibid, page 241.

[63] Jordan Peterson, '12 Rules', ibid at pages 93 and Rule 6 at page 147 and following 'Set your house in perfect order before you criticise the world.' And the Coda at page 364 'Perhaps our environmental problems are not best construed technically. Maybe they're best considered psychology. The more people sort themselves out, the more responsibility they will take for the world around them and the more problems they will solve…Maybe the environmental problem is ultimately spiritual. If we put ourselves in order, perhaps we will do the same for the world. Of course, what else would a psychologist think?'

[64] Ryan, ibid, page 60.

[65] Vlastos, ibid, page 248.

[66] Ryan, op cit, page 36.

[67] Professor Julia Annas, the Regents Professor of Philosophy at the University of Arizona in the book 'Plato', Oxford University Press, 2003, chapter two 'Socrates and the Academy'.

[68] See for example, Professor Julia Annas, the Regents Professor of Philosophy at the University of Arizona, a graduate of Oxford University and Harvard University in her book 'Plato', Oxford University Press, 2003, chapter two 'Thus we find, for example, the claim that Plato went on a journey to Egypt seeking wisdom. There is nothing implausible about this.'

[69] Johann Reuchlinn, 'On the art of the Kabbalah', 1517, republished 1993, Bison Book edition, University of Nebraska Press, page 175.

[70] Using the spelling favoured by C.G. Jung.

[71] Annas, op cit, chapter 7 'The nature of things – the Forms'.

[72] See also the discussion by Plato in his books 'Phaedo' and in 'Republic' and in 'Symposium' on the role of Forms in creating patterns on earth without coming into being on earth. This is pure Cabala.

[73] Ryan, op cit page 65.

[74] Jordan Peterson, 'Maps of Meaning: The Architecture of Belief', 1999, Routledge, Chapter 5 The Hostile Brothers: Archetypes of Response to the Unknown at page 339.

[75] Ryan, op cit, page 67.

[76] Julia Annas, op cit, chapter 5 'Virtue, in me and in my society'.

[77] Annas, op cit, chapter 6 'My soul and myself – Problems about the soul.'

[78] A.H.Almaas, 'The Inner Journey Home', Shambala Boston and London 2012, location 9914 of 13861 in the Kindle publication.

[79] Annas, ibid, chapter 6.

[80] Annas, ibid, chapter 6.

[81] A.H. Almaas, 'The Inner Journey Home', Shambala Boston and London 2012, locations 8164 and 8204 of 13861 – Appendix A – Western Concepts of Soul.

[82] Johann Reuchlinn, 'On the art of the Kabbalah', 1517, republished 1993, Bison Book edition, University of Nebraska Press, page 135.

[83] Ryan, op cit, page 71.

[84] Jonathan Barnes, Professor of Ancient Philosophy at Oxford University, 'Aristotle', Oxford University Press, 1982, chapter 1 'The man and his works'.

[85] Barnes, op cit, page 137.

[86] Arthur Fairbanks, 'Pythagoras and the Pythagoreans', 1898, London, K.Paul Trench Trubner & Co. Ltd, chapter 9, pages 132 to 144, particularly 'Simplicii in Aristotelis physicarum libros qua ores' edidit H.Diels, Berlin 1882; and Simplicius 'Commentary on Aristotle's De caelo'.

[87] Aristotle 'On the Soul' Book II chapter 2, the 'Delphi Complete Works of Aristotle', translated by J.A. Smith, Delphi Classics.

[88] Barnes, op cit, page 27.

[89] Barnes, op cit, page 28.

[90] Barnes, op cit, page 33, referring to Artistotle's 'Gryllus' and the criticism of it by Cephisodorus.

[91] Aristotle, 'Nicomachean Ethics' referred to by Barnes, op cit pages 26 to 29.

[92] Negayev, S 'The Revolutionary Catechism', ibid, paragraphs 23 to 25.

[93] The positioning from left to right of Pythagoras, Socrates, Plato, Aristotle then Euclid, presumably is intended to demonstrate an historical progression, the effluxion of time, the movement from the left hand side of the page to the right hand side of the page in Western style reading and writing.

[94] Ryan, op cit, page 32.

[95] Comprising 8 books.

[96] Ryan, op cit, page 71.

[97] Ryan, op cit, page 71.

[98] Ryan, op cit, page 71.

[99] Ryan, op cit, page 84.

[100] Ryan, op cit, page 88.

[101] Ryan, op cit, page 88.

[102] Ryan, op cit, page 88.

[103] Ryan, op cit, page 91.

[104] 'Political Man: The Social Bases of Politics' by Seymour Martin Lipset, Anchor Books, Garden City, New York, 1960, foreword pages 7 to 10.

[105] Ian McGilchrist 'The Master and his Emissary – the Divided Brain and the Making of the Western World', 2009, Yale University Press, New Haven and London.

[106] Professor Norman Doidge, University of Toronto and Columbia University New York, the author of 'The Brain that changes itself', quoted in 'The Master and his Emissary' in the forenotes.

[107] The Master and his Emissary, op cit, page 5.

[108] The Master and his Emissary, op cit, page 6.

[109] The Master and his Emissary, op cit, page 6.

[110] 'American Commonwealth' vol 1, by James Bryce, New York: Macmillan Company, 1911, at page 29; 'The Origin and Growth of the English Constitution' vol 1 by Hannis Taylor, Boston: Houghton, Miffline, 1889, at page 60.

[111] 'The Foundations of the Constitution' by David Hutchison, Secaucus, New Jersey: University Books, 1975, originally published 1928, at pages 20 to 21.

[112] 'Greek Ruins' by T.L. Simmons at page 43 in 'Polybius and the Founding Fathers: the separation of powers' by Marshall Davies Lloyd. See mlloyd.org, 22 September 1998. See also Ryan, op cit, chapter 4 'Roman Insights: Polybius and Cicero' pages 111 to 117 and 121.

[113] Patrick Keyzer 'The Americanness of the Australian Constitution: the influence of American constitutional jurisprudence on Australian constitutional jurisprudence' published in Australasian Journal of American Studies, vol 19 no 2 (December 2000) pages 25 to 35 at page 25.

[114] Pieter Labuschagne 'The doctrine of separation of powers and its application in South Africa', published in 'Politeia' vol 23 no 3, 2004, Unisa Press, at pages 84 to 102, at page 87.

[115] See the article by the Hon Justice Arthur Emmett, Challis Lecturer in Roman Law at the University of Sydney, in 'Roman Law' published in NSW Bar News, Winter 2008 at page 70, referring to Barton J.

[116] Ryan, ibid, page 129.

[117] John F. Kennedy Speeches, JFK Library, www.jfklibrary.org, speech at the Rudolph Wilde Platz, Berlin, 26 June 1963.

[118] Ryan, op cit, page 137.

[119] 12 Rules, ibid, Rule 2 'Treat yourself like someone you are responsible for helping' in the section 'A spark of the divine', pages 59 to 60.

[120] A.H. Almaas 'The Inner Journey Home', Shambala Boston and London 2012, chapter one page one. A.H. The book has been described by Richard Smoley as 'a brilliant synthesis of the best in traditional spirituality with the best in modern psychology'. This statement is set out in the descriptions of the book at location 37 of 13861 in the Kindle publication.

[121] Almaas 'The Inner Journey Home', ibid, location 309 of 13861 in the Kindle publication.

[122] Almaas, 'The Inner Journey Home', ibid, location 319 of 13861 in the Kindle publication.

[123] Ryan, ibid, at page 143.

[124] Ryan, ibid, at page 145.

[125] Dion Fortune, 'The Mystical Qabalah', op cit, page 34.

[126] 12 Rules, op cit, Rule 2 'The Domain, Not of Matter, but of What Matters'.

[127] In particular see the 'Nicomachean' and the 'Eudemian'.

[128]

[129] Barnes, op cit, page 126 referring to Nicomachean Ethics at 20.

[130] Carl Jung in 'The Conjunction', '5. The psychological interpretation of the procedure' in 'Collected Works' Volume 14, Chapter VI paragraph 706.

[131] There is a risk that pathworking may provide an addictive escape from daily life lived in The Kingdom. Dion Fortune, in her forthright manner, identified that risk in the following passage: '(The Kingdom) is the nadir of evolution, but it should be looked upon, not as the ultimate depth of unspirituality, but as the marking-buoy in a yacht race. Any yacht that puts about on the homeward course before it has rounded the marking-buoy is disqualified. And so it is with the soul. If we try to escape from the discipline of matter before we have mastered the lessons of matter, we are not advancing heaven-wards, but suffering from arrested development. It is these spiritual detectives who flock from one to another of the innumerable wildcat uplift organisations that come to us from the Far East and the Far West. They find in cheap idealism an escape from the rigorous demands of life. But this is not a way of advancement, but a way of retreat. Sooner or later they have to face the fence and clear it. Life brings them up to it again and again, and presently begins to use the whip and spur of psychological sickness; for those who will not face life, dissociate; and dissociation is the prime cause of most of the ills that mind is heir to.' For those interested in exploring The Kingdom of the Tree of Life via pathworking there are three useful books that I have identified in the endnotes. Dolores Ashcroft-Nowicki's book contains a useful introduction and a script that you can use for a pathworking along the Tree of Life pathways.

[132] Dr Liz Greene, 'Apollo's Chariot – the meaning of the astrological sun', 2001, The Centre of Psychological Astrology Press. Kindle Edition 2014 published by CPA Press, at location 181 of 4409.

[133] Pages 66 to 74.

[134] The introduction to the Penguin Classics Deluxe Edition of 'The Greek Myths', by Robert Graves, 2012, Kindle Edition, at page xix.

[135] 'The Golden Bough a study in comparative religion', James George Frazer, MacMillan and Co 1894.

[136] Op cit page 404.

[137] James George Frazer, ' The Golden Bough (Vol. 1 of 2) page 466 (Kindle Locations 5421-5429). Kindle Edition.

[138] Ibid, Kindle location at 7705.

[139] Ibid, page 406 and Kindle location 4100.

[140] Ibid, Kindle location 4563.

[141] A nod here to Dr Jordan Peterson's Rule 4 'Compare yourself to who you were yesterday, not to who someone else is today' from the fabulous '12 Rules for Life', referred to above.

[142] Ian McGilchrist 'The Master and his Emissary – the Divided Brain and the Making of the Western World', 2009, Yale University Press, New Haven and London.

[143] Professor Norman Doidge, University of Toronto and Columbia University New York, the author of 'The Brain that changes itself', quoted in 'The Master and his Emissary' in the forenotes.

[144] 'The Master and his Emissary', op cit, page 459.

[145] 'The Master and his Emissary', op cit, page 18.

[146] Ibid page 5.

[147] The Mystical Qabalah, op cit, at page 34 paragraph 5.

[148] There is a fifth sphere called D'aath. Some diagrams of the Tree of Life depict D'aath as being located in the Pillar of Equilibrium. D'aath is very significant and will be explored later.

[149] The Master and his Emissary, op cit, page 43.

[150] The Master and his Emissary, op cit, page 30.

[151] The Master and his Emissary, op cit, page 39.

[152] The Mystical Qabalah, ibid, at page 35 paragraph 9.

[153] The Master and his Emissary, ibid, at page 27.

[154] The Mystical Qabalah, ibid, at page 35 paragraph 9.

[155] The Master and his Emissary, ibid, page 27.

[156] The Mystical Qabalah, ibid, at page 148 paragraph 1.

[157] The Master and his Emissary, op cit, page 91.

[158] The Master and his Emissary, op cit, page 93.

[159] The Mystical Qabalah, at page 19 paragraph 6.

[160] Referred to in The Emerald Tablet of Hermes.

[161] The Mystical Qabalah, ibid, at page 49 paragraph 1.

[162] The Master and his Emissary, op cit, page 5.

[163] The Master and his Emissary, op cit, page 6.

[164] The Master and his Emissary, op cit, page 6.

[165] The Master and his Emissary, op cit, page 40.

[166] The Master and his Emissary, op cit, page 41.

[167] The Master and his Emissary, op cit, page 54.

[168] The Mystical Qabalah, op cit, page 19 paragraph 6.

[169] The Master and his Emissary, op cit, page 43.

[170] The Master and his Emissary, op cit, page 46.

[171] The Master and his Emissary, op cit, page 203.

[172] The Master and his Emissary, op cit, page 190.

[173] The Master and his Emissary, op cit, page 198.

[174] The Master and his Emissary, op cit, page 199.

[175] Published by Hodder & Stoughton in 2008.

[176] My Stroke of Insight, op cit, at page 1.

[177] My Stroke of Insight, op cit, at page 31.

[178] My Stroke of Insight, op cit, at page 47.

[179] My Stroke of Insight, op cit, at page 49.

[180] My Stroke of Insight, op cit, at page 63.

[181] My Stroke of Insight, op cit, at page 69.

[182] My Stroke of Insight, op cit, at page 69.

[183] My Stroke of Insight, op cit, at page 133.

[184] My Stroke of Insight, op cit, at page 170.

[185] My Stroke of Insight, op cit, page 140.

[186] My Stroke of Insight, op cit, page 159.

[187] My Stroke of Insight, op cit, page 166.

[188] 'The Master and his Emissary', op cit, page 459.

[189] Dion Fortune, 'The Mystical Qabalah', ibid, chapter 11 paragraph 1, chapter 15 paragraph 24.

[190] The nature of the Yetziratic Text is beyond the scope of my humble book. The Book of Creation aka the Book of Creation or the Book of Formation is a good place to start.

[191] Dion Fortune, 'The Mystical Qabalah', ibid, chapter 24 paragraphs 1 and 2.

[192] Dion Fortune, 'The Mystical Qabalah', ibid, chapter 24 paragraph 3.

[193] The full citation is set out in chapter one of this book.

[194] Marsha Linehan 'DBT Skills Training Manual', Guilford Publications, 2014, page 169.

[195] Linehan, op cit, at page 169.

[196] Linehan, op cit, at page 171.

[197] Linehan, op cit, at page 173.

[198] Dr J.B. Peterson '12 Rules for Life' op cit.

[199] Ibid page 47.

[200] Ibid.

[201] Dr Liz Greene 'The Seven Sins – The journey from shadow into light', published by Astrodienst AG, 2020, ebook, Conclusion, page 34.

[202] Richard Webster 'Communicating with Archangel Michael', Llewellyn Publications, Minnesota, 2004, page 12.

[203] The Hebrew word 'satan' means adversary or accuser. It was used to refer to human beings who played that particular role in court proceedings. See Psalm 109:1-6.

[204] Revelation 12: 9.

[205] John Milton 'Paradise Lost', Book VI lines 320 and following.

[206] Francis Yates, 'The Occult Philosophy in the Elizabethan Age', London: Routledge Classics, 2001 at page 208; Il Peneroso lines 85-90; Paradise Lost lines 474-481.

[207] Ibid page 47.

[208] Ibid.

[209] Chapter 17.

[210] Dion Fortune 'The Mystical Qabalah', ibid, Chapter 11 paragraph 1.

[211] Dion Fortune, 'The Mystical Qabalah'. Ibid, Chapter 23 paragraph 24.

[212] Dr Liz Greene 'The Seven Sins – The journey from shadow into light', published by Astrodienst AG, 2020, ebook, Conclusion, page 34.

[213] Dion Fortune, 'The Mystical Qabalah'. Ibid, Chapter 23 paragraph 32.

[214] Dion Fortune, 'The Mystical Qabalah', ibid, Chapter 23 paragraph 33.

[215] Sam Harris, 'Waking Up – A guide to spirituality without religion', 2014, Penguin Random House, chapter 4 and following.

[216] Almaas 'The Inner Journey Home – the Soul's realization of the unity of reality' 2004, Shambala Boston and London, location 6305 of 13861 and footnote 20 and following.

[217] Dion Fortune, 'The Mystical Qabalah', ibid, Chapter 23 paragraph 41.

[218] Rav P.S. Berg, 'The Essential Zohar', 2002, Bell Tower New York, Random House, page 20.

[219] Ibid.

[220] Rav P.S. Berg, 'The Essential Zohar', 2002, Bell Tower New York, Random House, page 20.

[221] Chapters 11 and 18.

[222] Dion Fortune, 'The Mystical Qabalah', ibid, paragraph 5 chapter 22.

[223] Dion Fortune, 'The Mystical Qabalah', ibid, paragraph 9 chapter 22.

[224] Bhagavad Gita at 3.36-43.

[225] See the translator's notes to the King James Translation of the Bible, www.heavenlypublishers.com.

[226] The Mystical Qabalah, ibid, at page 165 paragraphs 32 and 33.

[227] The Mystical Qabalah, ibid at page 166 paragraph 37.

[228] Ian McGilchrist, ibid, at page 5.

[229] Dr Liz Greene, 'Apollo's Chariot – the meaning of the astrological sun', 2001, The Centre of Psychological Astrology Press. Kindle Edition 2014 published by CPA Press.

[230] Dr Liz Greene, 'Apollo's Chariot – the meaning of the astrological sun', 2001, The Centre of Psychological Astrology Press. Kindle Edition 2014 published by CPA Press, at locations 161 and 166 of 4409.

[231] Ibid page 47.

[232] Dr Liz Greene, 'Apollo's Chariot – the meaning of the astrological sun', 2001, The Centre of Psychological Astrology Press. Kindle Edition 2014 published by CPA Press, at locations 500 and 505 of 4409.

[233] Dr Liz Greene 'The Seven Sins – The journey from shadow into light', published by Astrodienst AG, 2020, ebook, Conclusion, pages 23 and 34.

[234] Ibid page 47.

[235] Montserrat- tourist-guide.com.

[236] Sir James George Frazer, 'The Golden Bough – A study in Comparative Religion', 1894, MacMillan and Co., chapter 3 'Killing the God'.

[237] Dion Fortune, 'The Mystical Qabalah', op cit, chapter 20 paragraph 52.

[238] Dion Fortune, 'The Mystical Qabalah', op cit, chapter 20 paragraph 52.

[239] The jury is out as to whether Dionysus is the father or whether Zeus is the father. The Goddess Hera said it doesn't matter who the father was, what was important is that Aphrodite needed to be punished for not knowing who the father was and that Hera punished Aphrodite by endowing Priapus with the huge penis in order to remind Aphrodite of Aphrodite's excesses in that department.

[240] 'Italian Baroque Sculpture', 1998, in 'World of Art' by Bruce Boucher, Thames & Hudson, page 138.

[241] Dion Fortune, 'The Mystical Qabalah', op cit, chapter 20 paragraph 36.

[242] Dion Fortune, 'The Mystical Qabalah', op cit, chapter 20 paragraph 36.

[243] The Tree of Life seeks to use symbols like the Child-Christ to describe what is usually considered to be ineffable.

[244] Dr Jordan Peterson '12 Rules for Life: An Antidote to Chaos', 2018, Allen Lane part of Penguin Random House, in chapter one at page 32 of 370 in the ebook.

[245] Tobit chapter 12 verse 15.

[246] Dr Liz Greene in 'Apollo's Chariot – the meaning of the astrological sun', 2001, The Centre of Psychological Astrology Press. Kindle Edition 2014 published by CPA Press, at location 1401 of 4409.

[247] Dr Liz Greene in 'Apollo's Chariot – the meaning of the astrological sun', 2001, The Centre of Psychological Astrology Press. Kindle Edition 2014 published by CPA Press, at location s 1694 to 1699 of 4409.

[248] These characteristics were identified by Dr Liz Greene in her fabulous book 'Apollo's Chariot – the meaning of the astrological sun', 2001, The Centre of Psychological Astrology Press. Kindle Edition 2014 published by CPA Press, at location 293 of 4409 and following.

[249] Dr Liz Greene in 'Apollo's Chariot – the meaning of the astrological sun', 2001, The Centre of Psychological Astrology Press. Kindle Edition 2014 published by CPA Press, at location 305 to 314 of 4409.

[250] Dr Liz Greene in 'Apollo's Chariot – the meaning of the astrological sun', 2001, The Centre of Psychological Astrology Press. Kindle Edition 2014 published by CPA Press, at location 305 to 314 of 4409.

[251] Dr Liz Greene in 'Apollo's Chariot – the meaning of the astrological sun', 2001, The Centre of Psychological Astrology Press. Kindle Edition 2014 published by CPA Press, at locations 382 to 386 of 4409.

[252] Dr Liz Greene in 'Apollo's Chariot – the meaning of the astrological sun', 2001, The Centre of Psychological Astrology Press. Kindle Edition 2014 published by CPA Press, at location 519 of 4409.

[253] Dr Jordan Peterson '12 Rules for Life: An Antidote to Chaos', 2018, Allen Lane part of Penguin Random House, rule six, chapter six, page 159 of 389 in the ebook.

[254] Dr Liz Greene in 'Apollo's Chariot – the meaning of the astrological sun', 2001, The Centre of Psychological Astrology Press. Kindle Edition 2014 published by CPA Press, at location 2219, 2224, 2253 of 4409.

[255] Dr Liz Greene in 'Apollo's Chariot – the meaning of the astrological sun', 2001, The Centre of Psychological Astrology Press. Kindle Edition 2014 published by CPA Press, at location 2269 of 4409.

[256] Dr Liz Greene in 'Apollo's Chariot – the meaning of the astrological sun', 2001, The Centre of Psychological Astrology Press. Kindle Edition 2014 published by CPA Press, at location 2572 of 4409.

[257] Dr Liz Greene in 'Apollo's Chariot – the meaning of the astrological sun', 2001, The Centre of Psychological Astrology Press. Kindle Edition 2014 published by CPA Press, at location 598 of 4409.

[258] Dr Liz Greene in 'Apollo's Chariot – the meaning of the astrological sun', 2001, The Centre of Psychological Astrology Press. Kindle Edition 2014 published by CPA Press, at location 1664 of 4409.

[259] Dr Liz Greene in 'Apollo's Chariot – the meaning of the astrological sun', 2001, The Centre of Psychological Astrology Press. Kindle Edition 2014 published by CPA Press, at location 1653 of 4409.

[260] Dr Liz Greene in 'Apollo's Chariot – the meaning of the astrological sun', 2001, The Centre of Psychological Astrology Press. Kindle Edition 2014 published by CPA Press, at location 2194 of 4409.

[261] Dr Liz Greene in 'Apollo's Chariot – the meaning of the astrological sun', 2001, The Centre of Psychological Astrology Press. Kindle Edition 2014 published by CPA Press, at location 2093 of 4409.

[262] Ibid page 47.

[263] Ibid page 17.

[264] Ibid page 17.

[265] Ibid page 17.

[266] Dion Fortune ' The Mystical Qabalah' op cit chapter 19 paragraphs 13 and 14.

[267] Stanley McChrystal, Jeff Eggers and Jason Mangone, 'Leaders: myth and reality', chapter two 'The marble man: Robert E Lee', Penguin Random House 2018.

[268] First Book of Samuel chapter 17.

[269] Dion Fortune, 'Mystical Qabalah', op cit chapter 19 paragraph 48.

[270] Dion Fortune, 'Mystical Qabalah', op cit chapter 19 paragraph 25.

[271] Dion Fortune, 'Mystical Qabalah' op cit chapter 19 paragraphs 21 and 22.

[272] Dion Fortune, 'Mystical Qabalah' op cit chapter 19 paragraphs 21 and following.

[273] 'The Mars Quartet: Four Seminars on the Astrology of the Red Planet' by Liz Greene, Lynn Bell, David Costello, Melanie Reinhart. Gardners Books, 2001; Liz Greene and Howard Sasportas 'The Inner Planets', Samuel Weiser Books, 1993, Part 3 'Mars – The Warrior and the Womaniser'.

[274] Liz Greene, 'The Inner Planets (Seminars in Psychological Astrology)', p. 177, Red Wheel Weiser. Kindle Edition.

[275] Liz Greene, 'The Inner Planets (Seminars in Psychological Astrology)', p. 190, Red Wheel Weiser. Kindle Edition.

[276] Liz Greene, 'The Inner Planets (Seminars in Psychological Astrology)', p. 191, Red Wheel Weiser. Kindle Edition.

[277] Liz Greene, 'The Inner Planets (Seminars in Psychological Astrology)', p. 191, Red Wheel Weiser. Kindle Edition.

[278] Liz Greene, 'The Inner Planets (Seminars in Psychological Astrology)', p. 191, Red Wheel Weiser. Kindle Edition.

[279] 'The Mars Quartet: Four Seminars on the Astrology of the Red Planet' by Liz Greene, Lynn Bell, David Costello, Melanie Reinhart. Gardners Books, 2001.

[280] Liz Greene 'The Seven Sins' via Astrodienst at page 10 and following, prepared for CJ Leggat.

[281] Dr Carl Jung has described in 'Answer to Job', Routledge Classic, from the Introduction page 2 of 143, that the story of Job a being an 'unvarnished spectacle of divine savagery and ruthlessness'. Jung also stated at page 7 that the difference between, on the one hand, Yahweh / God's interaction with Job, and on the other hand, Zeus, was that Zeus had 'a benevolent and somewhat detached manner (and) allowed the economy of the universe to roll along on its accustomed courses and punished only those who were deranged. He did not moralise but ruled purely instinctively.'

[282] Dion Fortune 'The Mystical Qabalah', ibid, chapter 19 paragraphs 1 to 4.

[283] Dion Fortune 'The Mystical Qabalah', ibid, chapter 19 paragraph 4.

[284] Ibid.

[285] Ibid.

[286] Ibid.

[287] Dr Liz Greene 'The Seven Sins – The journey from shadow into light', published by Astrodienst AG, 2020, ebook, Conclusion, page 47.

[288] Per Liz Greene, 'Seven Sins', ibid, page 40.

[289] Ibid at page 40.

[290] Ibid.

[291] Dion Fortune 'The Mystical Qabalah', ibid, chapter 26 paragraph 15.

[292] Dr Liz Greene 'The Seven Sins – The journey from shadow into light', published by Astrodienst AG, 2020, ebook, Conclusion, page 47.

[293] Ibid page 5.

[294] A nod here to Dr Jordan Peterson's Rule 4 'Compare yourself to who you were yesterday, not to who someone else is today' from the fabulous '12 Rules for Life', referred to above.

[295] Dr Liz Greene 'The Seven Sins – The journey from shadow into light', published by Astrodienst AG, 2020, ebook, Conclusion, page 5.

[296] Ibid.

[297] Ibid.

[298] Ibid at page 47.

[299] Ibid at page 29.

[300] Ibid.

[301] Ibid page 47.

[302] Ibid.

[303] A nod here to the wonderful work of Dr Jordan Peterson, referred to earlier, and Rule 8 in '12 Rules for Life'.

[304] Dr Liz Greene 'The Seven Sins – The journey from shadow into light', published by Astrodienst AG, 2020, ebook, Conclusion, page 34.

[305] Ibid page 47.

[306] Ibid page 17.

[307] Ibid page 17.

[308] Ibid page 17.

[309] Ibid page 10.

[310] Ibid page 23.

[311] Ibid page 47.

[312] Ibid page 47.

[313] An inquisitive reader may be interested in the following ideas about Qliphoth. First, each of the sephiroth have a corresponding sephiroth, akin to being like the reverse side of the same coin. See Dion Fortune 'Mystical Qabalah' op cit, chapter 26 paragraph 6. Second, the corresponding sephiroth on the reverse side of the same coin, form the Qliphoth. See Dion Fortune ibid chapter 26 paragraph 15. Third, if a pendulum is swung between say, The Power and The Glory, and if that pendulum moved out of a two dimensional swing and into a three dimensional circular swing so that the pendulum swung around onto the reverse side of the Tree of Life, then that over-reaching or misplacement is called 'evil'. See Dion Fortune ibid chapter 26 paragraph 15. Fourth, evil is dealt with by its absorption back into the sephiroth from whence it came. Dion Fortune ibid chapter 26 paragraph 21.

[314] Leonard Cohen's beautiful song 'Hallelujah'.

[315] Page 166 of 'My Stroke of Insight', op cit.

[316] Encyclopaedia Britannica, on line, entry for 'Metatron – Angel', entries edited 20 July 1998 to 12 March 2020, Melissa Petruzzello, one of the Editors of Encyclopaedia Britannica.

[317] Dion Fortune 'The Cosmic Doctrine' at location 2735 of 3061 in the Kindle edition.

[318] Dion Fortune 'The Mystical Qabalah', op cit.